Road Traffic Law in Scotland

To my family, without whom
this book would have been
twice as long and finished in
half the time.

Road Traffic Law in Scotland

John Wheatley
Sheriff of Tayside Central
and Fife at Perth

Butterworths/Law Society of Scotland
Edinburgh
1989

United Kingdom	Butterworth & Co (Publishers) Ltd, 88 Kingsway, LONDON WC2B 6AB and 4 Hill Street, EDINBURGH EH2 3JZ
Australia	Butterworths Pty Ltd, SYDNEY, MELBOURNE, BRISBANE, ADELAIDE, PERTH, CANBERRA and HOBART
Canada	Butterworths Canada Ltd, TORONTO and VANCOUVER
Ireland	Butterworth (Ireland) Ltd, DUBLIN
Malaysia	Malayan Law Journal Sdn Bhd, KUALA LUMPUR
New Zealand	Butterworths of New Zealand Ltd, WELLINGTON and AUCKLAND
Puerto Rico	Equity de Puerto Rico, Inc, HATO REY
Singapore	Butterworth & Co (Asia) Pte Ltd, SINGAPORE
USA	Butterworth Legal Publishers, ST PAUL, Minnesota, SEATTLE, Washington, BOSTON, Massachusetts, AUSTIN, Texas and D & S Publishers, CLEARWATER, Florida

A CIP Catalogue record for this book is available from the British Library

ISBN 0 406 11225 8

Typeset by Phoenix Photosetting, Chatham
Printed and bound by Thomson Litho Ltd, East Kilbride

Preface

This book is based on an article submitted for the Laws of Scotland: Stair Memorial Encyclopaedia, and the author wishes to express his gratitude to the Editors of that work for their kind permission to reproduce this material. Thanks are also due to Butterworths for their traditional charm and comprehensive assistance; to the typists who helped with the typing of parts of the manuscript; to John Kirk and others of the Procurator Fiscal's Office in Perth; to John Smith of the Traffic Examiner's Department; to Ian Innes; and to various officers of the Perth Police for invaluable assistance. Any errors however are solely the author's.

An attempt has been made to state the law as at 15 May 1989, when the Road Traffic Act 1988, the Road Traffic Offenders Act 1988, and the Road Traffic (Consequential Provisions) Act 1988 came into force.

J Wheatley
July 1989

Introduction

The purpose of this book is to provide a simple manual of Road Traffic Law for Scottish practitioners, students and others whose business brings them into contact with the subject.

A large proportion of the cases calling before the sheriff and district courts relate to road traffic matters, and although the bulk of such cases are straightforward, there appears to be sufficient need for a comprehensive yet reasonably convenient handbook which looks at the law from a Scottish viewpoint, and which discusses those matters which chiefly engage the attention of the courts. Most university courses feature some instruction in road traffic law and this book may have a wider interest. However, it must be emphasised that, while it is hoped that the book will cover most areas of the subject which arise in practice, it is not intended to provide an exhaustive treatment of this particularly wide and complex field of law.

The history of road traffic legislation in this country effectively began with the Road Traffic Act 1930. This was the first attempt made by the legislature to provide a comprehensive set of rules governing road traffic matters. Prior to 1930, the use of motor vehicles on the roads had been subject mainly to common law duties of care and statutory provisions relating chiefly to highways and classes of vehicles. The 1930 Act contained *inter alia* definitions of motor vehicles, provisions for the licensing of drivers, age limits for drivers, insurance provisions, arrangements for the setting up of traffic areas and traffic commissioners, the requirements for public service vehicle licenses and road service licences, and driving offences such as speeding, reckless and careless driving, and driving under the influence of drink or drugs. This statute forms the basis of all successive principal Acts leading up to the Road Traffic Act 1972 (c 20) which remained the principal statute for road traffic until 1989.

On 15 May 1989, the 1972 Act was replaced by three pieces of legislation, namely the Road Traffic Act 1988 (c 52), the Road Traffic Offenders Act 1988 (c 53), and the Road Traffic (Consequential Provisions) Act 1988 (c 54). These Acts now form the basis of the provision of the road traffic law.

Since 1930 there has also been a continuous, and very substantial increase in the range of the legislation; the number of topics has expanded dramatically, because of the complexity of all aspects of traffic and transport by road. At the same time there has been a necessary and constant revision of all parts of this legislation. The volume of this legislation, both principal and secondary is now enormous, and a comprehensive treatment of the subject is quite outwith the scope of this book. For such detailed information, the practitioner or student will still have to resort to the voluminous loose-leafed encyclopedias which are regularly updated. In using this book, therefore, it is essential to remember that while every effort has been made to ensure that the contents accurately reflect the position at the time of publication, constant regard has to be given to the continuous process of change in both major and minor areas of the law.

The sources of road traffic law are the principal Acts embodied in the relevant statutes, secondary legislation enacted by means of regulations and orders and introduced by statutory instruments, the regulations of the European Economic Community, and reported case law. Consideration on occasion must also be given, when relevant, to common law duties of care. The bulk of primary and secondary legislation applies to the whole of the United Kingdom but there are significant areas of legislation which apply only to England or parts thereof, and other parts which apply exclusively to Scotland. The directives and regulations of the European Economic Community apply to the whole of the United Kingdom and indeed affect all member states. In terms of the Treaty of Rome, the European Economic Community is committed to the harmonisation of a number of important aspects of road transport law, such as the Construction and Use Regulations, Drivers' Hours and Conditions of Work, and so on. This process is undertaken on a continuing basis. The Minister of Transport has overall statutory responsibility for road traffic matters affecting the whole of the United Kingdom, while in matters exclusive to Scotland, the responsibility rests with the Secretary of State for Scotland.

Of the vast volume of reported case law on the subject in both Scotland and England, on matters common to both, most, though not all, decisions are normally accepted as being applicable and relevant to both jurisdictions. The Scottish and English courts appear to arrive at broadly similar results on similar topics, although the route followed to reach such a common result may radically differ in each jurisdiction. However, it must be remembered that the methods of criminal prosecution and the procedures there involved are fundamentally distinct in Scotland and England, and this can lead to separate or different approaches being taken in certain areas of the common legislation. Further, there are areas where the Scottish and English courts have taken fundamentally different approaches to identical subject matter.

Perhaps the most prominent example of such a difference is the definition given to the word 'reckless' in the two jurisdictions. In *Allan v Paterson* 1980 JC 87, 1980 SLT 77, the Appeal Court in Scotland defined in detail the formula for assessing whether or not a particular course of driving should be regarded as reckless. In the English case of *R v Lawrence (Stephen)* [1981] RTR 217, the English courts contemplated a somewhat different approach to the definition of reckless driving. While in practice it would appear that both definitions lead to approximately the same standards being applied to recklessness in each country, and although the Scottish definition appears to have an advantage in both clarity and logic, both jurisdictions continue to use their own definition in cases under section 1 or 2 of the Road Traffic Act 1972.

Further areas of difference can be found in the treatment of cases involving motorists who are alleged to be 'in charge' of a vehicle in terms of section 6(1)(b) of the 1972 Act. In England it has been held there must be someone 'in charge' of a vehicle unless that 'charge' has been effectively abandoned; in Scotland, the phrase 'in charge' has been restricted to situations where the driver exercises some measure of control over the vehicle (*Crichton v Burrell* 1951 JC 107). Again a person pushing a car along a road from outside the vehicle and controlling the steering wheel through an open window has been held in Scotland to be driving the vehicle within the meaning of section 6 of the 1972 Act (*Ames v McLeod* 1969 JC1); whereas a driver in England, in identical circumstances, was held not to be driving and was thus not convicted of driving whilst disqualified (*R v McDonagh* 1974 [RTR] 372).

Although it is not always safe to assume that reported English cases and the reasoning contained therein will assist in deciding matters at issue in Scotland, English authorities have been quoted to vouch propositions which would appear to apply to Scotland but which have not hitherto been covered by reported Scottish cases. It is interesting to note that a charge to the jury on the influence of automatism contained in *HMA v Ritchie* 1926 SC(J) 45 was endorsed by the Court of Appeal in England in *R v Quick* [1973] 3 All ER 347, but that this defence appears to have been rejected as incompetent in Scotland by *HM Advocate v Cunningham* 1963 SC(J) 80.

In addition to the principal reports of case law such as Session

Cases, Scots Law Times and Scottish Criminal Case Reports, reference will be made to Crown Office Circulars which sometimes report cases not otherwise available. Crown Office Circulars usually contain a brief rubric and the judgments of significant cases heard in the Appeal Court. Where such cases have been subsequently reported in any of the principal volumes of reports, reference will be made to the Crown Office circular for the sake of completeness. It is appreciated that normally only the courts, fiscals and the Crown Office have copies of these circulars, though it is thought that in principal there will be no reason for those who have copies to refuse access to solicitors or others seeking details of a particular case. Furthermore, copies of the circulars may be obtained from the Law Society.

Contents

Table of statutes

Table of cases

Chapter One

Definitions: identification of driver

1.1 GENERAL

The legislation provides a large number of statutory definitions and descriptions of terms used in road traffic law. Some of the most important of these have been considered and interpreted by the courts. Section 185 of the Road Traffic Act 1988 (c 52) provides a series of definitions of the term 'motor vehicle' and other expressions relating to vehicles. Sections 186–191 give a number of supplementary and additional descriptions relating to such vehicles. Section 192 of the Act sets out a number of general interpretations of words and phrases used throughout the Act, and s 194 provides a definition index. Section 11 gives a number of particular interpretations relating to ss 4–10; ss 85 and 86 are respectively an interpretation section and a definition index relative to Part II of the Act (Construction and Use provisions); s 108 is the interpretation section for Part III (Drivers' Licences); s 120 provides similarly for Part IV (HGV Drivers' Licences); and ss 161 and 162 are respectively the interpretation section and definition index for Part VI (Insurance). Further definition sections are found in ss 136–142 of the Road Traffic Regulation Act 1984 (c 27) and regulation 3 of the Road Vehicles (Construction and Use) Regulations 1986, SI 1986/1078. In addition, other words and phrases associated with driving offences have been the subject of judicial interpretation.

A description of some of the more commonly used statutory and other terms now follows. However, while the definition of a particular term will generally suffice for most of the occasions and purposes of its use in different contexts throughout the legislation, there are certain exceptions to this general rule which are indicated as appropriate in the text. In particular, special significance has been additionally applied to some of these terms in relation to the drink-related offences described in ss 4–10 of the Road Traffic Act 1988, and this is discussed in paragraphs 3.3:1 *et seq.*

1.2 MOTOR VEHICLES

1.2:1 General

A motor vehicle is defined in terms of s 185(1) of the Road Traffic Act 1988 as 'a mechanically propelled vehicle intended or adapted for use on the roads'. In other words, the vehicle must be constructed for the purpose of being used on the roads, or alternatively be altered or adapted to make it suitable for that purpose (*French v Champkin* [1920] 1 KB 76). Whether a vehicle has been 'adapted for use on the roads' will depend on the facts and circumstances in each case (*Taylor v Mead* [1961] 1 WLR 435, [1961] 1 All ER 626, a case where a commercial traveller adapted a private car to carry goods). In addition, in terms of the statutory definition it is essential that the vehicle is so constructed that it can be mechanically propelled. This qualification should be interpreted in an ordinary as opposed to a strictly technical sense. The definition may be applicable to a vehicle whether that vehicle is moving under its own power, whether it is capable of so moving, or whether it is temporarily out of order. However, if a vehicle is in such a condition that there are no reasonable prospects of it being mobile again, it is no longer a mechanically propelled vehicle (*Maclean v Hall* 1962 SLT (Sh Ct) 30; *McNeill v Ritchie* 1967 SLT (Sh Ct) 68). Equally a vehicle will not qualify for inclusion in the statutory definition if it has reached 'such a state of mechanical or structural decrepitude' that it would offend against common sense to describe it as a mechanically propelled vehicle (*Tudhope v Every* 1976 JC 42, 1977 SLT 2).

In considering the test to be used in determining whether any particular vehicle falls within this statutory definition, regard should principally be had to the construction of the vehicle rather than the use to which it is put. In *McEachran v Hurst* [1978] RTR 462, a broken down moped was being pedalled along a road; it was held that the vehicle was still a moped rather than a cycle. A vehicle therefore which is plainly not constructed or adapted or intended for use on the roads will not normally fall within this statutory definition. The fact that a vehicle is temporarily broken down or has had its engine removed does not necessarily take the vehicle outwith the statutory definition; even where a vehicle has its source of motor power removed it can still properly be described as being so constructed as to be mechanically propelled (*Newberry v Simmonds* [1961] 2 QB 345, [1961] 2 WLR 675, [1961] 2 All ER 318). But if the evidence demonstrates that essential parts of the vehicle such as the engine or gear box have been permanently removed and are unlikely to be replaced, then such a vehicle may no longer qualify as a motor vehicle in terms of the Act.

However, a further matter that may also have to be taken into account in considering whether a particular vehicle falls within the statutory definition or not is to decide if it can be said, on any reasonable view of the facts and circumstances, that one of the uses for which the vehicle was intended was a use on the public highway (*Burns v Currel* [1963] 2 QB 433; *Nichol v Heath* [1972] RTR 476; *O'Brien v Anderton* [1979] RTR 388). Accordingly, dumper vehicles used solely on building sites for construction work, and which are not in fact used or intended or designed to be used for carrying materials on public roads, will not be classed as motor vehicles (*McDonald v Carmichael* 1941 JC 27, 1941 SLT 8; *McLean v McCabe* 1964 SLT (Sh Ct) 39). This is so even though the vehicles in question could be driven on public roads or converted so that they might be appropriate for such use. The essential feature which excludes such vehicles from the statutory definition is that the vehicles are used solely off the public roads and are intended only for such use. It therefore follows that an agricultural tractor, which may well carry out many of its functions on private land and off the public roadway, but which is constructed and intended to be used for part of the time on the road, would fall within the statutory definition of a motor vehicle (*Woodward v James Young (Contractors) Ltd* 1958 JC 28, 1958 SLT 289).

In defining the term 'motor vehicle' s 185(1) draws specific attention to the special provision made for invalid carriages in terms of the Chronically Sick and Disabled Persons Act 1970 (see paragraph 1.6:8).

1.2:2   Towed vehicles

A motor vehicle does not cease to be classified as such when it is towed by another vehicle (*Cobb v Whorton* [1971] RTR 392). In terms of s 185(1) of the Act, a trailer means a vehicle drawn by a motor vehicle. Any kind of vehicle which is towed is liable to fall within the definition of a trailer; such a vehicle may therefore be at the same time both a motor vehicle and a trailer. Accordingly, the towed vehicle will also require to be covered by insurance, and will be subject to the requirements of the Vehicles (Excise) Act 1971 and the relevant Construction and Use Regulations. This is because the vehicle, although being towed, is still 'used' on the road. Trailers are described in paragraph 1.5:1.

1.2:3 General application

In terms of s 87 of the Road Traffic Act 1988, an appropriate licence is required before any person can drive a motor vehicle of any class on a road, and in terms of s 143 there is a requirement that the use of a motor vehicle on a road should be covered by a policy of insurance or other security. In both those instances it is submitted that the foregoing definition of a motor vehicle should be applied. Further, in terms of the Vehicles (Excise) Act 1971, an excise duty is charged in respect of every 'mechanically propelled vehicle' used or kept on a public road. The phrase 'mechanically propelled vehicles' is not defined in that Act, but it is considered that identical considerations should be applied to that definition as to the definition of the phrase 'motor vehicles' contained in paragraph 1.2:1 and used in other parts of the legislation.

1.2:4 Exceptions

In terms of s 189(1) of the Act, and s 140 of the Road Traffic Regulation Act 1984, certain vehicles such as grass-cutting machines which are controlled by a pedestrian and not capable of being used or adapted for any other purpose, and electrically assisted pedal cycles (see Electrically Assisted Pedal Cycles Regulations 1983, SI 1983/1168)) are not to be considered as motor vehicles. However, this exception would not apply to privately owned grass-mowers with a seat for the driver, which are used on a verge forming part of the road.

A cycle is taken to mean a bicycle, tricycle or cycle having four or more wheels, and is similarly not to be regarded as a motor vehicle (s 192(1); paragraph 1.6:7); neither, as indicated above, is an electrically assisted pedal cycle of such a class as is prescribed by regulations. Offences connected with the riding of cycles on the roadway are found in ss 24, 26 and 28–32 of the Act; reference should be made to paragraphs 2.7 and 2.17. A hovercraft is a motor vehicle whether or not it is adapted or intended for use on the road (s 188 of the Act), but it is not to be regarded as a vehicle of any of the classes as defined in s 185 of the Act.

Within these general guidelines the question of whether any vehicle does or does not come within the statutory definition of a motor vehicle will depend on the facts and circumstances of each case. In addition to the statutory definition of a motor vehicle, there are numerous regulations governing the construction and use of all kinds of such vehicles. The principal regulations in this respect are the Road Vehicles (Construction and Use) Regulations 1984, SI 1984/1078.

1.3   MOTOR CAR

A motor car is defined in terms of s 185(1) of the Road Traffic Act 1988 as–

a mechanically propelled vehicle, not being a motor cycle or an invalid carriage, which is constructed itself to carry a load or passengers and the weight of which unladen – (a) if it is constructed solely for the carriage of passengers and their effects, is adapted to carry not more than seven passengers exclusive of the driver, and is fitted with tyres of such type as specified in regulations made by the Secretary of State, does not exceed 3050 kilogrammes – (b) if it is constructed or adapted for the conveyance of goods or burden of any description, does not exceed 3050 kilogrammes, or 3500 kilogrammes if the vehicle carries a container or containers for holding for the purpose of its propulsion any fuel which is wholly gaseous at 17.5 degrees Celsius under a pressure of 1.013 bar or plant and materials for producing such fuel – (c) does not exceed 2450 kilogrammes in a case falling within neither of the foregoing paragraphs.

A similar definition is provided in s 136(2) of the Road Traffic Regulation Act 1984; and regulation 3 of the Road Vehicles (Construction and Use) Regulations 1984, SI 1984/1078 gives a simpler but essentially identical definition. The significance of the phrase 'mechanically propelled' is discussed in paragraph 1.2:1.

1.4   GOODS VEHICLES

1.4:1   General

A goods vehicle means a motor vehicle constructed or adapted for the carriage of goods, or a trailer so constructed or adapted (Road Traffic Act 1988, s 192(1)). In the Road Vehicles (Construction and Use) Regulations 1986, SI 1986/1078, reg 3(2), the definition is 'a motor vehicle or trailer constructed or adapted for use for the carriage or haulage of goods or burden of any description'.

Whether a vehicle has been constructed for the carriage of goods will normally be self-evident. The question of whether a vehicle has been adapted for such use is a question of fact and degree in each case, and is likely to depend chiefly on the nature of the use to which the vehicle is put in its altered state (*Taylor v Mead* [1961] 1 WLR 435; 1 All ER 626; *Backer v Secretary of State for Environment* [1983] 1 WLR 1485, [1983] 2 All ER 1021).

1.4:2 Goods

The term 'goods' includes goods or burden of any description; and the phrase 'carriage of goods' includes the haulage of goods (Road Traffic Act 1988, s 192(1)). It is not necessary that the goods carried on the vehicle are for sale; the term can include such diverse matters as workmen's equipment and effluent (*Clarke v Cherry* [1953] 1 WLR 268, [1953] 1 All ER 267; and *Sweetway Sanitary Cleaners v Bradley* [1962] 2 QB 108). However, if a vehicle is fitted with a crane, dynamo, welding plant or other special appliance or apparatus which is a permanent or essentially permanent fixture, the appliance or apparatus shall not be deemed to constitute a load, or goods or burden of any description, but shall be deemed to form part of the vehicle (Road Traffic Act 1988, s 186(3)).

1.5 TRAILERS

A trailer is a vehicle drawn by a motor vehicle (Road Traffic Act 1988, s 185(1)). This definition is general and extremely wide and includes virtually anything on wheels which is towed or drawn by a motor vehicle. For example, a poultry shed being moved for sale on wheels drawn by a car will be classified as a trailer (*Garner v Burr* [1951] 1 KB 31), as will a wheeled roadman's hut used as an office and taken onto the road (*Horn v Dobson* 1933 JC 1).

In *Johnston v Cruickshank* 1963 JC 5, 1962 SLT 409, a case under the Lighting Regulations, it was held that where a mechanically propelled vehicle was drawing a trailer, the vehicle doing the towing, and not the composite vehicle, was to be regarded as the motor vehicle in terms of the requirements of the regulations.

For the purpose of driver's hours and records, a trailer is defined as any vehicle designed to be coupled to a motor vehicle or a tractor (Regulation 543/69/EEC).

It is important to note that for the purpose of Driver's Hours and Records of Work (the tachograph legislation) the total weight of a commercial vehicle is to be calculated on the composite weight of both the towing vehicle and the trailer. If this total weight exceeds the statutory minimum (currently fixed at 3.5 tonnes) then the vehicle will require to be fitted with a tachograph, and the driver will be subject to the regulations concerned with the maximum hours which it is permitted to work. Small commercial vehicles below 3.5 tonnes, currently exempt, may therefore fall under these requirements during any periods when a trailer takes the total weight including its load over the statutory minimum (Road Traffic

Act 1988, s 108(1) – definition 'permissible maximum weight'). However, this applies only to cases where the trailer is not a 'small trailer' which is defined in the amended terms of s 60(4) of the Transport Act 1968 as one whose unladen weight does not exceed 1020 kilograms. Such small trailers can therefore be towed without bringing the composite vehicle within the tachograph rules.

A side-car attached to a motor cycle is not normally to be regarded as a trailer.

Regulations 83–93 of the Road Vehicles (Construction and Use) Regulations 1986, SI 1986/1078 supply detailed provisions in respect of trailers and side-cars drawn by various kinds of vehicles.

A semi-trailer is defined as a trailer which is constructed or adapted to form part of an articulated vehicle (and includes a vehicle which is not itself a motor vehicle but which has some or all of its wheels driven by the drawing vehicle – Road Vehicles (Construction and Use) Regulations 1986, reg 3).

Towed vehicles are described further in paragraph 1.2:2.

1.6   VARIOUS VEHICLES

1.6:1   Introduction

Throughout the general legislation there are definitions provided of a variety of sorts of vehicles for different purposes. The principal relevance of these definitions is in licensing, weight limits, and construction and use regulations generally. A general description of some of the most commonly used definitions are as follows:

1.6:2   Articulated vehicles

In terms of s 108(1) of the Road Traffic Act 1988, an articulated goods vehicle means 'a motor vehicle which is so constructed that a trailer designed to carry goods may by partial superimposition be attached thereto in such a manner as to cause a substantial part of the weight of the trailer to be borne by the motor vehicle'. By virtue of the same section, an articulated goods vehicle combination is defined as 'an articulated goods vehicle with a trailer so attached'. The same definition applies for the purposes of Part IV of the Act (s 120). The context in which these definitions are given in the Act is the licensing of drivers. For the purposes of the Road Vehicles (Construction and Use) Regulations 1986, SI 1986/1078 (reg 3) the term defined is an 'articulated vehicle', which is 'a heavy motor car or motor car, not being an articulated bus, with a trailer so attached that part of the trailer is superimposed on the drawing vehicle and, when the trailer is uniformly loaded, not less than 20 per cent of its load is borne by the drawing vehicle'. An articulated goods vehicle, or an articulated vehicle is therefore regarded, when not divided, as two separate vehicles, namely the drawing vehicle (which is either a motor car or a heavy motor car (depending on the individual weight), and the trailer. However, in terms of s 186(2), where a vehicle is so constructed that a trailer may by partial superimposition be attached to the vehicle in such a manner as to cause a substantial part of the trailer to be borne by the vehicle, that vehicle shall be deemed to be a vehicle itself constructed to carry a load. Further provision in the definition of articulated vehicles is found in s 187 of the Act.

As indicated in paragraph 1.5, there are restrictions on the number of trailers that can be drawn by a vehicle and various conditions applicable to their use.

1.6:3 Heavy motor cars

A heavy motor car for the purpose of the Road Traffic Act 1988 means 'a mechanically propelled vehicle, not being a motor car, which is constructed itself to carry a load or passengers and the weight of which unladen exceeds 2540 kg' (s 185(1)); a similar definition is provided for the Road Traffic Regulation Act 1984 (s 136(3)). For the purposes of the Road Vehicles (Construction and Use) Regulations a heavy motor car is defined as 'a mechanically propelled vehicle, not being a locomotive, a motor tractor, or a motor car, which is constructed itself to carry a load or passengers and the weight of which unladen exceeds 2540 kg' (reg 3(2)). Heavy motor vehicles are accordingly the heaviest class of motor vehicle and neither the statute nor the regulations provide an upper limit on their unladen weight. However, other regulations restrict the laden and total weights of such vehicles. The drawing unit of most articulated vehicles is therefore a heavy motor car, except where it does not exceed 2540 kg, when it is simply a motor car.

1.6:4 Commercial vehicles

A heavy commercial vehicle means any goods vehicle which has an operating weight exceeding 7.5 tonnes (Road Traffic Regulation Act 1984, s 138(1), (2), wherein also are described the methods of arriving at the operating weight). A similar definition is given in s 20 of the Road Traffic Act 1988 for the purposes of s 19 of that

Act (prohibition of parking on verges, dangerous positions etc).
See also paragraph 9.12:1.

Goods vehicles generally are described in paragraph 1.4:1, and
the term 'goods' is described in paragraph 1.4:2.

A large goods vehicle is defined in s 71 of the Transport Act 1968
for specific purposes of controlled and authorised use within the
terms of that Act.

A medium-sized goods vehicle means 'a motor vehicle which is
constructed or adapted to carry or to haul goods and is not adapted
to carry more than nine persons inclusive of the driver and the
permissible maximum weight of which exceeds 3.5 but not 7.5
tonnes' (Road Traffic Act 1988, s 108, which also provides a
number of definitions concerned with weight considerations
relating to commercial vehicles).

A small goods vehicle, by virtue of the same section, is 'a motor
vehicle (other than a motor cycle or invalid carriage) which is
constructed or adapted to carry or to haul goods and is not adapted
to carry more than nine persons inclusive of the driver and the
permissible maximum weight of which does not exceed 3.5
tonnes'. As indicated in paragraph 1.5:1, the permissible maximum weight of 3.5 tonnes is to be calculated by including the
weight of any trailer with an unladen weight exceeding 1020
kilograms and its contents drawn by such a vehicle at the relevant
time. This is of particular importance in the drivers' hours of work
and tachograph legislation, which comes into effect when a vehicle
qualifies as a small goods vehicle. Accordingly, a goods vehicle
which is under 3.5 tonnes in weight, and which is not therefore
subject to drivers' hours and tachograph requirements, may
exceed the minimum weight limit when a trailer in excess of 1020
kilograms is added; if this happens then the vehicle must be fitted
with a tachograph, and the driver and owner of the vehicle are
subject to the Drivers' Hours and Record of Work legislation.
'Motor Vehicle' is defined in paragraph 1.2:1.

1.6:5   Passenger and public service vehicles

A passenger vehicle means a vehicle constructed or adapted for use
solely or principally for the carriage of passengers (Road Traffic
Act 1988, s 187(4)). A passenger vehicle is also defined for the
purpose of the Construction and Use Regulations as 'a vehicle
constructed solely for the carriages of passengers and their effects'
(Road Vehicles (Construction and Use) Regulations 1986, SI 1986/
1078 reg 3(2)). For the purposes of Part III of the Road Traffic Act
1988, a small passenger vehicle, in terms of s 108, means 'a motor

vehicle (other than a motor cycle or invalid carriage), which is constructed solely to carry passengers and their effects and is adapted to carry not more than nine persons inclusive of the driver'.

A public service vehicle is defined in s 1 of the Public Passenger Vehicles Act 1981 for the purpose of that Act as 'a motor vehicle (other than a tramcar) which – (a) being a vehicle adapted to carry more than eight passengers, is used for carrying passengers for hire or reward; or (b) being a vehicle not so adapted, is used for carrying passengers for hire or reward at separate fares in the course of a business of carrying passengers'. There are further qualifications of this definition within s 1, and the topic is more fully discussed in paragraphs 9.2:1 *et seq.*

The term 'motor vehicle' is discussed in paragraph 1.2:1.

1.6:6 Motor cycles

A motor cycle is defined as a 'mechanically propelled vehicle, not being an invalid carriage, with less than four wheels and the weight of which unladen does not exceed 410 kg' (Road Traffic Act 1988, s 185(1); Road Vehicles (Construction and Use) Regulations 1986, SI 1986/1078 reg 3(2)). The definition of a motor cycle for these purposes includes a variety of vehicles, including three-wheelers, motor bicycles and mopeds, each of which is governed for various purposes by further legislation.

For the definition of 'mechanically propelled vehicle', see paragraph 1.2:1. Section 23 of the Road Traffic Act 1988 imposes restrictions on the carriage of persons on motor cycles. Regulation 102 of the Road Vehicles (Construction and Use) Regulations 1986, SI 1986/1078 requires that footrests are fitted for any passenger.

1.6:7 Cycles

A cycle is 'a bicycle, tricycle, or cycle having four or more wheels, not being in any case a motor vehicle' (Road Traffic Act 1988, s 192).

The Secretary of State has power to make regulations in respect of brakes, bells, etc on pedal cycles (s 81). Regulations made under the corresponding power in prior legislation, are the Pedal Cycles (Construction and Use) Regulations 1983, SI 1983/1176.

Reference should also be made to the Electrically Assisted Pedal Cycles Regulations 1983, SI 1983/1168. Offences concerned with the riding of cycles are found in ss 24, 26 and 28–32 of the Road

Traffic Act 1988; reference should be made to paragraphs 2.7 and 2.17.

A police officer has the power to stop any person riding a cycle on a road (Road Traffic Act 1988, s 163(2)).

1.6:8   Invalid carriages

An invalid carriage is 'a mechanically propelled vehicle the weight of which unladen does not exceed 254 kg and which is specially designed and constructed, and not merely adapted, for the use of a person suffering from some physical defect or disability and is solely used by such a person' (Road Traffic Act 1988, s 185(1); Road Vehicles (Construction and Use) Regulations 1986, SI 1986/ 1078 reg 3(2)). Special provision for the use of such invalid carriages on the roads is provided by s 20 of the Chronically Sick and Disabled Persons Act 1970; and s 21 of the same Act makes provision for the issuing by local authorities of badges for display on motor vehicles used by disabled persons. Wrongful use of a disabled person's badge is an offence (Road Traffic Regulation Act 1984, s 117). Special parking provisions for the disabled are discussed in paragraph 7.10:1.

For the phrase 'mechanically propelled vehicle', see paragraph 1.2:1.

1.6:9   General

It should be noted in considering the foregoing paragraphs that certain vehicle term definitions are provided for particular purposes such as construction and use regulations, licensing and so on. Care should therefore be taken in considering the context of any definition provided in the legislation. As indicated above, (paragraph 1.1), there are a large number of further statutory definitions of various kinds of vehicles and features relating thereto in the definition sections of the principal Acts and Regulations.

1.7   DRIVERS: DRIVING

1.7:1   General

The courts in Scotland have generally held that the driver of a motor vehicle is someone who is either in the driving seat or in control of the steering wheel, and in addition has something to do with (although not necessarily complete control over) the propulsion of the vehicle.

In *Ames v McLeod* 1969 JC 1, a man steered his car which had run out of petrol down an incline by walking beside it with his hand on the steering wheel, and in these circumstances he was held on appeal to be driving the vehicle at the material time. The Lord Justice General (Clyde) indicated (at page 3) that it was not essential for the purposes of determining whether a person was driving that it is established that the engine was running or that the accused should be sitting in the driving seat. The true test was whether the accused is 'in a substantial sense controlling the movement and direction of the car'; or, in other words, whether the extent of the accused's intervention with the movement and direction of the vehicle was sufficient to establish that he was driving. It should be noted however that in almost identical circumstances an opposite conclusion was reached in England (*R v MacDonagh* (sub nom *MacDonald*) [1974] QB 448, [1974] RTR 372, [1974] 2 All ER 257). *Ames v McLeod* (*supra*) was followed in *Lockhart v Smith* 1979 SLT (Sh Ct) 52; in that case a boy who on instruction from the milkman released the handbrake of a milk float so that it rolled downhill, but who did not touch the steering wheel, was held not to be driving.

Thus it would appear that a person who was merely directing or steering a car being towed by another might have a defence if charged with a moving traffic offence such as 'driving' recklessly or carelessly. This would be on the basis that while the driver of the towed vehicle exercised control over the steering he did not have any measure of control over the propulsion of the vehicle (see *Wallace v Major* [1946] KB 473 at 477, per Goddard LCJ). However, such a person will in ordinary course be convicted of driving whilst disqualified (*McQuaid v Anderton* [1980] 1 WLR 154, (1980) 3 All ER 540, [1980] RTR 371); and presumably also of driving without insurance or a licence. Accordingly, it is submitted that the court might well take the view in most cases that by agreeing to be towed, the driver of a towed vehicle was exercising some measure of control over the propulsion of the vehicle as well as control of the steering, and thus qualify as a driver for most purposes of the road traffic legislation. The case of *Wallace v Major* (*supra*), though not yet over-ruled, has been doubted on a number of occasions.

Whether or not a person is in fact driving at the material time, or is to be regarded as 'the driver' of a vehicle for the purposes of a particular prosecution, will depend on the facts and circumstances of each case, in the context of the particular offence in question. However, it has been decided that it is possible that at any one time, more than one person can fall within the definition of being the driver of the vehicle at that time (*Tyler v Whatmore* [1976] RTR 83). For example, a learner driver and an instructor may well be regarded as both driving at the same time if in practice both have some measure of control over both the steering and the propulsion of the vehicle (*Langman v Valentine* [1952] 2 All ER 803). Further, where a person acts as a steersman of a motor vehicle, the Road Traffic Act 1988, s 192(1) provides that he is to be included in the term 'driver' as well as any other person engaged in the driving of the vehicle. This provision is specifically excluded from applying to prosecutions under s 1 of the Act. However where a driver has been effectively prevented or persuaded from driving his vehicle, he can no longer be regarded as driving (*Edkins v Knowles* [1973] QB 748 at 757, [1973] 2 WLR 977). In *Farrell v Stirling* 1975 SLT (Sh Ct) 71, a case involving careless driving under summary procedure, a diabetic experienced for the first time an attack of hypoglycaemia shortly before an accident, and the court there concluded that he could not be described as driving his vehicle at the material time.

Further definition of the nature of driving in the context of the drink/driving legislation is found in paragraph 3.3:2.

1.7:2   Attempting to drive

The question of whether a motorist is attempting to drive his vehicle is a question of fact. The phrase has its principal significance in offences under ss 4(1) and 5(1) of the Act, and is more fully described in paragraph 3.3:3.

1.8   ROAD

1.8:1   General

The principal definition of the term 'road' is to be found in s 151(1) of the Roads (Scotland) Act 1984 (c 54). A road means 'any way (other that a waterway) over which there is a public right of passage (by whatever means) and includes the road's verge, and any bridge (whether permanent or temporary) over which, or tunnel through which the road passes and any reference to a road includes a part thereof'. This definition is applied to all relevant prior legislation, by Schedule 9 of the 1984 Act, and s 192(2) of the Road Traffic Act 1988 adopts the same definition. In general terms, the Roads (Scotland) Act 1984 makes a number of important provisions relating to the use of roads. A footway which is either separate or attached to a carriageway is part of a road (s 151(2)). A lay-by is also normally to be regarded as part of the road (*MacNeill v Dunbar* 1965 SLT (Notes) 79).

The definition makes it clear that the road need not necessarily be a public road. The question will be determined according to the facts and circumstances of each case and the nature of the offence, but the test normally applied is whether there is public access to the road. Thus in *MacNeill v Dunbar* 1965 (*supra*) a car parked contiguous to a service road was held to be parked on a public road. In *Harrison v Hill* 1932 JC 13, 1931 SLT 598, a road which formed the access from a public highway to a farm and which led only to the farmhouse, was not maintained by the local authority but by the farm tenant and serviced no other vehicle, but was used by the public as an access to the farm and sometimes for a place to walk was held to be a public road. In that case Lord Sands (at p 17) provided a definition which has subsequently often been applied in both Scotland and England: 'In my view, any road may be regarded as a road to which the public have access (and) upon which members of the public are to be found who have not obtained access either by overcoming a physical obstruction or in defiance of prohibition express or implied.' In *Hogg v Nicholson* 1968 SLT 265 a road which was marked 'Private Road', and which was not on the list of public highways but was entirely contained within an estate, was also held to be a road because, although it was used mainly by the inhabitants of the estate, other members of the public, such as the police and delivery vans, did have access to the road. In *Purves v Muir* 1948 JC 122, 1948 SLT 529, however, an area where the public did have limited access was held in all the circumstances not to be a public road. In *Henderson v Bernard* 1955 SLT (Sh Ct) 27, a courtyard to which access could be obtained by two entrances from the public road was held again in the circumstances not to be a road within the meaning of the [1930] Act. These last two authorities may now be doubtful in view of the current statutory definition. In *Davidson v Adair* 1934 JC 37, 1934 SLT 316, the drive to a private house was held to be a road, but this view was doubted by Lord Guthrie in *Hogg v Nicholson* (*supra*) at p 268.

Section 33 of the Road Traffic Act 1988 provides controls on the use of motor vehicle trials on footpaths and bridleways, and s 34 prohibits the driving of motor vehicles elsewhere than on roads, subject to certain exceptions (see also paragraph 2.4).

1.8:2 Other public place

In the drink and driving legislation, offences may take place on a road 'or other public place'. The phrase 'other public place' means a place to which the public may resort by express or implied permission, and to which they have access. This topic is more fully discussed in paragraph 3.3:5.

1.9   ACCIDENT

Whether or not an accident has occurred will depend on the facts and circumstances of each case. A satisfactory definition of the word is not easy to provide, having regard to the variety of circumstances under which what might be described as an accident can occur. No definition of the term appears anywhere in the legislation, and the courts have not been anxious to provide a general or all-purpose definition of the word, preferring normally to draw conclusions from the circumstances of each case. It has been suggested that an appropriate test might be to consider whether an ordinary man who witnessed what happened would say that in all the circumstances there had been an accident. It is however clear that an accident can arise out of a deliberate act, and need not involve another vehicle.

The matter was considered by the Appeal Court in *Pryde v Brown* 1982 SLT 314, 1982 SCCR 26, 1982 CO Circulars A/5, where two pedestrians walking on a main road were obliged to take evasive action when a vehicle came round a bend at speed on the wrong side of the road. In holding that this had been an 'accident', the Appeal Court said:

'We do not think that any precise definition of the word "accident" . . . can be formulated. We do not think that any of the tests adumbrated in the cases referred to are wholly satisfactory in every circumstance. We do not think that only unintended occurrences can be included in the word "accident", as the word may obviously include occurrences which may have been intended. We do not think it can be limited to untoward occurrences having an adverse physical result, because it is possible to visualise an "accident" having no adverse physical result at all. It seems to us to be more appropriate to proceed on the basis that it will depend on the circumstances of each case whether a happening can properly be described as an "accident". The test is one of common sense rather than conformity with a definition difficult to formulate and providing an exhaustive cover.'

The circumstances in which an accident can be said to have occurred are therefore wide and general. Incidents where a vehicle has been required to take avoiding action as a result of the conduct of another vehicle, where an obstruction, or object as opposed to another vehicle or person has been struck, or where something has happened as a result of the way a vehicle is being driven completely outwith the awareness of the driver, may all be termed as accidents. Section 170 of the Road Traffic Act 1988 envisages that an accident has occurred if injury is caused to any other party or damage is caused to any other vehicle, to specified animals or to any property constructed on, fixed to, growing in or otherwise forming part of the land on which the road is situated or land adjacent thereto. The *de minimis* rule would seem to have very little relevance, if any, in the interpretation of the word.

The question of whether or not an accident has taken place may be of particular importance *inter alia* in prosecutions under the breathalyser legislation (Road Traffic Act 1988, s 6(2)); in charges of failing to stop after an accident (s 170); and in respect of prosecution restrictions in terms of s 2(1) of the Road Traffic Offenders Act 1988. The duty on a driver to stop after an accident is discussed in paragraph 7:6.3.

1.10   USING, CAUSING AND PERMITTING

1.10:1   General

Throughout the legislation there are a number of offences which are committed when an accused person uses a vehicle, or causes or permits a vehicle to be used, in a particular way. The terms 'use' or 'using', 'causing' and 'permitting' have always to be considered in the context in which they are employed; however, certain general observations may be made on these terms.

1.10:2   Using

The most common offences involving use are those which contravene s 143 of the Road Traffic Act 1988 (compulsory insurance), s 87 of the same Act, (licensing of drivers) or the use of vehicles in a manner contrary to many of the Road Vehicle (Construction and Use) Regulations 1986, SI 1986/1078. An offence involving use as opposed to causing or permitting normally involves strict liability and the question of *mens rea* is irrelevant. The word has been interpreted in a wide sense, and for example convictions for using a car without insurance are commonplace where the only use made of the vehicle is to park it on the street. Even if a vehicle is broken down and unable to move by its own power, it will be regarded as being used on the road for the purpose of s 143. Driving involves the use of a vehicle.

A vehicle being towed will also be regarded as being used for all relevant purposes of the legislation (*Cobb v Whorton* [1971] RTR 392). A corporate entity may be guilty of an offence involving use of a vehicle, and because most of such offences carry absolute liability, the employer of a driver who drives or uses a vehicle which contravenes the construction and use regulations may well be guilty of an offence even although the employer had no direct or personal knowledge of the defect which caused the offence (*Swan v MacNab* 1977 JC 57, 1978 SLT 192, 1978 CO Circulars A/13). The word 'use' can also mean 'have the use of' and two people may therefore be using a vehicle at the same time (*Dickson v Valentine* 1989 SLT 19, 1988 SCCR 325, 1988 CO Circulars A/21).

However, the nature of 'use' has been qualified in certain circumstances. In *Hamilton v Blair and Meechan* 1962 JC 31, 1962 SLT 69, it was held that an owner of a vehicle who had hired it out for an excursion to a third party (who was to supply the driver) was not 'using' the vehicle at the material time, nor was the hirer 'using' the vehicle at a time when she was not within the vehicle. In the latter instance, Lord Carmont (at p 76) indicated that the hirer, although not using the vehicle, may have been causing or permitting its use. In *Valentine v MacBrayne Haulage Ltd* 1986 SCCR 692 (a sheriff court case) it was held that where a statute penalised both using and causing or permitting use of a vehicle, the category of 'user' should be confined to the driver of the vehicle and his employer at the material time, and should not be extended further. The report usefully considers the principal authorities on the term 'using'.

Whether a vehicle is being 'used' or not may depend upon the particular offence in question. Thus in *Tudhope v Every* 1976 JC 42, 1977 SLT 2 it was held that a vehicle which was immobile and parked on a road was being used in terms of s 143 of the Road Traffic Act 1972 (which required vehicles used on a road to be covered by insurance), but was not being used on a road in terms of s 44(1) of the same Act (which requires vehicles used on a road to be covered by a MOT Certificate).

The reason for this differing treatment of the same word is that the meaning of the term 'use' contemplated in the two sections of the Act, and the nature of the prohibition involved in each case, is different. A parked car, even when immobile, may cause or be involved in an accident; therefore it must be insured. However, the MOT Certificate is designed to cover other areas of use which an immobile vehicle could not perform, and accordingly such a vehicle is not being used for that purpose.

Nothing in the Road Traffic Acts authorises a person to use on a road a vehicle so constructed or used as to cause a nuisance, or affects the liability, under statute or common law of the driver or owner (Road Traffic (Consequential Provisions) Act 1988, s 7).

1.10:3 Causing or permitting

'Causing' and 'permitting' are two separate ideas. In practice their meanings may overlap. Corporate entities may be guilty of causing or permitting. The principal application of the terms is again in the Road Traffic Act 1988, s 87 (licensing of drivers), and s 143 (compulsory insurance) and in the Construction and Use Regulations.

The two words are used, normally together, in slightly different ways and contexts throughout the legislation, and consideration has to be given to the particular nature of the offence in each case. For general purposes, the term 'causing' involves some measure of direction or control by the accused towards or over a third party in a matter where the accused has the proper capacity to make such a direction or exercise such control. The most common example of 'causing' in practice is where an employer instructs an employee to drive the employer's vehicle.

For an accused to be convicted of causing a third party to commit an offence, the prosecution will normally have to establish both that the accused directed or controlled the substantive acts complained of, and that he was aware or should have been aware that those acts constituted an offence. This is notwithstanding that most of the offences in which the terms are used involved strict liability.

In *Smith of Madiston Ltd v Macnab* 1975 JC 48, 1975 SLT 86, 1975 CO Circulars 21 February 1975, a limited company was charged with using, or causing or permitting to be used, a vehicle with an insecure load. The company had hired out to a third party a vehicle and a driver to transport a load. The driver, who was experienced in such matters, elected to secure the load in an ineffective manner although he had been supplied with suitable securing material. The Appeal Court (overruling *Hunter v Clark* 1956 JC 59) held that the company could not be guilty of the offence as it neither knew nor should have known of the contravention of the relevant regulations, and could not therefore be said to have caused or permitted the use complained of.

In *Macdonald v Wilmae Concrete Co Ltd* 1954 SLT (Sh Ct) 33, it was held that a company was not guilty of causing or permitting a vehicle to be used with a defective brake in circumstances where it was not proved that any responsible official of the company knew of the defect. In particular, it was held to be insufficient for a conviction, simply to show that the company took no action or event that this system of inspection was not perfect. However, in *Brown v Burns Tractors Ltd* 1986 SCCR 146, it was held (following *Smith of Madiston Ltd v Macnab supra*) that knowledge, in relation to a statutory provision includes 'the state of mind of a man who shuts his eyes to the obvious and allows another to do something in circumstances where a contravention is likely, not caring whether a contravention takes place or not'. In other words, wilful blindness, or culpable ignorance, in respect of the relevant statutory provisions on the part of an accused in a charge of causing or permitting is not a defence. In this context, reference may also be made to *Clydebank Co-operative Society v Binnie* 1937 JC 17, 1937 SLT 114; *Mackay Bros v Gibb* 1969 JC 26, 1969 SLT 216; and *Farrell v Moggach* 1976 SLT (Sh Ct) 8.

Permitting means simply giving permission, or allowing a third party to do something. The permission must however be proved to be something which the accused can properly give. In addition, for conviction it must be shown, as in the case of 'causing' (*supra*), that the accused was aware that what was permitted constituted an offence. The same general considerations that apply to 'causing' described in the foregoing paragraph apply also to 'permitting'.

It is competent and common practice for accused persons or corporate entities to be charged with 'using' and 'causing or permitting' as alternatives.

1.11 IDENTIFICATION OF DRIVER

1.11:1 General

Except in some limited cases where there is specific statutory exemption, corroborative evidence of the identity of the driver of a vehicle is required for the purposes of prosecution of road traffic offences (*Mitchell v MacDonald* 1959 SLT (Notes) 74; *Sinclair v MacLeod* 1964 SLT (Notes) 60).

Accordingly if the only evidence of identification is two police officers who speak to an admission by the driver that he was driving at the material time, this is insufficient for conviction (*Sinclair v McLeod* (*supra*).

A car driver will not be considered in normal circumstances to be a person in a special capacity in terms of s 312(x) of the Criminal Procedure (Scotland) Act 1975 (*Cruickshanks v MacPhail* 1988 SCCR 165); however, an accused charged with driving while disqualified by reason of age will be regarded as being in such a special capacity and so in those circumstances the need for corroborative evidence does not arise (*Smith v Allan* 1985 SLT 565, 1985 SCCR 190, 1986 CO Circulars A/8).

An admission by a driver, made to a police officer or any other person, that he was driving at the time of alleged offence can be sufficient evidence of identification if the surrounding facts and circumstances confirm that identification (*Copeland v Shields* 1959 SLT (Sh Ct) 50; *Sinclair v Clark* 1962 JC 57 (per Lord Justice Clerk Thomson at 62, 1962 SLT 307; *Lockhart v Crockett* 1987 SLT 551, 1986 SCCR 685; see also *White v MacDonald* 1964 SCCR Supp 5; *Douglas v Pirie* 1975 at 61, 1975 SLT 206; *Miln v Fitzgerald* 1978 SCCR Supp 205, 1978 CO Circulars A/9; *McDonald v Smith* 1978 SCCR Supp 219; *MacNab v Culligan* 1978 SCCR Supp 222; 1978 CO Circulars A/26, *Lodhi v Skeen* 1978 SCCR Supp 197; *Wright v Tudhope* 1983 SCCR 403; *Cummings v Tudhope* 1985 SCCR 125; *Tudhope v Dalgleish* 1986 SCCR 559; *McClure v McLeod* 1987 SCCR 274; *MacLennan v Macdonald* 1988 SCCR 133; and *Cruickshanks v MacPhail* 1988 SCCR 165).

A statement made in reply to a caution, or a caution and charge, if properly administered by a police officer, is competent evidence both as to the identity of the driver and of any other relevant matters included in the statement.

1.11:2 Statement made in response to a question

At common law, an admission by an accused that he was the driver at the time of an alleged offence in response to a question from a police officer may be admissible in evidence (*Miln v Cullen* 1967 JC 21, 1967 SLT 35). The test as to whether such an answer is admissible or not is to be determined having regard, in all the circumstances, to the principle of fairness to the accused. In considering that test, regard must be given to the accused's circumstances and position, and also to the public interest in ascertaining the true facts of each case, and the detection of offences. If, having regard to all these matters, it is decided that the request for information imposes unfairness on the accused, the evidence will generally be inadmissible. Equally, if no unfairness is caused to the accused, the evidence will be allowed.

1.11:3 Duty to give information to police

In terms of s 172(2) of the Road Traffic Act 1988, where a driver of a vehicle is alleged to be guilty of any road traffic offence (apart from certain exceptions listed within the section), the keeper of the vehicle or any other person may be required by a police officer to give information as to the identity of the driver at the material time. The phrase 'any other person' includes the alleged driver himself (*Foster v Farrell* 1963 JC 46, 1963 SLT 182, overruling *Stewart v McLugash* (1962) 78 Sh Ct Rep 189). An admission by the driver under this sub-section is admissible in evidence (*Foster v Farrell* (*supra*) and as in the case of other forms of admission, can satisfy the test of corroborative evidence if there is supporting evidence from another credible source (*Galt v Goodsir* 1982 JC 4, 1982 SLT 94, 1981 SCCR 225, 1981 CO Circulars A/34). This and other duties to provide information are described in paragraph 2.6 and chapter 7.

Chapter Two

Reckless and careless driving

PART 1
RECKLESS DRIVING

2.1 RECKLESS DRIVING

Section 1 of the Road Traffic Act 1988 (c 52) provides that it is an offence to cause the death of another person by driving a motor vehicle on a road recklessly. Section 2 of the Act makes it an offence to drive recklessly. Section 1 therefore creates a specific and separate offence if death results from such driving. The term 'recklessly' has exactly the same meaning in both ss 1 and 2. Charges under s 1, however, must be taken on indictment; s 2 cases may be taken on summary complaint. Servants of the Crown are not exempted from prosecution under either section, or in respect of other driving offences (Road Traffic Act 1988, s 183).

The statutory offence of causing death by dangerous or reckless driving was introduced by the Road Traffic Act 1960 (c 16). Prior to 1960, the only method open for the prosecution of proceedings against a motorist where death resulted from the driving of a vehicle, was to charge him with culpable homicide. However, in many such cases, juries were disinclined to return with such a verdict, and a statutory alternative was therefore introduced. The offence of causing death by dangerous or reckless driving again appeared in the Road Traffic Act 1972 (c 20), s 1; the word 'dangerous' was deleted from the statutory definitions of ss 1 and 2 of the 1972 Act by the Criminal Law Act 1977, s 50(1). Cases prior to this amendment which relied on evidence of 'dangerous driving' are now of limited value in considering current charges.

2.2 CULPABLE HOMICIDE AND SECTION 1

2.2:1 Procedure and penalties

It is, however, still open to the Crown to bring charges of culpable homicide against a motorist rather than to undertake a prosecution under s 1. This procedure is normally adopted only in the most serious cases. It is submitted that the standard of driving to be considered on a charge of culpable homicide should nonetheless be for all practical purposes identical to the standard to be applied in the statutory charge. A charge of culpable homicide is taken on indictment. The penalties available to the court where culpable homicide is committed by the driver of a motor vehicle include obligatory disqualification and endorsement of the offending driver's licence (Road Traffic Offenders Act 1988, Schedule 2, Part II). Similarly, obligatory disqualification and endorsement follow a conviction under s 1 of the Act in terms of Part I of Schedule 2 of the Road Traffic Offenders Act 1988, which also allows for a sentence of up to five years' imprisonment. A statutory offence under s 2 of the Act can be charged as an alternative to culpable homicide (or to a charge under s 1) and this is normally done. In any event, a jury is specifically entitled to bring in such alternative verdicts (Road Traffic Offenders Act 1988, s 23(1), (2)).

2.2:2 Warning or notice of intended prosecution

In respect of such an alternative conviction in terms of s 2 of the Road Traffic Act 1988 to a charge of culpable homicide, it should be noted that the provisions of s 1 of the Road Traffic Offenders Act 1988 do not apply, (see s 2(5) of that Act). The provisions of that section, which require either that a police officer warns the accused at the time that the offence was committed that a prosecution may follow, or alternatively, that within 14 days of the incident a notice of intended prosecution should be served on the accused, are pre-requisites of any prosecution under s 2 (though not of s 1) of the Road Traffic Act 1988, and of the other offences specified in Schedule 1 to the Road Traffic Offenders Act 1988. The requirement in such cases for either a prosecution warning or the service of a complaint must be strictly observed; a verbal warning must be given at the time (*Cuthbert v Hollis* 1958 SLT (Sh Ct) 51) and the warning must be clear and specific (*Watt v Smith* 1942 JC 109, 1943 SLT 101). However, s 1(3) of the Road Traffic Offenders Act 1988 affords a presumption that the requirements have been observed in every case until the contrary is proved, and s 2(1) provides exemption from the general requirements in the cases of offences involving accidents. Further, s 2(3) provides that failure to observe the conditions set out in s 1(1) will not bar conviction where the accused cannot be traced despite the exercise of reasonable diligence or where the accused himself contributes to the failure.

Any fatal accident inquiry into the circumstances of an incident which subsequently gives rise to a prosecution under ss 1 or 2 of the Act, normally takes place after any criminal proceedings have been concluded.

2.3   SECTION 1 OF THE 1988 ACT

2.3:1   Proof

Section 1 of the Road Traffic Act 1988 provides:
'A person who causes the death of another person by driving a motor vehicle on a road recklessly shall be guilty of an offence'.

For a conviction against a motorist under s 1 of the 1988 Act, the Crown must prove that the driving complained of was (i) reckless; (ii) that it was a cause of the death of some other person (who may be a passenger in the car driven by the accused or indeed any other category of person); and (iii) that the driving took place in a 'motor vehicle' and on a 'road'.

2.3:2   Definitions

Driving:– see paragraph 1.7:1. The definition section of the Road Traffic Act 1988 (s 192) specifically excludes from s 1 prosecutions the extended provision of which includes a steersman in the category of driver, and which otherwise applies for the purpose of the statute.

Reckless driving: What constitutes 'reckless driving' was fully and definitively described in the case of *Allan v Patterson* 1980 JC 57, 1980 SLT 77, 1979 CO Circulars A/20. This definition is now regularly used by sheriffs, it would appear, in all cases of reckless driving, either considering for themselves the proper tests to be applied in considering the quality of the driving in question, and by judges in charging juries.

The full definition given by the Lord Justice General in the Appeal Court is as follows:

'Section 2 [of 1972 Act] as its language plainly, we think, suggests, requires a judgment to be made quite objectively of a particular course of driving in proved circumstances, and what the court or a jury has to decide using its common sense, is whether the course of driving in these circumstances had the grave quality or recklessness. Judges and juries will readily understand, and juries might well be reminded, that before they can apply the adverb "recklessly" to the driving in question they must find that it fell far below the standard of driving expected of the competent and careful driver and that it occurred either in the face of obvious and material dangers which were or should have been observed, appreciated or guarded against, or in circumstances which showed a complete disregard for any potential dangers which might result from the way in which the vehicle was being driven. It will be understood that in reaching a decision upon the critical issue a judge or jury will be entitled to have regard to any explanation offered by the accused driver designed to show that his driving in the particular circumstances did not possess the quality of recklessness at the material time'.

The court also approved the description of reckless driving submitted by the Crown. In the Crown's submission, reckless driving meant

'a piece of driving which, judged objectively, is eloquent of a high degree of negligence – much more than a mere want of due care and attention – and supports the inference that material risks were deliberately courted or that these risks which ought to have been obvious to any observant and careful drivers were not noticed by reason of gross inattention. Driving "recklessly", accordingly, is driving which demonstrates a gross degree of carelessness in the face of evident dangers'.

It is plain from the decision of the Appeal Court that reckless driving is not confined to driving which has been embarked upon wilfully or deliberately in the face of known risks of a material kind. Driving which occurs in circumstances where there are potential dangers, which are only liable to arise, can nonetheless be described as 'reckless'. Further, an examination of the state of knowledge of a driver charged with reckless driving, or of his intentions at the material time, is not relevant. Similarly, the particular skill, capacity or ability of the driver in question is not to be considered. In other words, the tests applied to the driving under consideration, must be regarded objectively in the context of the proved circumstances of the driving; and must relate purely to the quality of the driving in fact.

It should also be observed that the Appeal Court in *Allan v Patterson (supra)* made it clear that it was not prepared to follow the somewhat different approach to reckless driving which has been adopted in England, and which can be found in the subsequent cases of *R v Colville* [1981] 2 WLR 509, and *R v Lawrence (Stephen)* [1982] AC 510, [1981] RTR 217. Reference should also be made to paragraphs 2.3:4, 2.3:5 and 2.3:6.

Causes the Death: For a conviction for reckless driving under s 1, it must also be demonstrated that the death resulted from the driving complained of. The course of driving need not necessarily be the only or indeed the principal cause of the resulting death. Unless the cause or connection between the driving and death is '*de minimis*' a motorist can be convicted under this section if the driving is shown to be one of several causes which result in the death of the victim (*R v Hennigan* [1971] 3 All ER 133; *Watson v HM Advocate* 1978 SCCR Supp 192.) In *McCluskey v HM Advocate* 1989 SLT 175, 1988 SCCR 629, a driver who caused injuries to an unborn child which died as a result shortly after birth, was convicted under this section. In cases where there is some doubt, the alternative of a charge in terms of s 2 or even s 3 may be added.

Motor Vehicle: – see paragraph 1.2:1.

Road: – see paragraph 1.8:1.

2.3:3 Evidence

Is it competent to introduce evidence in the prosecution of a charge of culpable homicide that the motorist had consumed alcohol or drugs such as would be liable to affect adversely his ability to drive. In *McKie v HM Advocate* 1958 JC 24, 1958 SLT 152, an accused driver was charged, after an accident, with driving while unfit through drink. Subsequently it was discovered that another person had died as a result of the accident. The driver was charged with culpable homicide and at his trial, evidence of a medical examination in relation to the drunk driving charge was held admissible. In *Burrell v Hunter* 1956 SLT (Sh Ct) 75, it was held to be competent for a motorist to be charged with dangerous driving whilst suffering 'from a nervous disorder aggravated by the consumption of alcohol'. If such evidence of previous alcohol consumption is adduced, then it must be for the purpose of demonstrating that the consumption of alcohol affected or was liable to affect the driving complained of, or that it was in the circumstances a reasonable inference that the consumption of alcohol had adversely affected the driving. It is of course competent to charge a motorist with further offences in an indictment containing a charge under s 1 or s 2. Additional charges, such as driving a motor vehicle when under the influence of alcohol or with an alcohol concentration above the prescribed limit in terms of ss 4 or 5 of the Act, can, and regularly are, added to such indictments where appropriate. It is submitted that notwithstanding the rule of evidence in the cases of *McKie v HM Advocate* and *Burrell v Hunter* (*supra*), it is proper practice for the prosecution to libel such additional offences if reliance is to be placed on the consumption of alcohol in securing convictions under s 1 or 2 prosecutions.

Amendment of the locus of a charge by the Crown may be allowed at the discretion of the court (*Craig v Keane* 1981 SCCR 166; *Brown v McLeod* 1986 SCCR 615 CO Circulars A/58).

2.3:4 Section 2: Reckless driving

Section 2 of the 1988 Act provides:
'A person who drives a motor vehicle on a road recklessly shall be guilty of an offence'.

In terms of the Act, reckless driving is an offence by itself where no fatality occurs. Precisely the same standard and considerations apply in determining whether or not a particular course of driving should be described as reckless as apply in the cases brought under s 1. A charge under s 2 of the Act may be brought either under solemn or summary procedure, at the option of the Crown. The particular nature of the driving complained of as being reckless need not be specified in the charge although it is of course necessary to give sufficient details of the time and place of the alleged offence (*Todrick v Dennelar* 1904 7 F 8, (1904) SLT 573; see also *Watkin v HM Advocate* 1989 SLT 24, 1988 CO Circulars A/23). Careless driving may be and often is charged as an alternative to reckless driving on the same indictment or complaint. In terms of Part I of Schedule 2 to the Road Traffic Offenders Act 1988, disqualification following conviction under s 2 of the Act is obligatory only if the offence has been committed within three years of a previous conviction under ss 1 or 2. Endorsement is obligatory, and on conviction and in the absence of disqualification, penalty points must be imposed on the accused's licence in terms of Schedule 2, Part I, Column 7.

Whether or not driving in a particular case is to be regarded as reckless will of course depend upon the facts and circumstances that are proved to have prevailed in each case. However, it is not essential for a successful prosecution under this section that there should have been a collision involving another vehicle, or indeed an accident of any sort. Each case will depend on its own facts and all the aspects of the driving complained of require to be considered.

Reckless driving may be inferred from a given set of facts and circumstances where, for example, a vehicle behaves in an abnormal fashion without any explanation for that behaviour being proved.

As in cases under s 1, the matter has to be considered objectively, and the ability or state of mind of the motorist is not a relevant consideration. Driving which can properly be described as reckless as defined in the case of *Allan v Patterson (supra)* is not likely to arise from a momentary lack of attention, or a simple error of judgment. Similarly, the intentions of the driver are irrelevant. A test sometimes applied in these circumstances is for the judge or jury to satisfy themselves on the evidence as to what in fact took place, and then put themselves in the position of a bystander and from that viewpoint consider whether the driving proved to have taken place can properly be characterised as reckless in terms of the definitions found in *Allan v Patterson* (paragraph 2.3:2). Evidence of driving earlier in the course of a particular journey, prior to the conduct complained of in the indictment or complaint, may be admissible. However, it is considered good practice for the prosecutor to give full notice by way of the description of the *locus* where all of the driving complained of took place.

2.3:5   Highway Code

The most readily recognisable tests of reckless driving may be found within the provision of the Highway Code. Section 38(7) of the Road Traffic Act 1988 provides in effect that failure to observe the Highway Code may tend to establish liability for reckless driving; however, in terms of the subsection, a violation of any of the provisions of the Highway Code does not necessarily mean that the driver should be prosecuted. Clearly, therefore, a judge or jury in considering reckless driving, may competently have regard to the provisions of the Highway Code in determining whether or not a particular course of driving was reckless (see for example *McCrone v Normand* 1989 SLT 332), but equally the fact that a driver has failed to observe a particular rule in the Highway Code does not necessarily mean that he should be convicted. The Highway Code is published by Her Majesty's Stationery Office and some of the relevant provisions are reproduced in Appendix A.

2.3:6   Speed in reckless driving

Excessive speed may be the single most important constituent of a charge of reckless driving, but if so, it must occur in circumstances which allow the driving to be described as reckless. In *Frame v Lockhart* 1985 SLT 367, 1984 SCCR 377, 1984 CO Circulars A/31, a driver was travelling at 50 mph on an esplanade where the speed limit was 15 mph. Although there was no other traffic either vehicular or pedestrian on the esplanade at the material time, the circumstances were such that a large number of pedestrians were in the immediate area and were liable to pass over the esplanade. It was held that having regard to all the material facts, the speed at which the vehicle was being driven could properly be described as reckless. However, this was a majority decision of the Appeal Court and Lord Robertson's dissenting judgment is worthy of consideration for the contrary view.

Frame v Lockhart (*supra*) was followed in *O'Toole v McDougal* 1986 SCCR 56, 1986 CO Circulars A/16. In that case, a motorist drove for more than 11 miles on the A74 just before midnight at speeds between 100 and 120 mph, the speed limit for that part of the road being 70 mph. The road in question is a dual carriageway with many junctions and gaps in the central reservation and is used by pedestrians and vehicular traffic. While there was no evidence of any actual danger or inconvenience to any other road user, it was held that, in the circumstances, the driver showed a complete disregard for any potential dangers which might have arisen, and that accordingly the speed was so excessive that a conviction for reckless driving was justified. In delivering the opinion of the Appeal Court, the Lord Justice General (Emslie) (at p 59) said:

'If consideration is given to the time at which this chase took place in the hours of darkness, if consideration is given to the character of the roadway and the dangers presented by its particular features of construction which the sheriff has described, if attention is given to the fact that the road was carrying lorry traffic and motor traffic, it appears to us that the sheriff was entitled and indeed well entitled to conclude that anyone who drives on that stretch of road in the face of the potential dangers which it obviously carried at a speed of between 100 and 120 mph is driving recklessly, however skilful he may be in controlling the vehicle at whose wheel he sits. In our judgment the sheriff was perfectly right to be satisfied – not only entitled to be satisfied but we think right to be satisfied – beyond reasonable doubt that in all the circumstances in the findings in fact which are eloquent of potential danger, the appellant's speed was so excessive that it would be regarded as a piece of reckless driving as a whole'.

This case is therefore authority for emphasising that the material risks referred to in the case of *Allan v Patterson* (*supra*) which have to be observed, appreciated and guarded against are not confined to dangers which actually arise during the course of journey complained of, but include also potential dangers which are likely to or liable to arise.

In *Deans v Skinner* 1981 SCCR 49, a driver who had neither a licence nor insurance was driving at an excessive speed. He was pursued by a police car and panicked, going through a red light without being aware of doing so, and passed vehicles halted at traffic lights on the inside. This was considered to be a narrow case, but the driving was judged to be reckless.

2.3:7   Jurisdiction

In *R v Robert Millar (Contractors) Ltd* [1970] 2 QB 54, [1970] 2 WLR 541, [1970] 1 All ER 577, a lorry was driven in England with a defective tyre, and the driver and the company who employed him and who owned the vehicle, were both aware of the defect. An accident was caused by the defective tyre, and the court in England concluded that not only was the driver therefore guilty of dangerous driving, but that the directors of the company, which was situated in Scotland, were equally liable.

2.3:8   General

For other cases under ss 1 and 2 see *Watson v HM Advocate* 1978 SCCR Supp 192, *Earnshaw v HM Advocate* 1982 JC 11, 1982 SLT 179, 1981 SCCR 279, 1981 CO Circulars A/31; *Campbell v Johnston* 1981 SCCR 179; *Connorton v Annan* 1981 SCCR 307; *Cooper v HM Advocate* 1982 SCCR 87.

2.4   COMMON LAW

At common law the reckless or furious driving of a vehicle (or the riding of a cycle) is an offence only if it occurs to the danger of lieges (*Quinn v Cunningham* 1956 JC 22, 1956 SLT 55). This is a charge sometimes brought by the Crown where it cannot be proved that the driving took place on 'a road'; if the driving complained of does not have the quality of recklessness, the Crown may have recourse to s 34 of the Road Traffic Act 1988.

2.5   DEFENCES

In the case of *Allan v Patterson (supra)* it was emphasised that in reaching any decision on whether a particular course of driving should or should not be described as reckless, the judge or jury is entitled to have regard 'to any explanation offered by the accused driver designed to show that his driving in the particular circumstances did not possess the quality of recklessness at the material time'.

For a special defence, under solemn procedure in a case of reckless driving, to the effect that the motorist was not responsible for his actions, the test is that such a claim must amount to establishing insanity in the legal context. Thus it is not a competent defence to a charge of this kind for the motorist to claim that at the material time he was suffering from some temporary condition due to an epileptic fit or other pathological condition (*HM Advocate v Cunningham* 1963 JC 80, 1963 SLT 345). This case would appear to rule out a special defence of automatism in solemn procedure in Scotland. Such a defence may be available in England (*R v Quick* [1973] QB 910, [1973] 3 All ER 347; see also *Hill v Baxter* [1958] IQB 277, [1958] 2 WLR 76, [1958] 1 All ER 193); but the only reported case under solemn procedure in Scotland where such a defence has been considered as relevant was *HM Advocate v Ritchie* 1926 JC 45, which was specifically over-ruled by the case of *HM Advocate v Cunningham* (*supra*).

In summary procedure, the defence of automatism was considered but held not to be established in *Stevenson v Beatson* 1965 SLT (Sh Ct) 11. In *Farrell v Stirling* 1975 SLT (Sh Ct) 71, a diabetic who went into a state of hypoglycaemia (never having experienced such a condition in the past) just before an accident was held by the court not to be 'driving' and thus not guilty of careless driving. It is submitted that such a defence could not have succeeded if the accused had had previous experience of the condition and appreciated that it was liable to affect him while he was driving.

It may be possible to put forward a defence of mechanical defect, provided that it is shown that the way in which the vehicle was driven at the material time was due to a complete and unexpected loss of control as a result of some mechanical failure which was not caused in any way by the fault of the motorist. It is therefore considered that such a defence would be unlikely to succeed if the motorist knew or perhaps should have known by the exercise of reasonable diligence, that the fault existed (*R v Spurge* [1961] 2 QB 205, [1961] 3 WLR 23, [1961] 2 All ER 688; *R v Robert Millar Contractors* [1970] 2 QB 54, [1970] 2 WLR 541, [1970] 1 All ER 577.)

Whether a defence of necessity is available in cases of reckless driving was discussed, but not wholly resolved in *McNab v Guild* 1989 SCCR 138, 1989 CO Circulars A/4.

2.6   DUTY TO GIVE NAME

Any driver of a motor vehicle who is alleged to have been guilty of reckless driving in terms of ss 2 or 3 of the Road Traffic Act 1988 is obliged to give his name and address to any person having reasonable grounds for requiring this information (s 168). A failure to provide such information by the driver is an offence, and such a failure will make him liable to arrest without warrant by a police officer who considers that he has committed an offence of reckless or careless driving. See also paragraph 1.11:3 (duty of driver or keeper of a vehicle to give information). Such a request by the police for information if made in good faith, does not have to be accompanied by an allegation that an offence has taken place (*McMahon v Cardle* 1988 SCCR 556, 1988 CO Circulars A/42; see also *Galt v Goodsir* 1982 JC 4, 1982 SLT 94, 1981 SCCR 225, 1981 CO Circulars A/34 and *Duncan v McGillivray* 1989 SLT 48, 1988 CO Circulars A/41). Reference should also be made to paragraph 1.11:3.

2.7   RECKLESS CYCLING

It is an offence to ride a cycle recklessly on a road (Road Traffic Act 1988, s 28). The term 'recklessly' has the same meaning as in s 2 of the Act (paragraph 2.3:2). The word 'cycle' is defined in paragraph 1.6:7, and the word 'road' is defined in paragraph 1.8:1. Sections 167 and 168 of the Act apply in respect of such charges.

2.8   ART AND PART: AIDING AND ABETTING

That the accused in any case may be guilty either as principal actor or art and part is implied in all charges brought in Scotland whether on indictment or by means of summary complaint (Criminal Procedure (Scotland) Act 1975, ss 216 and 248). Any accused found guilty art and part is liable to the same penalties as the principal actor. However, it has been suggested that all members of a gang in a getaway car may not be guilty art and part of all of the offences committed by the driver in attempting to make good his escape (*Webster v Wishart* 1955 SLT 243).

The offence of aiding and abetting provided by s 176 of the Road Traffic Act 1972 is not repeated in the current legislation, presumably because it is considered to be unnecessary. What constituted the idea of aiding and abetting was discussed in *Valentine v Mackie* 1980 SLT (Sh Ct) 122, and *Manion v Smith* 1989 SLT 69.

2.9 CORPORATE LIABILITY

In *R v Robert Millar Contractors* [1970] 2 QB 54, [1970] 2 WLR 541, [1970] 1 All ER 577, a lorry was driven in England with a defective tyre. The driver and the company who employed him and who owned the vehicle were aware of the defect. An accident was caused by the defective tyre, and a court in England concluded that not only was the driver therefore guilty of dangerous driving but that the directors of the company, which was situated in Scotland, were equally liable.

PART 2
CARELESS DRIVING

2.10 CARELESS AND INCONSIDERATE DRIVING: SECTION 3

2.10:1 General

Section 3 of the Road Traffic Act 1988 provides:

'If a person drives a motor vehicle on a road without due care and attention or without reasonable consideration for other persons using the road, he shall be guilty of an offence.

Section 3 prosecutions are undertaken summarily; penalties on conviction are again found in Schedule 2, Part I of the Road Traffic Offenders Act 1988.

Section 3 provides for two quite separate descriptions of driving either of which, if proved against the motorist, constitute the offence. In the first place it is an offence for a motorist to drive a car on the road without due care and attention; secondly, it is also an offence for a motorist to drive a vehicle on a road without reasonable consideration for other persons using the road. A particular course of driving could conceivably contravene both aspects of the section. The scope of both aspects of this section is extremely wide.

2.10:2 Definitions

Driving. See paragraph 1.7:1.

Motor Vehicle. See paragraph 1.2:1.

Road. See paragraph 1.8:1.

Due care and attention: A formal definition of these words is not appropriate and has not been attempted by the courts. The question of whether a driver in any particular case has driven without due care and attention is invariably a matter of fact. Also, the circumstances which can produce such driving are virtually unlimited in nature. The words are therefore to be construed in their ordinary and everyday sense, having regard to the test described in paragraph 2.10:3 (*infra*).

Reasonable consideration: Similarly, no formal definition can be given for this phrase; the words must be considered in their normal sense having regard to the test described in paragraph 2.10:3 (*infra*).

Other persons using the road: This includes passengers in the accused's vehicle: *Pawley v Wharldall* [1966] 1 QB 373.

2.10:3   Character of offence: test to be applied

A description of the kind of situations in which careless or inconsiderate driving may arise would be virtually unlimited. For example, driving without due care and attention may arise out of simple acts of carelessness or failure to pay sufficient attention in the circumstances, a lack of judgment, momentary inattention or lack of concentration, or a simple mistake, up to and including all cases of extremely bad or objectionable driving which do not attain the high standard required for a charge of reckless driving.

Typical cases of driving without reasonable consideration for other persons using the road may include (among a wide variety of examples which might be given) the driving of a vehicle too close to the driver in front thus causing the preceding driver to be distracted, lose concentration and be liable to make driving errors; driving with full beam headlights at night, dazzling and inconveniencing oncoming drivers; driving needlessly in the outside lane of a motorway or dual carriageway, or overtaking in the inside lane, thus inconveniencing other road users; or even driving deliberately at high speed through pools of water causing pedestrians to be splashed with water. It does not appear to have been established in Scotland whether the prosecution is required to prove that actual inconvenience was caused to other road users, or whether such inconvenience was merely liable to occur. In England, it has been held that actual inconvenience must result (*Dilkes v Bowman Shaw* [1981] RTR 4). It is submitted that this authority might not be followed in Scotland.

The test to be applied in all cases is whether the particular course of driving proved in the circumstances, demonstrates that the driver was or was not exercising the degree of care, skill and attention which the reasonable, competent and prudent driver could be reasonably expected to show in the circumstances. The same general approach is applied whether the driver is alleged to have driven without due care and attention or without reasonable consideration for other persons using the road. The test as to whether a particular course of driving contravenes this section of the Act therefore involves the application of an objective and fixed standard, which means that the same requirements are imposed on all drivers irrespective of their status, capacity and experience. For example, no distinction is drawn, for the purpose of this section, between a learner driver and a qualified driver (*McCrone v Riding* [1938] 1 All ER 157). Driving carelessly, or without reasonable consideration for others may arise whether the driving complained of was deliberate or unintentional. It is not necessary for there to have been a collision between two vehicles, or contact between a vehicle and some other person or thing for careless driving to be established; charges may be brought where, for example, the conduct of the accused on the road requires another motorist or road user to take evasive or emergency action. Equally the fact that two vehicles have been in collision does not necessarily mean that either or both have been guilty of careless driving. Also, driving deliberately embarked upon to harass or intimidate other motorists or road users may found a contravention of the section.

2.11 CHARGES

In a charge of dangerous driving under the previous legislation, it was held to be competent for the prosecution to allege that the motorist had committed the offence while suffering from a nervous disorder aggravated by the consumption of alcohol (*Burrell v Hunter* 1956 SLT (Sh Ct) 75). However, in a case of careless driving, it is not competent to include in the complaint a reference to the effect that the victim has been killed as a result of the driving complained of (*McCallum v Hamilton* 1986 SLT 156, 1985 SCCR 368, 1985 CO Circulars A/28). In *Sharp v HM Advocate* 1987 SCCR 179, the Appeal Court said it was wrong for a sheriff to take into account the fatal consequences of a piece of careless driving in considering sentence. There is no limit to the number of charges which may be included in a complaint, as long as these charges represent distinct and different offences and each can individually be proved on the evidence (*Archibald v Keiller* 1931 JC 34, 1931 SLT 560; *Harris v Adair* 1947 JC 116, 1947 SLT 356).

No complaint should contain any charge which reveals that the accused has been disqualified by a court order or has any previous convictions (Criminal Procedure (Scotland) Act 1975, s 356(1)). A necessary and solitary exception to this rule is made only in charges of driving or obtaining a licence while disqualified in terms of s 103 of the Road Traffic Act 1988 (see for example *Moffat v Smith* 1983 SCCR 392, 1983 CO Circular A/25).

2.12   EVIDENCE: GENERAL RULES

Each case of driving carelessly or without consideration for other road users depends ultimately on its own facts and circumstances. However, there are a number of reported decisions which afford some general assistance by illustrating general rules. Some of these decisions are civil cases.

A driver who makes a signal for a manoeuvre which may lead to another person on the road observing and acting upon that signal may be under a duty to see that his signal has been appreciated and understood by that other person (*Sorrie v Robertson* 1944 JC 95, 1944 SLT 332). A motorist who signals to turn and then drives straight on and collides with another vehicle which had relied on that signal may be guilty of careless driving in respect that the other driver was entitled to rely on his false signal (*Another v Probert* [1968] Crim LR 564). A driver who follows another driver on the road is bound, in so far as is reasonably practicable, to adopt a position on the road and to drive in such a fashion that will allow him to deal successfully with all traffic exigencies reasonably to be anticipated, particularly in relation to the vehicle in front (*Brown & Lynn v Western SMT* Ltd 1945 SC 31). If a driver turns right into the path of an overtaking car, the test to be applied is whether he ought to have seen the overtaking vehicle (*Millar v Dean* 1976 SCCR Supp 134). Where a vehicle has skidded, this is not necessarily by itself evidence of carelessness on the part of the driver; however, the skid may well be a factor which has to be considered in all the circumstances of the case (*McGregor v Dundee Corpn* 1962 SC 15; *Thomson v Brankin* 1968 SLT (Sh Ct) 2). However, in circumstances where a vehicle went off a stretch of road, then travelled for 120 feet along the road side verge and thereafter collided with a rock face, it was held, on appeal, that there was on the face of such objective facts, evidence of faulty driving (*Pagan v Fergusson* 1976 SLT (Notes) 44; see also *Ryrie v Campbell* 1964 JC 33). There is no general rule of law to the effect that a driver requires to drive at night at a speed that will enable him to stop within the limit of vision supplied by his headlights (*Morris v Luton Corpn* 1946 KB 114).

If the evidence establishes that traffic lights are showing green in one direction then the court is entitled, in the absence of any contrary evidence, to assume that the traffic lights showing the other way are at red (*Pacitti v Copeland* 1963 SLT (Notes) 52). There may be circumstances where the driver on a major road may have to take into account the conduct of the driver on a minor road, if the conduct of the latter indicates that he is about to drive his vehicle in such a manner as will affect the driving of the vehicle on the main road, and the driver on the main road has reasonable opportunity to accommodate such interference (*Ramage v Hardie* 1968 SLT (Notes) 54). This case is of particular interest in this area because in the course of his opinion Lord Robertson considered in detail a number of earlier authorities on the respective duties of drivers on major and minor roads.

Where a driver drove off on his lorry despite the fact that children were playing thereon, he was found guilty of careless driving although not of reckless driving (*McDonald v Thomson* (1954) 70 Sh Ct Rep 288). Again, where the driver of a large articulated vehicle reversed slowly along a road without assistance, using only his mirrors, in an area where he was aware children were playing, and ran over one of the children, he was found guilty of careless driving because he had reversed without having clear vision to the rear, or assistance to allow him to reverse safely. This decision was reached notwithstanding that the lorry was showing a variety of lights, including hazard lights (*Farquhar v McKinnon* 1986 SCCR 524, 1986 CO Circulars A/49; followed in *McCrone v Normand* 1988 SCCR 551). The ordinary tests which apply to all cases of careless driving apply to a police officer answering an emergency call (*Wood v Richards* [1977] RTR 201; *Marshall v Osmond* [1983] 2 QB 1034, [1983] 2 All ER 225). The same considerations apply to the driver of an ambulance or others engaged in emergency work (*R v Lundt-Smith* [1964] 2 QB 167, [1964] 2 WLR 1063; [1964] 3 All ER 255).

It is not necessary in any charge under s 3 that a collision should have occurred as result of the way in which the offending vehicle has been driven. Moreover, the fact that there has been a collision between the two vehicles does not thereby imply that one of them is necessarily guilty of an offence of careless driving. However, it must be remembered that the facts and circumstances surrounding any particular course of driving may justify the inference that an offence under s 3 has been committed. Further, even where there are no eye-witnesses, the facts surrounding an incident may entitle the court to conclude that careless driving has taken place (*Ryrie v Campbell* 1964 JC 33; *Pagan v Fergusson* 1976 SLT (Notes) 44).

For other cases of careless driving for general purposes see *King v Cardle* 1981 SCCR 22; *Sigourney v Douglas* 1981 SCCR 302; *Holmes v Stewart* 1983 SCCR 446; *Dunlop v Allan* 1984 SCCR 329; *Melville v Lockhart* 1985 SCCR 242.

2.13   HIGHWAY CODE

As in the case of reckless driving, one of the most easily recognised tests of whether the driving in any particular case has been careless can be ascertained by reference to the provisions of the Highway Code. Section 38 of the Road Traffic Act 1988 provides that failure to observe the Highway Code may tend to establish liability for careless driving (see for example *McCrone v Normand* 1989 SLT 332). Equally, as in the case of reckless driving, the fact that the motorist has violated any of the provisions of the Highway Code does not necessarily mean that he should be prosecuted, and if he is prosecuted does not necessarily mean that he should be convicted.

The Highway Code is published by Her Majesty's Stationery Office, and some of the relevant provisions are reproduced in Appendix A.

2.14   COMMON LAW

At common law, the reckless or furious driving of a vehicle (or the riding of a cycle) is an offence only if it occurs to the danger of lieges (*Quinn v Cunningham* 1956 JC 22, 1956 SLT 55). This is a particularly useful charge for the Crown where it cannot be proved that the driving occurred on a 'road'.

Offences affecting or relating to traffic on the public roads are not confined to statutory offences. In *MacPhail v Clark* 1983 SLT (Sh Ct) 37, a farmer was charged at common law with culpable negligence and causing danger to the lieges by recklessly endangering the safety and lives of the occupants of two vehicles travelling on a road next to his farm. The accused had set fire to a quantity of straw, causing thick smoke to drift across the road so that the drivers of the two vehicles, whose vision was obscured, collided. It was held that this was a relevant charge and the accused was convicted and fined.

2.15   DEFENCES

As in the case of offences under ss 1 and 2 of the Act, the court must always take into account, in assessing whether or not the driving complained of was careless, any explanation tendered by the driver or any other person.

Defences are sometimes raised on the ground that the accused driver was confronted by an untoward incident or unforeseen emergency. Examples of such incidents are that the accused was dazzled by the headlights of an oncoming vehicle, was confronted suddenly by some vehicle, person or object which unexpectedly came into his path, or was stung by a wasp. As in the case of convictions, all such defences depend for their success on a consideration of all the material facts and circumstances. It is submitted that such defences can only succeed when it is shown that the unforeseen circumstances deprived the driver of control or vision and led directly to the accident or other consequences of the driving. Even if it is shown that some sudden or unexpected emergency occurred, the driver still has a duty thereafter, in so far as is reasonably practicable, to drive his vehicle with reasonable care; such emergencies will not necessarily excuse all further driving actions on the part of the driver. Further, it is submitted that an unforeseen emergency brought about by the driver's own negligence, such as carelessly dropping a lighted cigarette into his lap, or stepping on the accelerator rather than the brake, will render a defence of unforeseen emergency extremely difficult to establish. Any contribution to the unforeseen emergency by the accused will therefore proportionately reduce the effectiveness of any such defence. However, where a motorist has been placed in a position of emergency or difficulty through circumstances outwith his control, he may be able to argue in his defence that the standard of driving reasonably expected of him in the circumstances is lower than would normally be the case (*Johnston v National Coal Board* 1960 SLT (Notes) 84). Reference should also be made to the paragraph on defences to charges of reckless driving (paragraph 2.5:1) which are also relevant to charges of careless or inconsiderate driving.

2.16 DUTY TO GIVE NAME

Where there is an allegation that the driver of a motor car has driven recklessly or carelessly, the motorist is required by any person who has reasonable grounds for so requiring, to provide his full name and address (Road Traffic Act 1988, s 168). If a police officer considers that a driver has committed a contravention of s 3 of the Act, he may arrest that person without warrant unless the driver gives his name and address or produces his driving licence (s 167). See also paragraph 1.11:3 (duty of driver or keeper of vehicle to give information.)

2.17   CARELESS CYCLING

It is an offence to drive a cycle on a road carelessly or without reasonable consideration for other persons using the road (Road Traffic Act 1988, s 29). The terms 'without due care and attention' and 'without reasonable consideration for other persons using the road' have the same meaning as in motor vehicle offences (paragraphs 2.10:2 and 2.10:3). The word 'cycle' is defined in paragraph 1.6:7, and the word 'road' is defined in paragraph 1.8:1. Sections 167 and 168 apply in respect of such charges (see paragraph 2.16).

Chapter Three

Drink related offences

(**Road Traffic Act 1988, ss 4, 5**)

PART 1
INTRODUCTION AND SPECIAL DEFINITIONS

3.1 INTRODUCTION

Sections 4 to 11 of the Road Traffic Act 1988 deal with drinking and driving offences. These sections have generated a considerable number of reported cases and this area of law in particular, is constantly being considered and revised. A practitioner must keep abreast of all such developments by constant reference to the reports which contain road traffic material. Drinking and driving offences are among the most numerous of contested cases dealt with in the sheriff court, and are usually regarded as the most important and contentious of road traffic matters.

3.2 GENERAL

3.2:1 General scheme

It is helpful to have a general overall view of these seven important sections. Section 4 makes it an offence to drive or attempt to drive, or to be in charge, of a motor vehicle on a road or in a public place while unfit to drive through drink or drugs. In s 4 prosecutions there does not have to be any specimen taken for analysis from the motorist, although such specimens may properly be required during the police investigation of such a case. An offence under this section occurs simply if, in the judgment of others formed at the relevant time, the driver's ability to drive properly is for the time being impaired. It is not therefore necessary for conviction, to establish the precise level of alcohol in the accused driver. Section 5 makes it an offence for a person to drive or attempt to drive, or to be in charge of, a motor vehicle on a road or other public place after consuming so much alcohol that the proportion in his breath, blood or urine exceeds the prescribed limit. This offence is therefore established following the taking of such specimens from the driver. Section 6 of the Act makes general provision for breath samples to be required of drivers by a police officer as a preliminary step to further procedure. This is the process commonly known as the breathalyser or roadside test. This test must be carefully distinguished from the breath specimen supplied by the motorist to determine the level of alcohol in his body for the purposes of s 5 and in terms of s 7. Section 7 of the Act provides in detail for the provision of specimens of breath, blood or urine for analysis in the course of an investigation as to whether a person has committed an offence under ss 4 or 5. Section 8 provides that the lower of the two specimens given is to be used, and if that lower specimen contains not more than 50 microgrammes of alcohol in 100 millilitres of blood then the motorist may require that it be replaced by a specimen taken in terms of s 7(4). Section 9 contains special provisions for hospital patients in respect of the tests that may be required under ss 6 and 7. Section 10 allows the police to detain any person required to give a specimen of breath or blood or urine, at a police station until it appears that such a person would no longer be contravening ss 4 or 5. Section 11 is an interpretation section relating to s 4–10.

In addition, ss 15 and 16 of the Road Traffic Offenders Act 1988 (which replace s 10 of the Road Traffic Act 1972) contain significant evidential considerations relating to prosecutions under ss 4 and 5 of the Road Traffic Act 1988.

3.2:2   General procedure

It is still envisaged that the first step in normal circumstances will be the requirement by a constable for a motorist to take the preliminary breath test. This is sometimes known as the roadside test, and is carried out by the motorist blowing into an Alcotest, Alcolmeter or similar device. Thereafter the Act envisages that the principal method of procedure (other than in cases under s 4) will be the provision of a breath specimen for analysis by an accused driver. A blood or urine specimen can only be required if for whatever reason a reliable breath analysis device is not available, or if the lower of the two breath specimens given is below 50 microgrammes of alcohol in 100 millilitres. The current legislation places little emphasis on procedural, technical or formal requirements which were the subject of many reported decisions under previous law. In particular, it must be emphasised that the provision of a positive breath test in terms of s 6 and the arrest of the accused driver is not now a prerequisite before a specimen of blood, breath or urine may be required for the purpose of establishing whether an offence has been committed in terms of ss 4 or 5.

3.3   SPECIAL DEFINITIONS

3.3:1   Introduction

Sections 4(1) and 5(1)(a) of the Act contemplate an offence where a person drives or attempts to drive a motor vehicle on a road or other public place. Sections 4(2) and 5(1)(b) of the Act provide that an offence may occur if a person is in charge of a motor vehicle which is on a road or other public place. The definition chapter (chapter 1) provides general descriptions of the various terms used in ss 4 and 5, but in addition, for the purpose of these drink driving offences, special consideration has to be given to the words and phrases 'drives', 'attempts to drive', 'in charge of a motor vehicle' and 'road or other public place'.

3.3:2 'Drives'

The reported cases in recent years dealing with the question of whether a person is or is not driving in the context of prosecutions under ss 4 and 5 or their historical equivalents, have been concerned principally with three particular issues; firstly, whether in the proven circumstances of the case, a motorist was driving or not; secondly whether the motorist was driving as opposed to being in charge of the vehicle; and thirdly whether a driver in the circumstances was to be regarded as still driving his vehicle or whether his driving had come to an end.

On the first question as to whether a person is to be held as driving a vehicle as opposed to not driving it, the position for all practical purposes is as outlined in the definition chapter under the heading 'Drivers and Driving' (see paragraph 1.7:1). This means that a person will generally be held to be the driver of a vehicle if he is in the driving seat or in control of the steering wheel, and in addition has some measure of control over the propulsion of the vehicle (*Ames v McLeod* 1969 JC 1). More than one person may be driving the vehicle at a particular time (*Tyler v Whatmore* [1976] RTR 83; *Langman v Valentine* [1952] 2 All ER 803; Road Traffic Act 1988, s 192(1).) In England, it had been held that a steersman of a vehicle being towed by another was not driving (*Wallace v Major* [1946] KB 473); subsequently however, it has been further held that in such circumstances the steersman could be properly convicted of driving whilst disqualified (*Caise v Wright* [1981] RTR 49). It is submitted that the steersman of a towed vehicle in Scotland could properly be charged in terms of ss 4 or 5 of the Act on the view that there was control over the steering of the vehicle and the steersman had voluntarily accepted the propulsion of the vehicle from the principal driver.

It has also been held in England that to pedal a moped is driving, even although the engine was not operating or operational (*Floyd v Bush* [1953] 1 WLR 242, [1953] 1 All ER 265; *R v Tahsin* [1970] RTR 88); the moped did not cease to be a motor vehicle merely because there was or might have been a temporary loss of engine power.

The second category of cases involving drinking and driving in which the nature of the driving has been in issue, is concerned with whether the motorist was at the material time driving as opposed to being in charge. This distinction is not quite so significant as it was formerly. Under earlier legislation, a police constable had no power to require a roadside breathalyser test of a driver who was in charge of his vehicle rather than driving it. However, the current terms of s 6 of the Road Traffic Act 1988 (which repeats the terms of s 7 of the Road Traffic Act 1972 as amended by s 25(3) and Sch 8 of the Transport Act 1981 and introduced by virtue of the Transport Act 1981 Commencement Order 1983, SI 1983/576 on 6 May 1983) allows a police constable to require a driver to provide a roadside breathalyser test if he is in charge of a vehicle and the constable has reasonable cause to suspect that he has alcohol in his body or has committed a moving traffic offence. Accordingly, the significance chiefly attaching to the distinction between driving and being in charge of a vehicle prior to 6 May 1983 no longer applies. However, a complaint may libel an offence in terms of ss 4 or 5 in the alternative; that is to say, the driver may be charged with driving or alternatively being in charge of a vehicle in contravention of either of these sections. Having regard to the difference in penalties that may be imposed in respect of these alternatives, the distinction between driving and being in charge of a vehicle will remain of importance. Accordingly, reference should be made to paragraphs 1.7:1 and this paragraph for consideration of the nature of driving, and reference should be made to paragraph 3.3:4 (*infra*) for consideration of what is involved in being in charge. There appears as yet to be no Scottish authority dealing specifically with the distinction between driving and being in charge; the matter is generally one of fact which will be determined by the circumstances in each particular case.

The third question involving the nature of driving which the courts have considered in the past was whether a driver in the proven circumstances of the case was to be considered as still in the course of his journey and therefore driving his vehicle or whether his driving was to be regarded as having come to an end. Under previous legislation, the roadside breathalyser test could only be required of a motorist by a police constable if the constable had reasonable cause to suspect that the motorist had alcohol in his body while the vehicle was in motion and before the motorist had completed his journey. This issue was at the centre of a large number of cases decided between 1972 and 1983 (for example

Edkins v Knowles [1973] 1 QB 748, [1973] 2 WLR 977; *Ritchie v Pirie* 1972 JC 7, 1972 SLT 2). Apart from the question of whether there is reasonable cause for suspicion, these cases now have only marginal relevance, if any, because of the current terms of s 6(1)(b) and (c) of the Act. As indicated above, this section repeats the terms of the previous s 7 which came into force on 6 May 1983. In terms of s 6(1)(b), a breath test may be required of a person who 'has been driving or attempting to drive or been in charge of a motor vehicle on a road or other public place', and in terms of s 6(1)(c) where 'a person has been driving or attempting to drive or been in charge of a motor vehicle on the road or other public place and has committed a traffic offence whilst the vehicle was in motion'. It is therefore clear from the terms of the sub-sections that the question of whether a police officer makes the requirement for a breath test while the motorist is still engaged on his journey or whether he has completed his journey and is no longer driving, is now entirely academic. The section was specifically framed to exclude the defence, available to a driver before 1983, that he had completed his journey, and therefore could not thereafter be suspected of having alcohol in his body and thus be required to take a breath test. To underline this, the current legislation imposes no time limit of any kind on the right of a police constable in appropriate circumstances to require a roadside breathalyser specimen.

3.3:3 Attempting to drive

In terms of both ss 5(1) and 6(1) of the Act, it is a separate offence to attempt to drive a motor vehicle while affected by drink or drugs. It would appear to be the intention of the Act that this offence should cover the position when the vehicle is not in motion. The question of whether a motorist is attempting to drive at the material time is one of fact. In this context, the meaning of the word 'drive' has exactly the same meaning as in driving as described in the preceding paragraph. In assessing the proven facts in any case, regard will be had principally to the actions of the driver, and where appropriate, to his intentions expressed or implied. Thus, even where a car is *de facto* incapable of being driven through mechanical defect, anyone attempting to drive such a vehicle may be convicted under these subsections (*R v Farrance* [1978] RTR 225). Again, someone attempting to start a car with the wrong key is attempting to drive that vehicle (*Kelly v Hogan* [1982] RTR 352); the fact that the attempt failed because of ineptitude, inefficiency or insufficient means does not mean that the attempt to drive was not made.

Anyone who has been effectively stopped or dissuaded from driving cannot be considered as still being within the category of persons driving a vehicle (*Edkins v Knowles* [1973] QB 748 at 757, [1973] 2 WLR 977), or, it is submitted, of persons attempting to drive a vehicle.

3.3:4 'In charge'

Sections 4(2) and 5(1)(b) provide that offences occur when a motorist having consumed alcohol, is 'in charge' of, as opposed to driving, or attempting to drive, his vehicle. Being in charge of a vehicle therefore only arises before driving has started or after it has ceased. In *Crichton v Burrell* 1951 JC 107, 1951 SLT 365, a motorist who was standing beside his vehicle with the keys in his possession waiting for an employee to come and drive the vehicle, was held to be not in charge. The Appeal Court in that case held that to be 'in charge' meant that the motorist must be in some measure in *de facto* control of the vehicle. The circumstances of that case would therefore appear to indicate that by standing outwith the vehicle and making arrangements for another to drive, the accused had effectively surrendered control of the vehicle. In such a case, the statutory defence provided by s 4(3) would also now be available to the motorist.

The English courts have taken a fundamentally different approach to the idea of being 'in charge' of a vehicle; there, the view is taken that some person must be in charge of a vehicle unless that vehicle has been completely abandoned. It follows from this that a person remains in charge of a vehicle until he surrenders control thereof to some other person. Accordingly, the motorist in *Crichton v Burrell* (*supra*) would have been convicted in England. It is not thought that such an approach will be followed in Scotland; the large number of English cases on the subject are likely to be of little value.

The following are some examples of Scottish decisions: the supervisor of a learner driver has been held to be in charge of a vehicle (*Clark v Clark* 1940 SLT (Sh Ct) 68); a driver sitting in his vehicle (a taxi) which had broken down and was waiting for another vehicle to tow him away was held to be in charge (*MacDonald v Crawford* 1952 SLT (Sh Ct) 92); a mechanic repairing a broken down vehicle by the roadside was held not to be in charge of the vehicle (*Adair v McKenna* 1951 SLT (Sh Ct) 40). A person who was unconscious in the back of the vehicle which had been made mechanically incapable of being driven was held not to be in charge of the vehicle (*Dean v Wishart* 1952 JC 9, 1952 SLT 86). The owner of a vehicle who was sitting in the passenger seat at a time when the vehicle's engine was running and the person in the driver's seat was unlicensed, was held not to be in charge of the vehicle (*Winter v Morrison* 1954 JC 7). A driver who left his vehicle and gave a friend the keys to drive the car home was deemed not to be in charge of his vehicle (*Farrell v Campbell* 1959 SLT (Sh Ct) 43, (1959) 75 Sh Ct Rep 24). Reference may also be made to *MacDonald v Bain* 1954 SLT (Sh Ct) 30; *McDonald v Kubirdas* 1955 SLT (Sh Ct) 50; *MacDonald v MacDonald* (1955) 71 Sh Ct Rep 17; and *Thaw v Segar* 1962 SLT (Sh Ct) 63. It is not a coincidence, however, that all of these authorities pre-date the amended terms of the Road Traffic Act 1972. Although these cases are still relevant, the extended powers now available to the police to require breath tests in terms of s 6 means that the occasions when being in charge of a vehicle is of significance will become less frequent.

3.3:5 'Road or other public place'

This description clearly includes, but is significantly wider than, the definition of the term 'road' given in the definition chapter and applicable to the rest of the general legislation. A road may include a place where there is not a public right of way, but there is access for the public. The term 'public place' is in general a place which is not a road within the definition of s 151(1) of the Roads (Scotland) Act 1984, but can include a place to which the public may resort by express or implied permission, and to which they have access. For example, a field used as a car park at the Highland Show was held to be a public place (*Paterson v Ogilvy* 1957 JC 42, 1957 SLT 354). Similarly, a spare piece of ground used as an overflow parking area in a cattle mart was held to be a public place (*McDonald v McEwen* 1953 SLT (Sh Ct) 26). However, the prosecution may have to prove that the public do have the right to resort to a particular area (*Elkins v Cartlidge* [1947] 1 All ER 829; *Pugh v Knipe* [1972] RTR 286). A driveway from a public road to a hotel may be a public place even where the proprietors of the hotel reserved the right to exclude certain members of the public (*Dunn v Keane* 1976 JC 39). A lay-by or car park at the side of a road may be part of the road (*MacNeill v Dunbar* 1965 SLT (Notes) 79). In *Brown v Braid* 1985 SLT 37, 1984 SCCR 286, 1984 CO Circulars A/22, a motorist was discovered by police attempting to manoeuvre his vehicle off a low wall which separated a garage forecourt from an adjacent pavement. The motorist was initially acquitted on the ground that the garage forecourt was not a public place, in that other motorists would be unlikely to use the forecourt at that time. On appeal, however, it was held that the wrong test of what constituted a public place had been applied; the proper test was 'whether the forecourt was a place on which members of the public might be expected to be found and over which they might be expected to be passing, or over which they are in use to have access' (opinion of the court at p 38).

PART 2

DRIVING OR BEING IN CHARGE OF A MOTOR VEHICLE WHEN UNDER THE INFLUENCE OF DRINK OR DRUGS – SECTION 4

3.4 SECTION 4(1)

3.4:1 Introduction

Section 4(1) of the Road Traffic Act 1988 provides:

A person who, when driving or attempting to drive a motor vehicle on a road or other public place, is unfit to drive through drink or drugs shall be guilty of an offence.

This section is generally used in cases where for a variety of reasons it is not possible to determine the proportion of alcohol present in the motorist by reference to the analysis of specimens of breath, blood or urine. It may be that the accused is so drunk that he is incapable of being subjected to the various statutory procedures, or that such procedures for whatever reason cannot appropriately be carried out in the circumstances. There is a tendency also for prosecutors to use this section in respect of an accused who appears in custody and who wishes to plead guilty; such a charge can be prepared without first having an analyst's report on specimens which may have been provided. All prosecutions where the motorist is under the influence of drugs must be taken under s 4; s 5 makes no provision for driving while affected by drugs. Prosecutions under s 4 are normally taken under the summary procedure. The penalties following conviction are found in Schedule 2 of the Road Traffic Offenders Act 1988.

3.4:2 Definitions – general

'*Driving or attempting to drive*': see paragraphs 1.7:1, 3.3:2 and 3.3:3.

'*Unfit to drive*': see paragraph 3.5:1.

'*Motor vehicle*': see paragraphs 1.2:1 *et seq.*

'*Road or other public place*': see paragraphs 1.8:1, 1.8:2 and 3.3:5.

3.4:3 Special definitions: drink and drugs

In a prosecution under s 4, the issue is whether the motorist is unfit to drive through drink or drugs, as distinct from s 5 cases where the issue is whether the motorist exceeds the prescribed limits of alcohol in his breath, blood or urine. Although there is no definition of the word anywhere in the legislation, it has never been disputed that the word 'drink' means an alcoholic drink (see *Armstrong v Clark* [1957] 2 QB 391 at 394 per Lord Justice-Clerk Goddard). The question of what constitutes a drug is also not comprehensively defined in the legislation and prior to 1983 was not defined at all. In *Armstrong v Clark* (*supra*) it was held that insulin was included in the term 'drug', and that a motorist who had taken the correct and prescribed dose of insulin, but still thereafter became unfit to drive as a result, could properly be convicted in terms of s 5(1). However, in the broadly similar case of *Watmore v Jenkins* [1962] 2 QB 572, the Appeal Court declined to interfere with an acquittal in such circumstances imposed by a lower court; and in *Farrell v Stirling* 1975 SLT (Sh Ct) 71, a driver in similar circumstances to the accused in *Armstrong v Clark* was held not to be driving. In *Armstrong v Clark* (*supra*), the court decided that a drug meant medicine given for the purposes of treating a medical condition. It appears that the court did not intend that this definition should be exhaustive and it is clear that the meaning of the word is not confined to medicines designed to treat some medical conditions. In *Duffy v Tudhope* 1984 SLT 107, 1983 SCCR 440, 1983 CO Circulars A/26, the accused drove while under the influence of tuolene, which he had inhaled in the course of sniffing glue. The Appeal Court, following *Bradford v Wilson* [1983] Crim LR 482, held that as the substance had a drugging effect, it was clearly a drug and the accused could properly be convicted.

Following all of these cases, the Transport Act 1982, s 25(3) and Schedule 8 (which came into force on 6 May 1983 by virtue of SI 1983/576) introduced the current interpretation provisions now found in s 11 of the principal Act. *Inter alia*, these provide that 'a drug includes any intoxicant other than alcohol' (s 11(2)).

3.4:4 Driving under influence of drugs: special provision

If a constable arrests a motorist because he suspects that he has been driving or attempting to drive or been in charge of a vehicle while under the influence of drink or drugs, in terms of s 4 of the Act, and the constable is advised by a medical practitioner that the condition of the motorist may be due to some drug, the constable may require the provision of a blood or urine sample as opposed to the normal primary requirement of two specimens of breath for analysis (s 7(3)(c)). This requirement is competent even where the motorist has already provided, or has been required to provide, two specimens of breath for analysis. This provision is designed to cover the inability of the Camic Breath Analyser or similar device to detect the presence of drugs in the motorist; such drugs are more readily detected from the analysis of a blood or urine specimen. However, it will be noted that to take advantage of this power of requirement, the police constable must receive medical advice that the motorist's condition might be due to drugs and cannot opt to require a blood or urine specimen on his own initiative.

3.5   SECTION 4(1): THE TEST

3.5:1   General

The test of unfitness to drive in terms of this sub-section is whether the driver's ability to drive properly is for the time being impaired through drink or drugs (s 4(5)). The question is one of fact. The kind of evidence which is used to support such a charge, whether of driving or attempting to drive when under the influence of drink or drugs, is usually that of medical examination and tests (*Murray v Muir* 1950 SLT 41). General observations of the motorist's conduct may also be relevant to the charge.

The results of the analysis of specimens of breath, blood or urine taken in terms of other parts of the procedure may also be used. If the accused provides such an specimen of breath, blood or urine, the results of that analysis must in all cases be taken into account and it shall be assumed that the proportion of alcohol in the accused's breath, blood or urine at the time of the alleged offence was not less than in the specimen (s 15(2) of the Road Traffic Offenders Act 1988). However, in terms of s 4(5) the test is whether the ability to drive is impaired, and, accordingly, it is theoretically possible (although perhaps highly unlikely in practice) that a motorist could be acquitted of the charge even where there is evidence that the results of analysis of a blood or other specimen proved to be in excess of what is permitted in terms of s 5 of the Act. In *McNeill v Fletcher* 1966 JC 18, an accused was found to have nearly four times the permitted maximum of alcohol in his blood, he was unsteady on his feet, his eyes were glazed, and his breath smelt of alcohol; nonetheless, the police surgeon refused to certify the driver as unfit to drive. On appeal it was held that he was entitled to do so. However, in *Murray v Muir* 1950 SLT 41, the evidence demonstrated that a motorist had driven along a main road without any cause for criticism shortly before being taken for an examination by a police surgeon, and this was held not to create any presumption of sobriety which could not be overcome by medical or other evidence.

In *Reid v Nixon; Dumigan v Brown* 1948 JC 68, 1948 SLT 295, a Full Bench laid down general guidelines which are to be followed in cases where the evidence turns on a medical examination by a police surgeon. As cases might arise out of a great variety of circumstances it was recognised that rigid rules for universal application could not be imposed; however, any departure from these guidelines normally requires to be justified. The procedure to be adopted in terms of the guidelines is as follows:

Firstly, the suspect should be cautioned in the usual way by the police and invited formally to give his consent to a medical examination. If he is not first cautioned without good reason, the medical evidence is inadmissible (*Gallacher v HM Advocate* 1963 SLT 217.) The accused should be advised of his right to refuse to consent to such medical examination, and it is proper practice that this intimation should be established by full corroborative evidence, although the evidence of one witness only on this matter has been held to be sufficient (*Farrell v Concannon* 1957 JC 12, 1957 SLT 60). However, the requirement to advise the accused of his right to refuse to consent to medical examination may be rendered unnecessary when the accused specifically states that he has no objection to undergoing such an examination (*Taylor v Irivine* 1958 SLT (Notes) 15). It should also be made clear to the accused that the results of such examinations and tests may be used in evidence.

Secondly, the accused should be told that he has the right to summon a doctor of his own choice, and given facilities for doing so (overruling *Harris v Adair* 1947 JC 116). However, the police examination is not to be delayed until this other doctor is present.

Thirdly, the medical examination should normally proceed outwith the presence of the police officers.

Fourthly, any questioning of the accused by the doctor in respect of recent events must be directed solely to testing the accused's memory and coherence and not to eliciting information bearing on his guilt and any such information incidentally obtained must not be communicated by the doctor to the police officers.

Fifthly, if the accused refuses to consent to the examination, his refusal can be spoken to in evidence, and if the police doctor has been summoned, he should confine himself to observing the accused and should not carry out any examination or tests.

3.5:2   Evidence

In practice, evidence in support of a prosecution under s 4 is usually given by police and medical evidence. However, there is nothing to prevent such cases proceeding on the basis of lay evidence provided that such testimony is sufficient in quality and quantity to allow the court to conclude beyond reasonable doubt that the accused's ability to drive at the material time had been impaired through drink or drugs. For a case on the sufficiency of evidence in a charge of this kind, see *Wallace v McLeod* 1986 SCCR 678, 1986 CO Circulars A/72.

3.5:3   Procedure and penalties

Proceedings under s 4(1) are normally summary, and the penalties are found in Schedule 2, Part I of the Road Traffic Offenders Act 1988.

3.6   SECTION 4(2): IN CHARGE OF A MOTOR VEHICLE

3.6:1   General

Section 4(2) of the Road Traffic Act 1988 provides:

Without prejudice to sub-section (1) above, a person who, when in charge of a motor vehicle which is on a road or other public place, is unfit to drive through drink or drugs, is guilty of an offence.

The sub-section is designed to cover the situation when the vehicle in question is not in motion, and when the driver is not in the process of concluding a driving operation, and does not fall into the category of a person attempting to drive the vehicle. Whether a motorist is in charge of his vehicle, as opposed to not being in charge, or as opposed to driving or attempting to drive, is a matter of fact and evidence.

3.6:2   Definitions

'*In charge*' – see paragraph 3.3:4.

'*Motor vehicle*' – see paragraph 1.2:1 *et seq.*

'*Road or other public place*' – see paragraphs 1.8:1, 1.8:2 and 3.3:5.

'*Unfit to drive*' – see paragraphs 3.5:1 and 3.5:2.

'*Drink or drugs*' – see paragraph 3.4:3.

3.6:3 Procedure and penalties

Prosecutions under s 4(2) are normally taken summarily, and may be changed as an alternative to s 4(1). Penalties are given in Schedule 2, Part I of the Road Traffic Offenders Act 1988.

3.7 SECTION 4(3): STATUTORY DEFENCE (1): NO LIKELIHOOD OF DRIVING

3.7:1 General

Section 4(3) of the Road Traffic Act 1988 provides:

For the purposes of sub-section (2) above, a person shall be deemed not to have been in charge of a motor vehicle if he proves that at the material time the circumstances were such that there was no likelihood of his driving it so long as he remained unfit to drive through drink or drugs.

Section 4(3) therefore provides a statutory defence in prosecutions under s 4(2). A driver will be regarded as not being in charge of a vehicle if he proves that at the material time there was no likelihood of him driving during the period that he remained unfit to drive through drink or drugs. Whether such a defence can be successfully established will be a question of fact and evidence. Once a *prima facie* case is made out by the prosecution the burden of proof in this defence rests on the accused, and the standard of proof is on the balance of probabilities (*Neish v Stevenson* 1969 SLT 229). If this standard is not reached, but the defence case in any way casts a reasonable doubt on the guilt of the accused in the circumstances of the case, the accused will be entitled to an acquittal. Where appropriate, this defence may be established by uncorroborated evidence, including testimony from the accused driver himself.

For a successful defence of this kind, the accused requires to demonstrate that there is no likelihood of him driving so long as he is affected by drink or drugs to the extent that his ability to drive is impaired. Put another way, the accused has to establish when his ability to drive would no longer be impaired in addition to showing that there was no likelihood of him driving up to that point. In considering such a defence, the court will have regard to the accused's intentions, express or implied, in the light of all the other facts and circumstances of the case (*Morton v Confer* [1963] 1 WLR 763, 2 All ER 765). Reference should be made to paragraph 3.8:1 (defence of post-incident consumption of alcohol in terms of the Road Traffic Offenders Act 1988, s 15(3)) for evidential considerations relating to the time when a driver may be said to be no longer unfit to drive).

The circumstances in which a defence under s 4(3) may be presented can conceivably overlap with some of the earlier cases where it was found that an accused was not in charge of the vehicle (paragraphs 3.3:2 and 3.3:4), and these authorities may be of assistance in determining whether a motorist can demonstrate that he is not likely to drive while affected by drink or drugs.

The statutory defence under s 4(3) is only relevant in prosecutions in cases where the accused is in charge of the vehicle under s 4(2), and does not apply to s 4(1) (cases of driving or attempting to drive). In addition, in considering this defence, regard has to be had to s 4(4) (paragraph 3.7:2).

3.7:2   Section 4(4): Injury and damage to be disregarded

Section 4(4) of the Road Traffic Act 1988 provides:

The court may, in determining whether there was such a likelihood as is mentioned in subsection (3) above, disregard any injury to him and any damage to the vehicle.

In determining whether there is any likelihood that the accused will drive his vehicle while his ability to do so is impaired, the court may disregard any injury to the driver or damage to the vehicle. Thus it is not necessarily fatal to a prosecution if the evidence shows that either the driver or the vehicle in question is not in a condition to proceed further; the accused may in such circumstances still be deemed to be in charge of the vehicle.

3.8   SECTION 15(3) OF THE ROAD TRAFFIC OFFENDERS ACT 1988 – STATUTORY DEFENCE (2): POST INCIDENT DRINKING

Section 15(2) of the Road Traffic Offenders Act 1988 provides:

Evidence of the proportion of alcohol or any drug in a specimen of breath, blood or urine provided by the accused shall, in all cases, be taken into account and, subject to sub-section (3) below, it shall be assumed that the proportion of alcohol in the accused's breath, blood or urine at the time of the alleged offence was not less than in the specimen.

Section 15(3) of that Act provides:

If the proceedings are for an offence under s 5 of (the) Act or, where the accused is alleged to have been unfit through drink, for an offence under s 4 of (the) Act, that assumption shall not be made if the accused proves –
  (a) that he consumed alcohol after he had ceased to drive, attempt to drive or be in charge of a motor vehicle on a road or other public place and before he provided the specimen; and
  (b) that had he not done so the proportion of alcohol in his breath, blood or urine would not have exceeded the prescribed limit and, if proceedings are for an offence under s 4 of that Act, would not have been such as to impair his ability to drive properly.

The Act referred to in s 15(3) is the Road Traffic Act 1988. The assumption referred to in s 15(3) is the assumption made by s 15(2).

Section 15(3) therefore furnishes the guidelines for what is often referred to as the defence of post-incident drinking. In English authorities, this has sometimes been described as the hip-flask defence, although this is usually an inappropriate title. Unlike s 4(3) of the Road Traffic Act 1988, which provides a defence only to s 4(2) prosecutions, a s 15(3) defence can be applied in charges under both sub-sections (1) and (2) of s 4, as well as to charges under s 5(1)(a) and (b). Accordingly, this defence is available in all cases where the prosecution relies in any way on the results of an analysis of breath, blood or urine specimens. Although such specimens are normally used as the basis of prosecutions in terms of s 5, they can be, and sometimes (for the purposes of particular cases) are, used in s 4 cases. The sub-section in addition specifically contemplates the possibility of such a defence in s 4 cases generally.

To establish a defence in terms of s 15(3), the motorist has to prove not only that he had ceased to drive, attempt to drive, or be in charge of the vehicle, and thereafter consumed alcohol, but in addition he must establish that but for the amount of alcohol which is proved to have been so consumed, his ability to drive would not have been impaired. The onus of proof therefore lies on the accused to establish this defence in normal circumstances in the face of the evidence of impairment to drive (whether by specimen analysis or more commonly by other evidence) offered by the

Crown. The standard of proof required in these circumstances is that of the balance of probabilities (*Neish v Stevenson* 1969 SLT 229, overruling *Thaw v Seger* 1962 SLT (Sh Ct) 63). Where this standard of proof is not reached, it may be in the circumstances of a particular case that the defence evidence demonstrates that there is a reasonable doubt about the Crown case that the accused was unfit to drive through drink or drugs at the material time; if so, the accused will be entitled to an acquittal. In appropriate circumstances the accused may not have to prove the exact amount of alcohol subsequently consumed (*Hassan v Scott* 1989 SLT 380, 1989 SCCR 49).

It is submitted that in the normal case in prosecutions under s 4(1) or (2) where the accused seeks to establish this defence, the following considerations will apply. Firstly, the accused will have to show in evidence, with a substantial degree of accuracy, the amount and nature of the alcohol, if any, that has been consumed prior to the time when, in terms of the section, he ceased to drive, attempt to drive, or be in charge of the vehicle. In particular, it will normally be of considerable importance for the accused to provide detailed information as to exactly when or over what period any such alcohol was consumed. Alternatively, if it is claimed that no alcohol was consumed prior to the cessation of any driving operation, this too will have to be proved. The accused will then have to demonstrate that he ceased to drive, attempt to drive or be in charge of his vehicle and when this cessation took place. Next, the accused will require to prove the amount and nature of the alcohol which he thereafter consumed before the specimen was given or the observations on the impairment of his ability to drive occurred, and the period of time over which this consumption took place. Finally, the accused will have to demonstrate on the balance of probabilities, that but for the intake of the alcohol subsequently consumed, his ability to drive, attempt to drive or be in charge of the vehicle would not have been impaired at the material time. In most cases in practice, it will be essential that expert evidence be given on the effect and consequences of the subsequent drinking proved to have taken place. It is possible to envisage circumstances where the accused can establish that he had consumed no alcohol at all prior to the material time, and that his subsequent condition was wholly accounted for by post-incident drinking, but in practice such cases appear to be relatively unusual. However reference should be made to *Hassan v Scott supra*).

In such cases, expert evidence is usually adduced in respect of a number of aspects. The effect of the consumption of alcohol varies significantly depending on the amount and nature of the alcohol consumed, the height and weight of the motorist, and other factors. Expert witnesses have recourse to tables indicating the given effect of given quantities and types of alcohol on persons of differing physiques. Further, once consumed, alcohol begins thereafter to metabolise within the body and the level of alcohol therefore reduces, after the consumption of alcohol has ceased. Again, expert witnesses have recourse to tables which indicate in general terms the rate at which the body absorbs alcohol and levels reduce accordingly. These tables have not apparently been challenged by the Crown when produced by the defence, on the basis that such evidence is given by properly qualified experts who are entitled to consult such tables as being referable to their particular expertise.

A successful defence of post-incident drinking therefore depends on the consideration of a number of matters which taken together will establish that at the material time an offence in terms of the Act has not been committed. Careful preparation and proper presentation of this evidence is essential, and each case will depend upon its own facts and circumstances. It should also be remembered that even in cases where a motorist successfully establishes that he has consumed alcohol after he has ceased to drive or attempt to drive a motor vehicle on a road or other public place, he may well, if he is still in the vicinity of his vehicle, be regarded as 'in charge' of that vehicle.

It is also extremely important to note that, while it may be open to an accused to establish a defence on the basis as above described, there would appear to be nothing to prevent the Crown from proving, on the same principles, that a specimen analysis which was taken some time after a driving operation had ceased and which was lower than the permitted limit, could nonetheless demonstrate that at the time the motorist was shown to be driving, attempting to drive, or was in charge of his vehicle, his ability to drive was impaired (see paragraph 5.4).

The principal authorities are *Ritchie v Pirie* 1972 JC 7, 1972 SLT 2; *Sutherland v Aitchison* 1975 JC 1; 1979 SLT (Notes) 37; *Tudhope v Miller* 1978 JC 26; *Ferns v Tudhope* 1979 SLT (Notes) 23, 1978 CO Circulars A/28; *Campbell v Mackenzie* 1981 SCCR 341.

3.9 DEFENCE AT COMMON LAW

Apart from the normal non-statutory defences (which usually are concerned with an error or failure in the procedure, or with an error or failure in the identification of the driver), coercion, or necessity, where a driver is genuinely compelled to drive where otherwise he would not have done so, may provide a successful defence to a charge of driving while unfit through drink or drugs (*Tudhope v Grubb* 1983 SCCR 350). However this defence is not available indefinitely (*MacLeod v MacDougall* 1989 SLT 154, 1988 SCCR 519). Equally, driving in a medical or other emergency may provide a defence, but normally the court will have to be satisfied that no other reasonable alternative method of dealing with the emergency has been ignored; alternatively such a crisis may allow the court not to disqualify the driver (*Watson v Hamilton* 1988 SLT 316, 1988 SCCR 13).

3.10   SECTION 4(5): DEFINITION OF UNFITNESS TO DRIVE

Section 4(5) of the Road Traffic Act 1988 provides:

For the purposes of this section, a person shall be taken to be unfit to drive if his ability to drive properly is impaired.

The test of whether the ability to drive is impaired is therefore a question of fact to be determined by the court on the evidence. Reference should be made to paragraph 3.5:1 for the circumstances under which a medical examination should be conducted. In arriving at its conclusions the court may properly have regard to the subjective opinion of witnesses, whether police, medical or anyone else. The phrase 'for the time being' means the time at which the driving took place; however, evidence of the driver's conduct before and after the driving occurred is both competent and relevant.

3.11   SECTION 4(6): POWER OF ARREST

Section 4(6) of the Road Traffic Act 1988 provides:

A constable may arrest a person without warrant if he has reasonable cause to suspect that that person is or has been committing an offence under this section.

This sub-section therefore gives a constable wide powers of arrest, and such an arrest is usually effected in proceedings under s 4. What is reasonable cause will depend on the facts and circumstances of the case. The test as to whether a person is properly arrested in terms of this sub-section is whether the constable has reasonable grounds for his suspicions that the motorist is or has been committing an offence in terms of the section, and not whether the suspicion turns out to be justified or unjustified. If a constable arrests a motorist without reasonable cause, that arrest will be invalid even if subsequent investigations establish that the motorist has committed an offence under the section; equally, the fact that a motorist is shown not to have committed an offence will not invalidate an arrest made by a constable who properly has reasonable cause to suspect that an offence has been committed. Reference should also be made to paragraph 4.2:2.

Further, the sub-section makes it clear that the suspicion does not have to arise in the constable's mind while the alleged offence is in the course of being committed; the suspicion may equally be that the accused has been committing an offence under the section but is no longer doing so. Accordingly, the case of *Breen v Pirie* 1976 JC 60, 1976 SLT 136, which decided under previous legislation that an arrest could not properly be made if the suspicion had arisen in the constable's mind after the driver's journey had been completed, is no longer applicable. The power of arrest may under the current provisions be exercised after the driver has left the vehicle, or at any time after the suspicion has been correctly formed in the constable's mind. The sub-section does not prescribe any time limit within which the power of arrest may be exercised.

The question of corroboration is not relevant to the power of arrest; the suspicion and the subsequent entitlement to arrest can be carried out by one officer acting alone. Cases in which the matter of what constitutes reasonable grounds for suspicion was noted are *McLeod v Shaw* 1981 SLT (Notes) 93, 1981 SCCR 54, 1981 CO Circulars A/6 and *Smith v Ross* 1983 SLT 491, 1983 SCCR 109, 1983 CO Circulars A/8.

A valid arrest is not a prerequisite of further procedure under the legislation; if the arrest is judged to be improper the motorist may still be convicted under s 4 or 5 of the Act if the other evidence in the case shows that he has committed an offence. See also paragraph 5.3:3.

3.12   SECTION 4(7) AND (8): NON-APPLICATION TO SCOTLAND

These sub-sections provide firstly that in order to exercise the right to arrest without warrant contained in s 4(6) the constable may enter (if need be by force) any place where that person is, or where the constable has reasonable cause to suspect him to be. Section 4(8) provides that s 4(7) does not extend to Scotland and nothing in that section shall affect any rule of law in Scotland concerning the right of the constable to enter any premises for that purpose. It would appear that the express statutory power to enter premises conferred by s 4(7) on the constable was excluded from application in Scotland because it was considered by Parliament that the police in Scotland already have such powers at common law. This view was given substantial support in the case of *Cairns v Keane* 1983 SCCR 277, where the police entered the accused's home without invitation and in pursuit of the accused, whom they suspected of having driven while under the influence of alcohol. The court held that the urgency of the situation justified the invasion or trespass of the accused's house. This decision was upheld on appeal, although the High Court declined to deliver any opinion on the matter.

PART 3

DRIVING OR BEING IN CHARGE OF A MOTOR VEHICLE WITH ALCOHOL CONCENTRATION ABOVE PRESCRIBED LIMIT (S 5)

3.13 SECTION 5

3.13:1 General

The broad purpose of this part of the present legislation is to provide a method of ascertaining the proportion of alcohol present in a specimen of breath, blood or urine. Underlying all of the current provisions is the intention that the principal method of determining the proportion of alcohol should be by way of a specimen of breath at a police station in terms of s 7(1)(a) of the Act. The wording of s 7, read as a whole, makes it clear that a police officer must always, in the first instance, require a breath specimen, unless a reliable device is not available at the police station. The only qualification to this rule is found in s 8(2). This topic is discussed more fully in chapter 4. Parliament, in considering the present terms of ss 7 and 8 of the Act, was intent on diminishing the previous significance of procedural and technical requirements which were features of earlier legislation and which had proved to be a fruitful source of contention in drink driving prosecutions. The current terms of ss 7 and 8 were grafted onto the Road Traffic Act 1972 by s 25(3) and Schedule 8 of the Transport Act 1981, which came into force on 6 May 1983 by virtue of SI 1983/576. Case law in respect of formal requirements concerning s 5 prosecutions arising before 6 May 1983 is therefore of limited relevance.

3.13:2   Preliminary test

The provision of a preliminary breath test in terms of s 6 of the Act (sometimes known as the roadside or preliminary breath test and conducted by means of a breathalyser) is still seen as being normally the first step in the statutory procedure. However, it should be emphasised that in terms of the current provisions, such a roadside test is by no means an essential prerequisite for a prosecution in terms of s 5. A description of what is involved in roadside tests is described in paragraphs 4.1:1 *et seq.*

3.13:3   Section 5(1)

Section 5(1) of the Road Traffic Act 1988 provides:

If a person –
(a) drives or attempts to drive a motor vehicle on a road or other public place, or
(b) is in charge of a motor vehicle on a road or other public place,
after consuming so much alcohol that the proportion of it in his breath, blood or urine exceeds the prescribed limit he is guilty of an offence.

3.13:4   Special definitions

'*Drives*'. See paragraphs 1.7:1 and 3.3:2.

'*Attempting to drive*'. See paragraph 3.3:3.

'*Motor vehicle*'. See paragraph 1.2:1.

'*Road or other public place*'. See paragraphs 1.8:1, 1.8:2 and 3.3:5.

'*In charge*'. See paragraph 3.3:4.

3.13:5   The prescribed limits

The prescribed limits as provided in s 11(2) of the Act are 35 microgrammes of alcohol in 100 millilitres of breath, 180 milligrammes of alcohol in 100 millilitres of blood, and 107 milligrammes of alcohol in 100 millilitres of urine. Unlike the original provisions of s 6 of the Road Traffic Act 1972, which required that the readings be 'ascertained from a laboratory test' for the purpose of which the specimen was given, the present provisions impose no restriction or qualification, technical or procedural, on the method of determining levels of alcohol. Further, s 15(2) of the Road Traffic Offenders Act 1988 requires that all such readings, irrespective of how they are obtained, must be considered; the section provides:

Evidence of the proportion of alcohol or any drug in a specimen of breath, blood or urine at the time of the alleged offence shall, in all cases, be taken into account, and . . . it shall be assumed that the proportion of alcohol in the accused's breath, blood or urine at the time of the alleged offence was not less than in the specimen.

Accordingly, it is in general open for the court in a prosecution under s 5 to ignore any defects, omissions or failures in any procedural aspect of the Act involving the taking of the specimens. The only express exception to this is provided by s 15(4) of the Road Traffic Offenders Act, which requires that

A specimen of blood shall be disregarded unless it was taken from the accused with his consent by a medical practitioner.

However, it is submitted that while s 15(2) provides that evidence of the proportion of alcohol or drug in a specimen of breath, blood or urine shall be taken into account in all cases, the phrasing of the section leaves it open to a court to discount such evidence if for example it is established that the specimen had been obtained illegally, by deception or under duress (*R v Fox* [1985] RTR 337 (per Lord Fraser at 343), [1985] 1 WLR 1126).

The rules governing the provision of specimens of breath, blood or urine for analysis are found in s 7 of the Road Traffic Act 1988, and are discussed more fully in chapter 4. These rules should be read in the context of the evidential provisions of ss 15 and 16 of the Road Traffic Offenders Act 1988, which are discussed in chapter 5.

3.14 PUBLIC POLICY

In *Lockhart v Deighan* 1985 SLT 549; 1985 SCCR 204, the Crown Office had indicated publicly that prosecutions would not be taken in cases where the level of alcohol determined by a breath test in terms of s 6 did not exceed a certain level. The prosecution in the case based its charge on a specimen taken shortly before this public announcement which did not exceed that level. On appeal it was held that nonetheless the charge was based on a specimen properly and competently taken, and the motorist was convicted. However, in *Benton v Cardle* 1988 SLT 310, 1987 SCCR 738, and *McConnachie v Scott* 1988 SLT 480, 1988 SCCR 176, a motorist provided two specimens of breath of less than 50 microgrammes of alcohol which were also lower than the level below which the Crown Office had indicated proceedings would not be taken. In these circumstances it was held to be incompetent for a police officer to require the motorist to provide a specimen of blood or urine in terms of s 8(6) of the Road Traffic Act 1972 (now s 8(2) of the Road Traffic Act 1988).

3.15 SECTION 5(2): STATUTORY DEFENCE (1): NO LIKELIHOOD OF DRIVING

3.15:1 General

Section 5(2) of the Road Traffic Act 1988 provides:

It is a defence for a person charged with an offence under sub-section 1(b) above to prove that at the time he is alleged to have committed the offence, the circumstances were such that there was no likelihood of his driving the vehicle whilst the proportion of alcohol in breath, blood or urine remained likely to exceed the prescribed limited.

Section 5(2) therefore provides a statutory defence to a charge under s 5(1)(b). It will be noted that the defence is not available in charges under s 5(1)(a). If a driver who is proved to have been, or accepts that he has been, in charge of a vehicle after consuming so much alcohol that the proportion of it in his blood, breath or urine exceeds the prescribed limit, he is entitled to escape conviction if he proves that at the time the offence alleged against him was committed, there was no likelihood of his driving the vehicle whilst the proportion of alcohol in his breath, blood or urine remained likely to exceed the prescribed limit. Whether such a defence can be successfully established will in each case be a question of fact and evidence. It is submitted that such a defence, where appropriate, may be established by uncorroborated evidence, including testimony from the accused driver himself. It should be noted, however, that for a successful defence of this kind to be established, the accused requires to demonstrate that there is no likelihood of him driving, so long as the proportion of alcohol in his body exceeds or remains likely to exceed the prescribed limit. The accused therefore has to demonstrate when the proportion of alcohol in his body would have diminished to below the prescribed limit, as well as proving that there was no likelihood of him driving up to that point. In virtually all cases of this kind, proof of when the level of alcohol in the accused's body decreased to a point below the prescribed limit will depend on expert evidence, the general nature of which is discussed in paragraphs 3.8:1 and 3.13:2.

It is submitted that the standard of proof on the accused in these circumstances is on the balance of probabilities (*Neish v Stevenson* 1969 SLT 229). In considering this defence, the court will have regard to the accused's intentions, express or implied, in the light of all the other circumstances of the case (*Morton v Confer* [1963] 1 WLR 763; [1963] 2 All ER 765). In deciding the issue, the court may disregard any injury to the driver or damage to the vehicle (s 5(3)). Thus it is not necessarily fatal to a prosecution if the evidence shows that either the driver of the car, or the car itself, was not in a condition to proceed further; the accused even in those circumstances may still be deemed to be in charge of the vehicle.

The circumstances in which a defence under s 5(2) may be presented can conceivably overlap with some of the earlier cases where it was found that the accused was not in charge of the vehicle (paragraphs 3.3:2 and 3.3.:4).

3.6   SECTION 15(3) OF THE ROAD TRAFFIC OFFENDERS ACT 1988 – STATUTORY DEFENCE (2): POST INCIDENT DRINKING

3.16.1   General

Section 15(2) of the Road Traffic Offenders Act 1988 provides:

Evidence of the proportion of alcohol or any drug in a specimen of breath, blood or urine provided by the accused shall in all cases, be taken into account and subject to sub-section (3) below, it shall be assumed that the proportion of alcohol in the accused's breath, blood or urine at the time of the alleged offence was not less than in the specimen.

Section 15(3) of the Road Traffic Offenders Act 1988 provides:

If the proceedings are for an offence under section 5 of (the) Act, or for an offence under section 4 of (the) Act in a case where the accused is alleged to be unfit through drink, that assumption shall not be made if the accused proves –
(a) that he consumed alcohol after he had ceased to drive, attempt to drive or be in charge of a motor vehicle on a road or other public place and before he provided the specimen; and

(b) had he not done so the proportion of alcohol in his breath, blood or urine would not have exceeded the prescribed limit and, if proceedings are for an offence under section 4 of this Act, would not have been such as to impair his ability to drive properly.

The Act referred to within this section is the Road Traffic Act 1988. The assumption in the third line is that the proportion of alcohol in the accused's breath, blood and urine at the time of the offence was not less than indicated by the specimen. Section 15(2) therefore furnishes the guidelines for what is often known as the defence of post-incident drinking. In English authorities this has sometimes been referred to as the hip-flask defence, although this is usually an inappropriate and misleading title. Unlike s 5(2) of the Road Traffic Act 1988, which provides a statutory defence only to s 5(1)(b) prosecutions, a defence under s 15(2) of the Road Traffic Offenders Act 1988 can be applied to charges under both sub-sections (1)(a) and (1)(b), as well as to a prosecution under s 4 of the Road Traffic Act 1988 where that prosecution relies in any way on the results of specimen analysis.

3.16:2 Onus and standard of proof

To establish a defence under this section therefore, the motorist has to prove not only that he had ceased to drive, attempt to drive, or be in charge of the vehicle and thereafter consumed alcohol, but in addition he must establish that but for the amount of alcohol which is proved to have been consumed, the analysis of any specimen which he has provided would not have exceeded that limit as specified in s 11(2) of the Act. The onus of proof therefore lies on the accused to establish this defence in the face of the evidence of specimen analysis produced by the Crown. The standard of proof required in these circumstances is that of the balance of probabilities (*Neish v Stevenson* 1969 SLT 229 (overruling *Thaw v Segar* 1962 SLT (Sh Ct) 63.); see also *Ritchie v Pirie* 1972 JC 7; SLT 2; *Sutherland v Aitchison* 1975 JC 1; *Tudhope v Miller* 1978 JC 26; *Campbell v Mackenzie* 1988 SCCR 341.

It is submitted that in the normal case in prosecutions under ss 4, 5(1)(a) or 5(1)(b), the accused will have to establish with a substantial degree of accuracy the amount and nature of the alcohol, if any, that has been consumed, prior to the time when, in terms of the relevant section, he ceased to drive, attempt to drive or be in charge of his vehicle. In addition, it will normally be of considerable importance for the accused to provide as much detail as possible as to exactly when all of this alcohol was consumed. It will then have to be established that the accused in fact ceased to drive, attempt to drive, or be in charge of his vehicle, and when this cessation took place. The accused will then require to prove the amount and nature of the alcohol he thereafter consumed, and during what period of time this consumption occurred. Finally, the accused will have to prove that but for the intake of the alcohol subsequently consumed, he would not have exceeded the prescribed limits at the material time, that is to say, the time when he ceased to drive, attempt to drive, or be in charge of the vehicle. In most cases in practice it will be essential that expert evidence be given on the effect and consequences of the subsequent drinking proved to have taken place. In appropriate circumstances, the accused may not have to prove the exact amount of alcohol subsequently consumed (*Hassan v Scott* 1989 SLT 380, 1989 SCCR 49). It is of course possible to envisage circumstances where the accused can establish that he had consumed no alcohol prior to the material time, and that his subsequent condition was wholly accounted for by post-incident drinking, but in practice such cases appear to be relatively unusual.

Expert evidence is usually considered in respect of a number of issues. The effect of the consumption of alcohol varies significantly depending on the amount and nature of the alcohol consumed, the height and weight of the motorist, and many other factors. Expert witnesses have recourse to tables indicating the effect of given quantities of alcohol on different types of persons of different physiques. Further, once consumed, alcohol begins thereafter to metabolise within the body, and the level of alcohol therefore reduces after consumption of alcohol has ceased. Again, expert witnesses have recourse to tables which indicate in general terms the rate at which the body absorbs the alcohol and levels reduce accordingly. These tables have not been challenged by the Crown when produced by the defence presumably on the basis that such evidence is given by properly qualified experts who are entitled to consult such tables as being referable to their particular expertise.

A successful defence of post-incident drinking therefore depends on the consideration of a number of things which taken together will establish that at the material time an offence in terms of the Act has not been committed. In particular, the defence will have to show clearly that but for the post-incident consumption of alcohol, the amount of alcohol in the driver's body would not, at the material time, have exceeded the prescribed limit. Careful preparation and proper presentation of this evidence is essential, and each case will depend upon its own facts and circumstances. It should also be remembered that even in cases where a motorist successfully establishes that he has consumed alcohol after he has ceased to drive or attempt to drive a motor vehicle on a road or other public place, he may well, if he is still in the vicinity of his vehicle, be regarded as 'in charge' of that vehicle.

It is also important to note that while it may be open to an accused to establish a defence on the basis as above described, there would appear to be nothing to prevent the Crown from proving, on the same principles that a specimen analysis which was taken some time after a driving operation has ceased and which was lower than the permitted limit, could nonetheless demonstrate that at the time the motorist was driving, attempting to drive, or was in charge of his vehicle he had more than the permitted level of alcohol, and is thus liable to conviction (see paragraph 5.4).

3.17 Defence at common law

Apart from the normal non-statutory defences put forward (which are usually concerned with failure or mistake in the identification of the driver, or an error in the procedure), coercion or necessity, where a driver is genuinely compelled to drive in circumstances where otherwise he would not have done so, may provide a successful defence to a charge under s 5(1)(a) of the Act (*Tudhope v Grubb* 1983 SCCR 350). However, if such a defence is available, it cannot be extended indefinitely, and in particular will not extend to a point where clearly the emergency no longer applies (*McLeod v McDougall* 1989 SLT 151, 1988 SCCR 519).

Chapter Four

Preliminary breath tests and provision of specimens for analysis

Sections 6, 7 and 8 of the Road Traffic Act 1988

PART 1
PRELIMINARY BREATH TEST

4.1 SECTION 6: GENERAL

Section 6(1) and (2) of the Road Traffic Act 1988 allows a police constable to require a motorist to provide a specimen of breath for a breathalyser test in a wide variety of situations. This procedure is variously referred to as the preliminary breath test, the breathalyser test or the roadside breath test, and is completely distinct from (and is given into an entirely different device from), the specimens of breath for analysis described in s 7, and which form the basis for conviction in charges under s 5 of the Act. The provision of a preliminary breath test in terms of s 6 is seen as normally the first step in the statutory procedure. The test is undertaken by the motorist giving a breath specimen into an approved device. If the device registers that the specimen is positive, the constable administering the test will proceed to require a specimen of breath, blood or urine in terms of s 7 of the Act. However, notwithstanding the current terms of the legislation, the provision of a positive preliminary breath test is not an essential step before the procedure under s 7 is embarked upon; a constable may require any motorist to provide a specimen in terms of s 7 even though no preliminary test under s 6 has been taken, or presumably even where such a test has been taken and proved negative.

4.2 PRELIMINARY BREATH TEST

4.2:1 Section 6(1)

Section 6(1) provides:

Where a constable in uniform has reasonable cause to suspect –
(a) that a person driving or attempting to drive or in charge of a motor vehicle on a road or other public place has alcohol in his body or has committed a traffic offence while the vehicle was in motion; or
(b) that a person has been driving or attempting to drive or been in charge of a motor vehicle on a road or other public place with alcohol in his body and that that person still has alcohol in his body; or
(c) that a person has been driving or attempting to drive or been in charge of a motor vehicle on a road or other public place and has committed a traffic offence whilst the vehicle was in motion;
he may, subject to s 9 of this Act, require him to provide a specimen of breath for a breath test.

4.2:2 Definitions

A constable. A constable means any member of the police force irrespective of rank.

A constable in uniform. This phrase has not been judicially considered in terms in Scotland. However, it is submitted that the matter is essentially one of fact. In English cases, a constable otherwise in uniform but without his helmet (*Wallwork v Giles* [1970] RTR 117); and an officer with a raincoat over his uniform (*Taylor v Baldwin* [1976] RTR 265), were both held to be entitled to make the requirement. If the question of whether the constable was in uniform is not raised specifically in the evidence, there must be facts and circumstances from which the court can infer that the constable was in uniform (*Richards v West* [1980] RTR 215; *Cooper v Rowlands* [1971] RTR 291). In a case under s 2 of the Road Safety Act 1967 (c 30) it was held that a uniformed constable could make the requirement on the basis of information supplied by a plain clothes officer (*Copeland v McPherson* 1970 SLT 87).

Reasonable cause to suspect. It has to be established that, before requiring the specimen for a breath test, the constable has to have reasonable cause for his suspicion. Whether or not such cause is reasonable is a matter of fact in each case and depends upon the proven facts and circumstances. In the case of *Copeland v McPherson* (*supra*), the suspicion was held to be reasonable when it arose out of information given to the constable by another officer. In *Dryburgh v Galt* 1981 SLT 151, 1981 SCCR 26, 1981 CO

Circulars A/4, the information came from an anonymous phone call. The suspicion may arise from the way in which the vehicle is being driven, but it is clear that the conduct of the vehicle is not the only method by which such suspicions may arise (*Sinclair v Heywood* 1981 SCCR 63). In particular, the suspicion in the constable's mind may arise after the vehicle has been stopped for whatever proper and legal purpose.

A police constable has wide powers to stop motor vehicles in terms of s 163 of the Road Traffic Act 1988 and the only qualification on these powers would seem to be that they are not exercised capriciously or oppressively. It would therefore seem to be in order that a constable may stop a motorist purely with the intention of seeing whether or not he had been drinking (*Chief Constable of Gwent v Dash* [1985] Crim LR 674) so long as there is no question of mispractice, malice or caprice. However, once the vehicle has been stopped, the constable must then have reasonable cause to suspect that the motorist has alcohol in his body. The usual reasons given are that alcohol is smelt on the motorist's breath, or that his speech is slurred, his eyes glazed or his movements are unco-ordinated. A constable need not indicate to the motorist the reason for his suspicions; and if in all the circumstances the requirement is legally and properly made, it does not matter if a constable claims to have relied at the time upon grounds for his suspicion that subsequently proved to be improper (*McNaughton v Degnan* 1981 SLT (Notes) 105 1981 SCCR 97, 1981 CO Circulars A/5). It therefore follows that the constable's suspicion, whatever it may be, does not have to be subsequently confirmed as accurate or justified; all that has to be established is that the constable's suspicions were at the material time reasonable in the circumstances. It would accordingly not be a defence to a charge of failing to provide a specimen in terms of this section that the driver has not been drinking or even that he was not the driver at the material time, provided that the constable's suspicions are reasonable (see *McNaughton v Degnan supra*; and *McNicol v Peters* 1969 SLT 261). A constable, in making the requirement, does not have to indicate to the motorist at the time what the grounds of his suspicion are, and if he purports to make the requirement on an unjustified basis but proper grounds exist, then the requirement will be held to have been properly made (*McNaughton v Degnan* (*supra*)).

Driving or attempting to drive. See paragraphs 1.7:1, 3.3:2 and 3.3:3.

In charge. See paragraph 3.3:4.

Motor vehicle. See paragraphs 1.2:1 *et seq.*

Road or other public place. See paragraphs 1.8:1, 1.8:2, and 3.3:5.

A traffic offence. This is defined in s 6(8) and means 'an offence under–

(a) any provision of Part II of the Public Passenger Vehicles Act 1981,

(b) any provision of the Road Traffic Regulation Act 1984,

(c) any provision of the Road Traffic Offenders Act 1988 except Part III or

(d) any provision of this Act except Part V.'

Require. To require means to ask (*Milne v McDonald* 1971 JC 40 (per Lord Justice-Clerk Clyde at p 42); 1971 SLT 291). The requirement must be corroborated (*Carmichael v Gillooly* 1982 SCCR 119.)

A specimen of breath for a breath test. By virtue of s 11(2) of the Act, a breath test means 'a preliminary test for the purpose of obtaining, by means of a device approved by the Secretary of State, an indication of whether the proportion of alcohol in a person's breath or blood is likely to exceed the prescribed limit.'

The evidence should indicate that the device is approved; however in the absence of challenge this may be presumed (*McIlhargery v Herron* 1972 JC 38 1972 SLT 185).

4.2:3 General application

Section 6(1)(a), (b) and (c) therefore allow a police constable to require a motorist to provide a specimen of breath for a breath test in a wide variety of circumstances. The only qualifications on this power are that the constable must have reasonable grounds for his suspicions, and that the test must be administered at or near the place where the requirement is made, or in the case of an accident where the requirement is made in terms of s 6(2), at a police station (s 6(3)). Apart from these considerations, s 6(1) allows a constable to make the requirement of any person who is, or who has been, driving, attempting to drive, or in charge of a vehicle when the constable has reasonable cause to suspect that the person has alcohol in his body, or (after completing his journey) that he still has alcohol in his body, or that he has committed a moving traffic offence. Accordingly, the requirement may be made where the constable has reasonable cause to suspect that the motorist has been driving, in the absence of direct evidence on that matter, as well as having reasonable cause to suspect that the motorist has alcohol in his body. Further, there is specifically no time limit imposed in respect of the making of the requirement; so long as the constable has reasonable cause to suspect that the motorist has been driving, and that he has, or has had, alcohol in his body or has committed a traffic offence, the requirement can be made at any time thereafter.

The test must be carried out in accordance with the device manufacturers' instructions (see Appendix B and paragraphs 4.14:4 and 5.8:4). However, the provision of a specimen of breath for a breath test is not a prerequisite of further procedure under ss 4 or 5, and any failure in the procedure, either by the constable or the motorist, has relevance only in a charge of failing to provide a specimen in terms of s 6(4).

4.2:4 Procedural nature of test

The administration of the preliminary breath test is essentially a procedural matter, and can therefore be spoken to in evidence by one witness only (*McLeod v Nicol* 1970 JC 8, 1970 SLT 304; *Wither v McLennan* 1978 CO Circulars A/30). However, a charge of failing to provide a specimen will have to be supported by the corroborated evidence.

4.2:5 Safeguards for hospital patients

All the provisions of s 6(1) and (2) are subject to the safeguards for hospital patients described in s 9 (see paragraphs 6.1:1 *et seq.*)

4.3 REQUIREMENT FOR BREATH TEST FOLLOWING ACCIDENT (S 6(2))

4.3:1 Section 6(2)

Section 6(2) of the Road Traffic Act 1988 provides:

If an accident occurs owing to the presence of a motor vehicle on a road or other public place, a constable may, subject to section 9 of this Act, require any person who he has reasonable cause to believe was driving or attempting to drive or in charge of the vehicle at the time of the accident to provide a specimen of breath for a breath test.

4.3:2 Definitions

Accident. See paragraph 1.9:1.

Reasonable cause to believe. It should be noted that in terms of this sub-section the requirement imposed on the constable is significantly higher than in s 6(1). In particular, in terms of s 6(1) the constable may require a specimen of breath for a breath test in a variety of circumstances if he has reasonable cause to suspect that the accused has been driving and has alcohol in his body. In terms of s 6(2) however, the constable must have reasonable cause to believe that the accused was driving or attempting to drive or be in charge of a vehicle at the time of an accident. It is submitted that clearly the word 'believed' is intended to convey a higher standard of conviction on the part of the police constable than the word 'suspect'. In *Merry v Docherty* 1977 JC 34, 1977 SLT 117, 1977 CO Circulars A/2, the High Court discussed in some detail both the need for the prosecution to establish that an accident has taken place as a result of the presence of the vehicle on the road, and further what has to be established in order that it can be shown that a constable has reasonable cause to believe that the accused was driving at the time. In particular, in view of the way in which the section is now phrased, it would seem to be essential for any requirement under this particular sub-section that the constable knows of the accident in question at the time when he makes the requirement for a breath specimen. However, the nature and extent of the constable's knowledge of the accident need not be prescribed in any way, and in a case where police officers had received an anonymous call describing the circumstances of the accident, and the accused's vehicle was found to be in a condition consistent with that description, it was held that the police could have reasonable cause to believe that the accused had been driving his motor vehicle at the time of the accident (*Glass v Milne* 1977 CO Circulars A/7; *Allan v Douglas* 1978 JC 7, 1977 CO Circulars A/28; *Topping v Scott* 1979 SLT (Notes) 21; but see also *Breen v Pirie* 1976 JC 60, 1976 SLT 136). English cases that may be of assistance in comprehending this phrase are *inter alia Baker v Oxford* [1980] RTR 315; *Moss v Jenkins* [1975] RTR 25 and *Johnson v Whitehouse* [1984] RTR 38.

In terms of s 6(2), the constable does not have to be in uniform, nor does he have to have any suspicion that the accused has had alcohol in his body. Again, as in s 6(1) requirements, there are no time limits imposed by the sub-section on when the requirement must be made.

In *Binnie v Donnelly* 1981 SLT 294, 1981 SCCR 126, 1981 CO Circulars A/20, a motorist was involved in an accident on the Scottish side of the Scotland/England border, then drove his car across the border to where he was involved in a further accident. In these circumstances it was decided that there was nothing to

stop Scottish police officers pursuing the accused over the border
and requiring a breath specimen when he was apprehended.

4.4   THE LIMITS: PLACE WHERE TEST TO BE GIVEN
(S 6(3))

As indicated above, once the reasonable grounds for suspicion have
been properly established in the constable's mind, there is no time
limit within which either the requirement be made, or the test
administered. However, in terms of s 6(3) the specimen of breath
must be given at or near the place where the requirement is made.
This phrase does not appear to have been judicially considered in
Scotland; it is thought that the sub-section will be construed with
reasonable strictness, and if the specimen is provided at a place
which is in any way significantly distant from the place where the
requirement is made, then the specimen will be regarded as
invalid.

Section 6(2) provides no restriction on where the requirement to
provide a specimen in terms of that sub-section should be made;
normally the requirement will be made where the suspicion in the
constable's mind was formed. If the requirement is made at a
police station, the test need not be administered at the same station
(*Milne v McDonald* 1971 JC 40, 1971 SLT 291).

4.5   FAILURE TO PROVIDE A SPECIMEN OF BREATH
(S 6(4))

4.5:1   Section 6(4)

Section 6(4) of the Road Traffic Act 1988 provides:

A person who, without reasonable excuse, fails to provide a
specimen of breath when required to do so in pursuance of this
section shall be guilty of an offence.

4.5:2   Definitions

Fail. In terms of s 11(2) of the Act, the word 'fail' includes refuse.

Further, in terms of s 11(3) of the Act, 'a person does not
provide a specimen of breath for a breath test or for analysis unless
the specimen (a) is sufficient to enable the test or the analysis to be
carried out, and (b) is provided in such a way as to enable the
objective of the test or analysis to be satisfactorily achieved'.

There is no requirement on the constable administering the test to advise the motorist that failure to comply with the procedure may result in prosecution; however the Appeal Court has recommended that such a warning be given (*O'Sharkey v Smith* 1982 SLT 91, 1981 SCCR 189, CO Circulars A/24).

Breath test. See paragraph 4.2:2.

4.5:3 Approved devices

The principal devices approved by the Secretary of State for use in Scotland are the Alcotest 80/A, the Alcolyser, and the Lion Alcolmeter (see the Breath Test Device (Approval) (Scotland) Orders 1975 and 1987). In respect of the Alcotest, the device must be correctly assembled in accordance with the manufacturer's instructions printed thereon, and it must not be out of time in respect of the expiry date which is also printed on the device. In respect of the Alcotest 80/A, the Alcolyser, and the Lion Alcolmeter, the constable must explain clearly to the motorist the method by which the test is to be administered, in accordance with the manufacturer's instructions. Any failure in respect of the foregoing matters will invalidate the test. However, if the instructions have been complied with, the motorist must properly and correctly carry through the test, unless he has a reasonable excuse for not doing so (see paragraph 4.5:4). An offence under s 6(4) will accordingly be committed if the motorist fails to co-operate with the request to provide a specimen in any material way or if he fails to comply with the manufacturer's instructions in respect of the particular device used at the material time. A description of these devices and their operating instructions is given in Appendix B.

4.5:4 Reasonable excuse

It can in general terms be a reasonable excuse to fail to provide such a specimen only if the person concerned is physically or mentally unable to provide it, or that to do so would involve a substantial risk to their health (*R v Lennard* [1973] 1 WLR 483, [1973] RTR 252; *Williams v Critchley* [1979] RTR 46; *McGregor v Jessop* 1988 SLT 719, 1988 SCCR 339, 1988 CO Circulars A/29). Once the prosecution have established that the accused has failed to provide a specimen, and there were no, or insufficient, reasons for the refusal, it is for the accused to demonstrate that his failure was justified. However once the issue of reasonable excuse has been sufficiently raised by the defence, it is for the prosecution to rebut it, and in that event the court will have to determine on the basis of all the evidence led, whether or not it has been established beyond reasonable doubt that the motorist failed to provide the specimen without reasonable excuse (*Earnshaw v HM Advocate* 1982 JC 11, 1982 SLT 179, 1981 SCCR 279, 1981 CO Circulars A/31; *McGregor v Jessop supra; Pringle v Annan* 1988 SLT 899, 1988 SCCR 423, 1988 CO Circulars A/26). In the normal case, the accused may well have to lead medical or other evidence in support of his claim that he had a reasonable excuse to refuse to take the test. However the uncorroborated evidence of the accused if accepted can be sufficient to establish a defence. In exceptional cases it may be possible to proceed on the basis of a statement of facts agreed between the prosecution and defence, preferably by way of a joint statement of admissions.

It must be emphasised that the reasonable excuse claimed by the accused must relate to the taking of the test, and not to any other matter. It is therefore not a reasonable excuse for the driver to maintain that he has not in fact consumed alcohol as a reason for refusing to take the test (*McNicol v Peters* 1969 SLT 261), or that he was not in fact the driver at the material time (*McGrath v Vipas* [1984] RTR 58). Nor is it a reasonable excuse that an earlier requirement to give a specimen was made but properly withdrawn (*Nelson v McGuillivray* 1981 SCCR 701, 1981 CO Circulars A/8). Further, the fact that the reasonable cause of suspicion or belief entertained by the constable turns out in the event to be unjustified, unfounded or inaccurate will not invalidate the request to justify the refusal on the grounds of reasonable excuse. Reference should also be had to the cases described in paragraphs 4.14:3 and 4.14:7 (onus of proof and reasonable excuse in charges of failing to provide a specimen for analysis in terms of s 7(6)).

English cases that may be relevant are *Bryant v Morris* [1972] RTR 214; *R v Kelly* [1972] RTR 447; *Parker v Smith* [1974] RTR 500; *Williams v Critchley* [1979] RTR 46; *Mallows v Harris* [1979] RTR 404 and *Teape v Godfrey* [1986] RTR 213.

4.6   ARREST: SECTION 6(5)

Section 6(5) of the Road Traffic Act 1988 provides:

A constable may arrest a person without warrant if–

(a) as a result of a breath test he has reasonable cause to suspect that the proportion of alcohol in that person's breath or blood exceeds the prescribed limit; or

(b) that person has failed to provide a specimen of breath for a breath test when required to do so in pursuance of this section and the constable has reasonable cause to suspect that he has alcohol in his body, but a person shall not be arrested by virtue of this sub-section when he is at a hospital as a patient.

The phrase 'reasonable cause to suspect' is defined in paragraph 4.2:2.

This section gives a police officer the power to arrest an accused if he has given a positive breath test or failed to give a breath test. It should be noted, however, that neither the provision of a positive breath test, nor the failure to provide a specimen of breath, nor the arrest itself is now a necessary prerequisite of further procedure in prosecutions under ss 5 or 6 of the Act. The officer who effects the arrest is usually, but need not necessarily be, the same officer who required the specimen of breath; but if a different officer arrests the accused, then that officer must have been in a position to have observed the requirement taking place (*Stewart v Fekkes* 1977 JC 85, 1977 CO Circulars A/27).

In the latter case one constable administered a breath test to a motorist and the procedure was observed by another constable who then arrested the motorist. It was held that in fact the test had been carried out by both constables within the meaning of the Act as they were both clearly acting together, and it was observed that the underlying purpose of the section was to give power of arrest only to a constable who observed the test and its positive result.

4.7 GENERAL

4.7:1 Powers of entry: (s 6(6) and 6(7))

Section 6(6) gives a police constable in England the power to enter (if need be by force) any property or place where he has reasonable cause to suspect a person to be in order to effect an arrest under s 6(5). Section 6(7) specifically excludes this provision from applying to Scotland, presumably on the grounds (as in the similar provisions contained in s 4(7) and (8)), that in Scotland a police constable already has common law powers to effect such entry in these circumstances (*Cairns v Keane* 1983 SCCR 277).

4.7:2   Traffic offences (s 6(8))

Traffic offences are defined in this sub-section for the purpose of s 6(1)(a) and (c). The sub-section provides:

In this section 'traffic offence' means an offence under–
(a) any provision of Part II of the Public Passenger Vehicles Act 1981,
(b) any provision of the Road Traffic Regulation Act 1984,
(c) any provision of the Road Traffic Offenders Act 1988 except Part III, or
(d) any provision of this Act except Part V.

4.7:3   Procedure and penalties

A charge of failure to provide a specimen of breath in terms of s 6(4) is normally taken on summary complaint and the penalties are found in Schedule 2 of the Road Traffic Offenders Act 1988. Unlike s 7(7) of the Act, there is no provision in s 6 which requires the constable administering the test to warn the motorist that failure to comply with the procedure may lead to prosecution.

PART 2
PROVISION OF SPECIMENS FOR ANALYSIS

4.8   INTRODUCTION

4.8:1   Section 7

Section 7 of the Road Traffic Act 1988 provides as follows:

(1) In the course of an investigation into whether a person has committed an offence under section 4 or 5 of this Act a constable may, subject to the following provisions of this section and section 9 of this Act, require him–
(a) to provide two specimens of breath for analysis by means of a device of a type approved by the Secretary of State, or
(b) to provide a specimen of blood or urine for a laboratory test.

(2) A requirement under this section to provide specimens of breath can only be made at a police station.

(3) A requirement under this section to provide a specimen of blood or urine can only be made at a police station or at a hospital, and it cannot be made at a police station unless –

(a) the constable making the requirement has reasonable cause to believe that for medical reasons a specimen of breath cannot be provided or should not be required, or

(b) at the time the requirement is made a device or a reliable device of the type mentioned in sub-section (1)(a) above is not available at the police station or it is then for any other reason not practicable to use such a device there, or

(c) the suspected offence is one under section 4 of this Act and the constable making the requirement has been advised by a medical practitioner that the condition of the person required to provide the specimen might be due to some drug;

but may then be made notwithstanding that the person required to provide the specimen has already provided or been required to provide two specimens of breath.

(4) If the provision of a specimen other than a specimen of breath may be required in pursuance of this section the question whether it is to be a specimen of blood or a specimen of urine shall be decided by the constable making the requirement, but if a medical practitioner is of the opinion that for medical reasons a specimen of blood cannot or should not be taken the specimen shall be a specimen of urine.

(5) A specimen of urine shall be provided within one hour of the requirement for its provision being made and after the provision of a previous specimen of urine.

(6) A person who, without reasonable excuse, fails to provide a specimen when required to do so in pursuance of this section is guilty of an offence.

(7) A constable must, on requiring any person to provide a specimen in pursuance of this section, warn him that a failure to provide it may render him liable to prosecution.

4.8:2   General application

This section (subject to the provisions of ss 8 and 9) governs the provision of specimens for analysis in the course of an investigation as to whether a person has committed an offence under ss 4 or 5 of the Act. It is clearly intended that the principal procedure under this section is to be the provision by the motorist of two breath specimens into an approved device situated in a police station. The higher of these two readings is to be disregarded (s 8(1)). Only where any one of the three sets of circumstances described in s 7(3) applies, the requirement of the breath specimens cannot be made, and the constable in charge of the procedure must turn instead to the alternative requirement of a specimen of blood or urine. It is however open to a motorist who has provided two specimens of breath, where the lower of such specimens does not exceed 50 microgrammes of alcohol in 100 millilitres of breath, to claim that the breath specimen should be replaced by a specimen of blood or urine (s 8(2)). Unlike the provision of a preliminary breath test under s 7 of the Act, the constable making the requirement must warn the accused that failure to provide a specimen in terms of this section may render him liable to prosecution (s 7(7)).

4.9   PROVISION OF SPECIMENS FOR ANALYSIS (S 7(1))

4.9:1   Section 7(1)

Section 7(1) of the Act provides:

In the course of an investigation into whether a person has committed an offence under section 4 or section 5 of this Act a constable may, subject to the following provisions of this section and section 9 below, require him –
   (a) to provide two specimens of breath for analysis by means of a device of a type approved by the Secretary of State, or
   (b) to provide a specimen of blood or urine for a laboratory test.

4.9:2   Definitions

In the course of an investigation. This phrase has not come to the notice of the courts; it is submitted that the question is one of fact and that the meaning of the words is plain.

A constable. See paragraph 4.2:2. For the purpose of administering the provision of breath specimens into an approved device, only certain police officers have been trained in the use of such devices and are authorised by the Chief Constable for the area to use them. There is nothing in s 8 which says that the officer administering the test and requiring the two specimens of breath has to be appropriately trained or authorised; however, if the evidence indicates that the operator of the device is unskilled or unauthorised, the Crown may have difficulty in proving, for example, that the device was unreliable. There is no requirement that the constable supervising the procedure be in uniform.

To require. To require means to ask (*Milne v McDonald* 1971 JC 40 at 42 (per LJC Clyde) 1971 SLT 291.) The requirement of a specimen is something different from the provision of a specimen. The requirement must be corroborated (*Carmichael v Gillooly* 1982 SCCR 119).

Specimen of breath. Section 11(3) of the Act provides that a person does not provide a specimen of breath for a breath test or for analysis unless the specimen (a) is sufficient to enable the test or analysis to be carried out, and (b) is provided in such a way as to enable the object of the test to be satisfactorily achieved.

Section 7(2) makes it clear that a specimen of breath can only be provided at a police station; in other words an approved device cannot be located anywhere else.

An approved device. The breath specimen analysis devices currently approved for use in Scotland are the Camic Breath Analyser (S) and the Lion Breath Analyser (Sc), both of which were endorsed by virtue of the Breath Analysis Devices (Approval) (Scotland) Order 1983, made on 4 May 1983, and which came into force with Schedule 8 of the Transport Act 1981 on 6 May 1983. It is thought that the only device which is in daily use in Scotland is the Camic Breath Analyser Device. The prosecution are entitled to a presumption that the Camic Breath Analyser is an approved device within the meaning of the section but there must at least be oral evidence from the police that the Camic device was used (*Knox v Lockhart* 1985 SLT 248, 1984 SCCR 463, 1984 CO Circulars A/33; *Davidson v Aitchison* 1986 SLT 402, 1985 SCCR 415, 1986 CO Circulars A/31; *Valentine v Macphail* 1986 SLT 598, 1986 SCCR 321, 1986 CO Circulars A/24), and it is unnecessary to produce the relevant Approval Order (*Lee v Smith* 1982 SLT 200, 1981 SCCR 267, 1981 CO Circulars A/29). Further, where the device has done what it should have done if it was in proper working order, there is a presumption that the machine is in proper working order and has been correctly maintained (*Tudhope v McAllister* 1984 SLT 395, 1984 SCCR 182, 1984 CO Circulars A/15).

A description of the Camic Breath Analyser Device and its operating instructions are given in Appendix C.

Specimen of blood. Section 11(4) of the Road Traffic Act 1988 provides: 'A person provides a specimen of blood if and only if he consents to its being taken by a medical practitioner.' This definition is applied for the interpretation of ss 4–10 of the Act (s 11(1)).

Section 15(4) of the Road Traffic Offenders Act 1988 provides: 'A specimen of blood shall be disregarded unless it was taken from the accused with his consent by a medical practitioner.' This definition is provided for the purposes of proceedings under ss 4 or 5 of the Road Traffic Act 1988 (s 15(1)).

Section 16(2) of the Road Traffic Offenders Act 1988 provides: 'Subject to subsections (3) and (4) below, evidence that a specimen of blood was taken from the accused with his consent by a medical practitioner may be given by the production of a document purporting to certify that fact and to be signed by a medical practitioner'. Sub-sections (3) and (4) are concerned with the requirements of service.

Section 11(3) of the Road Traffic Act 1988 provides that a specimen for analysis must be sufficient and provided in a way to enable the objective of the analysis to be satisfactorily achieved.

'*Specimen of urine.*' The procedure for the provision of a specimen of urine is described in s 7(5) of the Road Traffic Act 1988.

'*Laboratory test.*' Although this phrase is not defined in the legislation, s 16(1)(b) of the Road Traffic Offenders Act 1988 describes the evidential procedure in respect of findings of the proportion of alcohol or any drug found by an authorised analyst in a specimen of blood or urine; and section 16(7) gives a definition of an authorised analyst.

4.9:3   General application (s 7(1))

As indicated above, it is the intention of the Act that the principal method of procedure should be by the way of two specimens of breath for analysis by means of an approved device. It is only where any of the circumstances described in s 7(3) apply that the alternative procedure of providing a specimen of blood or urine can be invoked. Any of such specimens of breath, blood or urine may be used to found a charge under s 4 as well as s 5. The provisions of s 7(1) must of course be read in the context of the other subsections of s 7, and are also qualified by the provisions for hospital patients contained in s 9.

4.9:4   Previous procedure unnecessary

It is not necessary that the procedural requirements of the preliminary breath test under s 6 of the Road Traffic Act 1988 (including the power of arrest) need be observed before this section can apply, although in practice such a test normally will and should be taken. If not, the court will no doubt look closely into the circumstances of how these preliminary steps were not followed in the light of any defence offered by the accused. However, it is submitted that even an illegal arrest will not make the provision of the specimens obtained under this section inadmissible in evidence; the arrest of the motorist in terms of s 4(6) or 6(5) is not required before the procedure under s 7 is embarked upon. Reference should be made to paragraph 4.6.

4.9:5 Where only one breath specimen given

Although the requirement in terms of s 7(1)(a) is to provide two breath specimens, a conviction has been upheld on the strength of one only, where the accused, in a considered attempt to frustrate the procedure, failed to provide a second specimen (*Reid v Tudhope* 1986 SLT 136, 1985 SCCR 268, 1985 CO Circulars A/20). On the other hand, where a driver gave a successful first specimen at the first attempt, but was refused a second chance after failing in his first attempt to give a second specimen in circumstances where both failures were genuine, it was held that in declining to give the accused a second chance to provide the second specimen the police had not given him a fair opportunity for the provision of the specimen (*Douglas v Stevenson* 1986 SCCR 519, 1986 CO Circulars A/57). In this respect the relevant test as to whether a proper opportunity has been given to the accused to provide a specimen is considered to be that of fairness to the accused in the light of his own actings.

4.9:6 Right to contact solicitor

An accused has the right to contact a solicitor on being arrested in terms of s 305 of the Criminal Procedure (Scotland) Act 1975, but it is not a reasonable excuse in terms of s 7(6) of the Act to refuse to give a specimen until that solicitor arrives (*Manuel v Steward* 1986 SLT 593, 1986 SCCR 121, 1986 CO Circulars A/15).

4.10 REQUIREMENT FOR A BREATH SPECIMEN TO BE MADE AT A POLICE STATION (S 7(2))

Section 7(2) of the Act provides:

A requirement under this section to provide specimens of breath can only be made at a police station.

This does not necessarily mean that both the requirement and the subsequent provision of the specimens need be made at the same police station; where the requirement was made at one station and it was then discovered that the approved device was not working there, it was held to be in order to take the specimens at another station (*Milne v McDonald* 1971 JC 40, 1971 SLT 291; *Tudhope v Fulton* 1986 SCCR 567).

4.11 CIRCUMSTANCES WHERE A BREATH TEST IS NOT APPROPRIATE (S 7(3))

4.11:1 General

This important sub-section in effect prescribes the only circumstances under which breath specimens are not to be provided; in other words, unless one of the circumstances described in the sub-section applies, the provision of breath specimens must be required. The first situation described in the sub-section is where the constable making the requirement has reasonable cause to believe that for medical reasons a specimen of breath can not or should not be provided. The second situation is where an approved device is not present in the particular police station or alternatively where there is such a device but it is not reliable or it is not for any other reason practicable to use the device. A third situation exclusively relates to s 4 prosecutions and arises where the constable making the requirement had been advised by a medical practitioner that the accused's condition might be due to some drug. All these situations however are subject to the important proviso that if they arise after the provision of two breath specimens or after just the requirement to provide them has been made, the police constable making the requirement is not precluded from then requiring a specimen of blood or urine.

4.11:2 Section 7(3)

Section 7(3) of the Road Traffic Act 1988 provides:

A requirement under this section to provide a specimen of blood or urine can only be made at a police station or at a hospital; and it can not be made at a police station unless—
  (a) the constable making the requirement has reasonable cause to believe that for medical reasons a specimen of breath cannot be provided or should not be required; or
  (b) at the time the requirement is made a device or a reliable device of the type mentioned in sub-section (1)(a) is not available at the police station or it is then for any other reason not practicable to use such a device there; or
  (c) the suspected offence is one under s 4 of this Act and the constable making the requirement has been advised by a medical practitioner that the condition of the person required to provide the specimen might be due to some drug;
but may then be made notwithstanding that the person required to provide the specimen has already provided or been required to provide two specimens of breath.

4.11:3 Medical reasons (s 7(3)(a))

A breath specimen will not be required if the constable making the requirement has reasonable cause to believe that the specimen cannot or should not be provided for medical reasons. This section has not been considered in the courts in Scotland but it is submitted that the following considerations are relevant.

Firstly, the test is that the constable must have reasonable cause to believe that the medical reasons do exist, not simply that he may have reasonable cause to suspect that such medical reasons may exist. The decision of the constable is intended to be an entirely subjective one and the Act does not require him to consult medical advice (*Dempsey v Catton* [1986] RTR 194). However, there do have to be grounds for the constable's decision. The term 'medical reasons' is therefore thought to be subject to a reasonably broad interpretation, and can include physical causes such as asthma, and psychological causes such as repugnance (*Johnson v West Yorkshire Metropolitan Police* [1986] RTR 167). It has been held in England that an accused has a duty to bring any medical condition he may have which might affect the provision of the sample to the notice of the officer making the requirement (*Teape v Godfrey* [1986] RTR 213 at 221; see also *Horrocks v Binns* [1986] RTR 202). It is thought that this consideration will also be applied in Scotland; however reference should be made to paragraph 4.14:7.

4.11:4 No device or reliable device available (s 7(3)(b))

Secondly, the requirement to provide two specimens of breath is set aside when there is not an approved device at a particular station, or where at the material time the device is not 'reliable', or where it is for any other reason not practicable to use the device.

Not all police stations are currently equipped with a breath analyser device. Further, as indicated above, only certain officers in any police force are trained in and authorised to work the device, and it appears that if no such officer is on duty at the material time then that will constitute 'any other reason' that it is not practicable to use the device and the alternative procedure should be adopted (*Chief Constable of Avon & Somerset v Kelliher* [1986] Crim LR 635).

Alternatively it may be that the device in the particular station is not 'reliable' usually because at the material time it is not properly operational or functioning. Whether the device is or is not reliable will be a question of fact decided by the court. In terms of the proviso to this section, it may be that the fact that the machine is not functioning correctly will become evident while the two specimens of breath are being provided, and if this is so, it will not preclude a further requirement to provide a specimen of blood or urine. However, the prosecution have to prove that the machine is not reliable in the course of evidence if they are to rely on the alternative procedure. The principal issue in such circumstances as demonstrated by the reported cases, is whether the information shown within the statement or printout automatically produced by the device is of such a character that, by virtue of that information alone, the device can be considered not reliable. This topic is more fully discussed in paragraphs 5.8:5 *et seq*. The question of the reliability of the machine may also have to be considered in the light of the manufacturer's instructions in respect of the proper operation of the machine (see eg *Allan v Miller* 1986 SLT 3, 1985 SCCR 227, 1985 CO Circulars A/15; *McLeod v Fraser* 1987 SLT 142, 1986 SCCR 271, 1986 CO Circulars A/27). These instructions are given in Appendix C.

If the Crown claim that the device is unreliable they also have to show that it is the only such device available in the police station (*Houston v McLeod* 1986 SCCR 219, 1988 CO Circulars A/27).

4.11:5   Section 7(3)(c)

This section has not so far come to the attention of the court, and its application is essentially a matter of fact. It should be noted that this part of the sub-section is restricted to s 4 prosecutions. This situation can arise only once a medical practitioner has suggested that the accused's condition may be due to some drug. The Act appears to impose no obligation on the constable to seek such medical advice; however, once the constable has received such advice from a medical practitioner, he must act on that advice whatever the circumstances, and has no discretion to do otherwise.

4.11:6   Definition: medical practitioner

The legislation does not provide a definition of what is meant by a medical practitioner. However, it is submitted that a medical practitioner is an appropriately qualified doctor who is authorised to be in medical practice in this country. There appears to be no reported case where the status of the medical practitioner has been challenged.

4.12 PROVISION OF SPECIMEN OF BLOOD OR URINE (S 7(4))

4.12:1 Section 7(4)

Section 7(4) of the Act provides:

If the provision of a specimen other than a specimen of breath may be required in pursuance of this section the question whether it is to be a specimen of blood or a specimen of urine shall be decided by the constable making the requirement, but if a medical practitioner is of the opinion that for medical reasons a specimen of blood cannot or should not be taken a specimen shall be a specimen of urine.

4.12:2 Definitions

See paragraph 4.9:2.

4.12:3 General application

It is clear from this sub-section that the option of which specimen the accused is to provide in circumstances where a breath specimen is not to be taken, rests entirely at the discretion of the constable making the requirement. This officer does not have to be the same constable who required any previous breath specimen under s 7(3). The only qualification to the constable's power is where a medical practitioner expresses the opinion that for medical reasons a blood sample should not be required. There is, however, again no apparent obligation on the constable to seek out such a medical opinion in this matter. Neither does the Act require a constable to justify his choice of the specimen required. Unless a doctor is of the opinion that, for medical reasons, a breath specimen cannot or should not be taken, the constable has complete discretion as to whether the motorist should in these circumstances be required to provide a sample of blood or urine.

In *Bain v Tudhope* 1985 SCCR 412, 1986 CO Circulars A/17, an accused who gave a breath specimen reading of 42 microgrammes elected to exercise his right under s 8(2) to provide an alternative specimen under s 7(4). He was required to provide a urine sample and failed to do so. He was accordingly convicted on the original breath specimen reading. The accused appealed on the ground that he should have been required to give a blood specimen; but this was rejected on the ground that the decision of which of the two specimens should be given under s 7(4) should in all circumstances be left wholly to the discretion of the constable. Reference should also be made to paragraphs 4.16:2 and 4.16:3. However, the driver must be informed of his statutory right to have the breath specimen replaced by one of blood or urine; an intimation that he may elect to give a sample of blood only will vitiate the procedure (*Hamilton v Jones* 1989 SCCR 1).

4.12:4   Other provisions

Section 7(4) does of course have to be read in the context of the other provisions of s 7, and is subject to the provisions of s 11(3) and 11(4) of the Road Traffic Act 1988 and ss 15(4) and 16(2) of the Road Traffic Offenders Act 1988.

4.13   PROVISION OF URINE SPECIMEN (S 7(5))

4.13:1   Section 7(5)

Section 7(5) of the Act provides:

A specimen of urine shall be provided within one hour of the requirement for its provision being made and after the provision of a previous specimen of urine.

4.13:2   General application

In terms of this sub-section, two specimens of urine have to be given within one hour of the requirement. While the two samples have to be given within an hour of the requirement, there is no stipulation as to when, during the hour, the samples must be given. For practical reasons, the first sample is usually given at the beginning of the period, and the second one towards the end. Unlike the previous legislation, there is no express provision that the first specimen shall be discarded. Reference again requires to be had to s 11(3) of the Road Traffic Act 1988.

The terms of this sub-section are simpler than under the previous legislation which also required the provision of two samples of urine and described the circumstances under which a failure would arise.

In a prosecution under the former legislation, where the second urine specimen was provided just over an hour after the requirement, but exactly an hour after the first specimen was provided, it was held to be competent to convict the accused on the basis of the second specimen (*Tudhope v Stevenson* 1980 SLT (Notes) 94, 1980 CO Circulars A/14; (following *Roney v Matthews* [1975] RTR

273)). However, the accused was convicted on the basis of the specimen which he had provided, not on his failure to provide a specimen within the terms of s 9(5) of the former [1972 Act] legislation. As the present sub-section requires that the requirement and both specimens shall be given within an hour, it may be that the particular circumstances of *Tudhope v Stevenson* (*supra*) would lead under the present law to an acquittal.

4.14   FAILURE TO PROVIDE A SPECIMEN (S 7(6))

4.14:1   Section 7(6)

Section 7(6) of the Act provides as follows:

A person who, without reasonable excuse, fails to provide a specimen when required to do so in pursuance of this section is guilty of an offence.

4.14:2   General application

Failure includes refusal (s 11(2)). The specimens provided must be sufficient to enable the analysis to be carried out. Section 11(3) of the Act makes it clear that if the specimen given either for a preliminary breath test or for analysis is not sufficient to enable the test or analysis to be carried out, or further is not provided in such a way as to enable the objective of the test or analysis to be satisfactorily achieved, then the person will be deemed not to have provided a specimen and thus be liable to conviction under this section.

If the Crown alleges that the specimen provided is not sufficient to allow proper analysis to be carried out in terms of s 11(3) of the Act, expert evidence to this effect will normally be required (*Carmichael v Gillooly* 1982 SCCR 119; *Aitchison v Johnstone* 1987 SCCR 225).

If a reliable device is not available at the police station to which the accused is first taken, the test can competently be carried out at another police station (*Tudhope v Fulton* 1986 SCCR 567).

4.14:3   Reasonable excuse: onus of proof

The Crown must prove that the motorist had no reasonable cause for refusing to provide the specimen of whatever kind. This is normally done by police officers testifying that no apparent cause existed for the refusal. Alternatively the officers may describe the reasons, if any, given by the accused for declining to give the sample and thereafter the Crown require to justify the proposition that such reasons did not amount to a reasonable excuse in the circumstances (*Earnshaw v HM Advocate* 1982 JC 11, 1982 SLT (Notes) 179, 1981 SCCR 279; *McLeod v Murray* 1986 SCCR 369; *McGregor v Jessop* 1988 SLT 179; 1988 SCCR 339; 1988 CO Circulars A/29). At the same time, while it is for the prosecution to demonstrate that no reasonable excuse exists for the refusal, if the accused wishes the court to consider the question of whether he has a reasonable excuse, or whether his excuse is reasonable, then he must raise the issue at the time of the requirement being made, if he is asked why he cannot provide a specimen. (*Stewart v Aitchison* 1984 SCCR 357; *Singh v McLeod* 1986 SCCR 656). However, if the motorist is not asked why he is unable to give a specimen he is not obliged to volunteer this information (*Pringle v Annan* 1988 SLT 899, 1988 SCCR 423, 1988 CO Circulars A/26). Reference should also be made to paragraphs 4.5:4 and 4.14:7.

4.14:4 Instructions to provide specimen

The Act does not indicate what instructions are to be given by the police officers to the motorist to enable him to provide the specimens properly. However, it seems clear that sufficient and proper instructions should be given, and whether or not that is done in any case is a matter of fact for the court to decide on the evidence (*Kelly v McKinnon* 1985 SLT 487, 1985 SCCR 97, 1985 CO Circulars A/6; *Fleming v Tudhope* 1987 CO Circulars A/16); it therefore appears to follow that, if inadequate instructions are given, and this can be related to the failure to provide a specimen, the accused may be able to claim that he had a reasonable excuse for not providing the specimen required. Cases which feature instructions in respect of particular devices are *Jeffrey v MacNeill* 1976 SLT 134; *Sloan v Smith* 1978 SLT (Notes) 27, 1977 CO Circulars A/5, and *Hogg v Smith* 1978 CO Circulars A/37.

The operating instructions are given in Appendix C.

4.14:5 Agreement to provide sample

An accused must unequivocally agree to provide a specimen or sample, otherwise he will be deemed to have failed to comply with the provisions of the Act. It is therefore insufficient for the accused, in response to a request for a sample, merely to say 'please yourself' and such an answer will constitute the offence of failure to provide a specimen (*MacPhail v Forbes* 1975 SLT (Sh Ct) 48;

Milne v Elliot 1974 SLT (Notes) 71; *MacDonald v MacKenzie* 1975 SLT 190; *Beveridge v Allan* 1986 SCCR 542, 1986 CO Circulars A/56. Which part of the body a sample of blood is taken from is at the discretion of the doctor (*Cader v Galt* 1976 SCCR Supp 116).

A conditional acceptance is also not sufficient and will be deemed to be a refusal (*Solesbury v Pugh* [1969] 1 WLR 1114; [1969] 2 All ER 1171), a case where the driver agreed to give a sample but insisted that it be taken from his big toe (*Rushton v Higgins* [1972] RTR 456 and *Pettigrew v Northumbria Police Authority* [1976] RTR 177). Immediately a failure or refusal occurs, the offence is committed and complete, and the situation cannot be redeemed by the accused changing his mind and offering subsequently to comply with the request to provide a specimen (*Harris v Tudhope* 1985 SCCR 305; *Beveridge v Allan (supra)*).

4.14:6 Reasonable opportunity to provide specimen

The accused motorist must be given a fair and reasonable opportunity of providing the specimens required. What is a fair and reasonable opportunity is a matter for the court. In *Douglas v Stevenson* 1986 SCCR 519; 1986 CO Circulars A/57, a driver failed at his first attempt to provide a breath specimen into a Camic device, but succeeded at his second attempt. He then failed at his first attempt at providing a second specimen, and was not given a second chance to provide the second specimen. It was held that the police had not acted fairly in refusing the accused a second opportunity to provide the second specimen, and he was acquitted.

4.14:7 Reasonable excuse

Apart from the possibility that insufficient instruction might justify a refusal, as described in paragraph 4.14:4, it has been held that a reasonable excuse is in effect limited to cases where the accused is physically or mentally incapable of providing a specimen or sample or that to do so will involve a serious risk to the accused's health (*Glickman v McKinnon* 1981 JC 81 (fear of needles not an excuse); see also *R v Lennard* [1973] 1 WLR 483, [1975] RTR 252; and *Williams v Critchley* [1979] RTR 46 (not a reasonable excuse to provide a specimen after a signficant period had elapsed following an accident); *Palmer v Killion* [1983] RTR 138 (embarrassment not a reasonable excuse); and *Cotgrove v Cooney* [1987] RTR 124 (physical inability to provide specimen may be a reasonable excuse). However, reference should also be made to *McLeod v Murray* 1986 SCCR 369, where an accused who alleged that he had been assaulted by the police refused to give a specimen for analysis because he said he could not trust the police not to tamper with it (but see also *Gallacher v Scott* 1989 SLT 397, 1989 SCCR 61, CO Circulars A/1).

The courts have however normally regarded the standard of proof which the accused has to reach in order to demonstrate that he was not capable of giving a sample, to be a high one. For example, in *Hogg v Lockhart* 1973 SLT (Sh Ct) 40, it was established that the accused had a very powerful repugnance to blood and hypodermic needles and in those circumstances the court held that his refusal to give a specimen was reasonable. In *McGregor v Jessop* 1988 SLT 719, 1988 SCCR 339, it was held that a motorist who made several genuine attempts to provide a second urine sample but was unable to do so could be said to have a reasonable excuse for failing to provide a specimen. Where an accused did have a medical condition but deliberately refused to provide a specimen, he is liable to be found guilty under this sub-section (*Singh v McLeod* 1987 SLT 550; 1986 SCCR 656, 1987 CO Circulars A/5). However, in *Pringle v Annan* 1988 SLT 899, 1988 SCCR 423, 1988 CO Circulars A/26, a driver who was unable to provide a specimen because of injuries sustained in an accident was held to be under no general duty to inform the police of his own volition, of the reasons for his inability to produce a specimen (see also *McLory v Thomas* 1989 CO Circulars A/11).

It is not a reasonable excuse that the accused was not in fact driving or in charge of the vehicle (*McLellan v Tudhope* 1984 SCCR 397). In such a case, even when it is subsequently proved that the accused was not driving or in charge of the vehicle at the material time, and refuses to provide this specimen when required, disqualification is obligatory in terms of Schedule 4 of the 1972 Act (*McLellan v Tudhope supra*); nor is a refusal justified because the accused wishes to wait until his solicitor arrives (*Manuel v Stewart* 1986 SLT 593, 1986 SCCR 121, 1986 CO Circulars A/15). It would appear from the terms of this section that a failure to arrest the accused under s 6(6) would not constitute a reasonable excuse for the accused to provide a specimen. However, if the requirement to provide a sample of blood or urine is refused following what the police consider was a failure by the accused to provide a proper second breath specimen, the Crown will be required to prove that the breath analyser device is unreliable before it can proceed to hold that the accused refused to provide a specimen of blood or urine (*Tudhope v Quinn* 1984 SCCR 255). In that case, police officers considered that the accused had failed to provide a proper specimen, and charged him under s 7(6). Thereafter, they discovered that the breath analysis device had produced proper readings, but the printout was inaccurate in other respects. It was held that before the Crown could secure a conviction in these circumstances, it was necessary to prove that the machine was unreliable before they could properly require a blood or urine sample. As the Crown had not proved this, the accused was acquitted.

It should be noted that if in terms of s 7(4) and 7(6) a motorist has a reasonable excuse for failing to supply one or other of a specimen of blood or urine, then it is still open for the police to further require a specimen of the remaining alternative (*Hall v Allan* 1984 SLT 199, 1983 SCCR 520, 1983 CO Circulars A/31). What may be a reasonable excuse for failing to provide one kind of specimen will not necessarily (or indeed normally) be a reasonable excuse for failing to provide a different kind of specimen.

In *McLeod v Murray* 1986 SCCR 369, it was held that it could be reasonable grounds for a refusal if the accused had been assaulted by the police and apprehended that the officers would interfere with any specimens provided. Reference should also be made to *Gallacher v Scott* 1989 SLT 397, 1989 SCCR 61. See also paragraph 4.5:4.

4.14:8 Procedure and penalties

Proceedings for refusal to provide a specimen are taken summarily, and the penalties are given in Schedule 2 of the Road Traffic Offenders Act 1988. It would appear from the Schedule that obligatory disqualification only applies in cases where the accused was driving or attempting to drive. If it is established that the accused was not in fact driving or attempting to drive, disqualification is discretionary (see also *Aird v Valentine* 1986 SCCR 353, 1986 CO Circulars A/34).

Where the charge libelled is a failure to provide a specimen of breath, the Crown cannot amend the complaint at the end of their case to a charge of failure to supply a specimen of blood (*McArthur v McNeill* 1987 SLT 299, 1986 SCCR 552, 1986 CO Circulars A/62). However, where an accused was taken to a police station where it was discovered that the Camic device was not working, and was then taken to another police station, the Crown was allowed to amend the locus in the complaint to include the second police station (*Tudhope v Fulton* 1986 SCCR 567; see also *Belcher v MacKinnon* 1986 CO Circulars A/55).

4.15 WARNINGS (s 7(7))

4.15:1 Section 7(7)

Section 7(7) provides as follows:

A constable must, on requiring any person to provide a specimen in pursuance of this section, warn him that a failure to provide it may render him liable to prosecution.

4.15:2   General application

It seems clear that the Act intends that the accused will be warned at the same time as the requirement is made that failure to provide the specimen in terms of the requirement may result in prosecution. The Act however provides no sanction in the event of such a failure. It must be assumed that if the constable making the requirement fails to give a clear and unequivocal warning that such failure to provide a specimen may lead to prosecution, then this will then invalidate the entire procedure and lead to the specimen being considered inadmissible in evidence. This is despite the terms of s 15(2) of the Road Traffic Offenders Act 1988 which provides that evidence of the proportion of alcohol or any drug in a specimen of breath, blood or urine provided by the accused shall be taken into account 'in all cases'. The provisions of s 15(2) must presumably be construed as meaning that such specimens will be taken into account in all cases so long as the specimens are taken in accordance with the provisions of the Act (*R v Fox* [1985] RTR 337 at 343, per Lord Fraser; [1985] 1 WLR 1126).

4.16   CHOICE OF SPECIMENS OF BREATH (S 8)

4.16:1   Section 8

Section 8 of the Road Traffic Act 1988 provides:

(1) Subject to subsection (2) below, of any two specimens of breath provided by any person in pursuance of section 7 of this Act that with the lower proportion of alcohol in the breath shall be used and the other shall be disregarded.

(2) If the specimen with the lower proportion of alcohol contains no more than 50 microgrammes of alcohol in 100 millilitres of breath, the person who provided it may claim that it should be replaced by such specimen as may be required under section 7(4) of this Act and, if he then provides such a specimen, neither specimen of breath shall be used.

(3) The Secretary of State may by regulations substitute another proportion of alcohol in the breath for that specified in subsection (2) above.

4.16:2   General application

This section contains two significant provisions. Firstly, the Crown case can only proceed on the basis of the lower of the two readings produced by the breath analyser device, the higher one being ignored for the purposes of prosecution. Secondly, if that lower reading is not higher than 50 microgrammes of alcohol in 100 millilitres of breath, the accused may exercise the option of having the breath specimen replaced by one of blood or urine in terms of s 7(4), and if such an alternative specimen is given, then that is used and both breath specimens are ignored. However, if for any reason the alternative specimens are not given, the Crown may still secure a conviction on the basis of the original breath specimens (*Bain v Tudhope* 1985 SCCR 412, 1986 CO Circulars A/17).

4.16:3   Choice of blood or urine specimen

If the lower of the two breath specimens is below the 50 microgrammes level, then it is for the police constable to indicate to the accused that the option of giving a blood or urine sample is open to him, and this alternative choice must be given fairly and fully. It is incorrect for the police officer to give the accused advice about which option he should choose, but such advice will not necessarily invalidate the conviction if the accused was not subject to improper pressure, and the constable did not act in bad faith (*Woodburn v McLeod* 1986 SLT 325, 1986 SCCR 107, 1986 CO Circulars A/4). However, if the police go further and exert pressure on the accused which results in him being forced to make a choice, a conviction is not thereafter competent on the basis of the specimen of blood or urine thus produced (*Green v Lockhart* 1986 SLT 11, 1985 SCCR 257, 1980 CO Circulars A/25). See also paragraph 4.12:3.

Once the motorist has elected to undergo the alternative procedure in terms of s 8(2), the choice of whether a blood or urine specimen is to be given is entirely within the discretion of the constable administering the test (*Bain v Tudhope (supra)*).

If the lower of the two breath specimens is also below the level at which the Crown Office have indicated proceedings will not in practice be taken, it would appear to be incompetent for this alternative procedure to be adopted (*Benton v Cardle* 1986 SLT 310, 1987 SCCR 738; *McConnachie v Scott* 1988 SLT 480, 1988 SCCR 167; see also paragraph 3.14).

4.16:4 Insufficiency of specimen

Where the Crown claims that an alternative specimen provided by the accused is insufficient to allow proper analysis to be carried out, this is normally established by expert evidence (*Carmichael v Gillooly* 1982 SCCR 119; *Aitchison v Johnstone* 1987 SCCR 225). Once it is established that such a specimen is not capable of analysis, the Crown may revert to the lower of the two original breath specimen readings (*Bain v Tudhope* (*supra*)).

Chapter Five

Use of specimens and evidence in proceedings under the Road Traffic Act 1988, sections 4, 5

5.1   THE ROAD TRAFFIC OFFENDERS ACT 1988, S 15

Sections 15 and 16 provide important evidential considerations in prosecutions under ss 4 and 5 of the Road Traffic Act 1988. In the previous legislation, the general provisions now in ss 15 and 16 of the Road Traffic Offenders Act 1988 were found in ss 8(6) and 10 of the Road Traffic Act 1972 (as amended by s 25(3) and Schedule 8 of the Transport Act 1981).

Section 15 of the Road Traffic Offenders Act 1988 reads in full as follows:

(1) This section and section 16 of this Act apply in respect of proceedings for an offence under section 4 or 5 of the Road Traffic Act 1988 (motor vehicles: drink and drugs); and expressions used in this section and section 16 of this Act have the same meaning as in sections 4 to 10 of that Act.

(2) Evidence of the proportion of alcohol or any drug in a specimen of breath, blood or urine provided by the accused shall, in all cases, be taken into account and, subject to subsection (3) below, it shall be assumed that the proportion of alcohol in the accused's breath, blood or urine at the time of the alleged offence was not less than in the specimen.

(3) If the proceedings are for an offence under section 5 of that Act or, where the accused is alleged to have been unfit through drink, for an offence under section 4 of that Act, assumption shall not be made if the accused proves–

(a) that he consumed alcohol after he had ceased to drive, attempt to drive or be in charge of a motor vehicle on a road or other public place and before he provided the specimen, and

(b) that had he not done so the proportion of alcohol in his breath, blood or urine would not have exceeded the prescribed limit and, if the proceedings are for an offence under section 4 of that Act, would not have been such as to impair his ability to drive properly.

(4) A specimen of blood shall be disregarded unless it was taken from the accused with his consent by a medical practitioner.

(5) Where, at the time a specimen of blood or urine was provided by the accused, he asked to be provided with such a specimen, evidence of the

proportion of alcohol or any drug found in the specimen is not admissible on behalf of the prosecution unless—

(a) the specimen in which the alcohol or drug was found is one of two parts into which the specimen provided by the accused was divided at the time it was provided, and

(b) the other part was supplied to the accused.

Section 15(1) repeats and amplifies s 10(1) of the Road Traffic Act 1972 (as amended); s 15(2) reflects the terms of the first part of s 10(2) of the 1972 Act; s 15(3) repeats the statutory defence formerly found in the second half of s 10(2) of the 1972 Act; s 15(4) restates the first part of s 10(4) of the earlier Act; and s 15(5) repeats the provisions relating to the supply of part of a specimen of blood or urine to the accused previously found in s 10(6) of the 1972 Act.

5.2   THE ROAD TRAFFIC OFFENDERS ACT 1988, S 15(1)

Section 15(1) reads as follows:

This section and section 16 of this Act apply in respect of proceedings for an offence under section 4 or 5 of the Road Traffic Act 1988 (motor vehicles: drink and drugs); and expressions used in this section and section 16 of this Act have the same meaning as in sections 4 to 10 of that Act.

The terms of this section are self-evident and simply make it clear that the same evidential considerations apply in terms of this and the following section to both section 4 and section 5 prosecutions.

5.3   EVIDENCE OF SPECIMEN TO BE TAKEN INTO ACCOUNT IN ALL CASES, S 15(2)

5.3:1   General

Section 15(2) provides:

Evidence of the proportion of alcohol or any drug in a specimen of breath, blood or urine provided by the accused shall, in all cases, be taken into account and, subject to subsection (3) below, it shall be assumed that the proportion of alcohol in the accused's breath, blood or urine at the time of the alleged offence was not less than in the specimen.

This sub-section is clearly designed to diminish the importance of formal or procedural requirements. In particular, notwithstanding the circumstances under which such specimens have been taken, the Act appears to provide that the evidence of the proportion of alcohol or drug in such specimens must be taken into account 'in all cases'. It is however not yet entirely clear what the effect of this will be in the variety of situations that will arise in practice. It has been suggested that the effect of this provision will be to render admissible in evidence even specimens which have been unlawfully obtained. However, it is submitted that the effect of this section can only at best cure procedural or technical requirements imposed by other parts of the legislation. Firstly, the Act provides specifically in s 15(4) that a specimen of blood is to be disregarded unless it was taken from the accused with his consent by a medical practitioner. Further, s 11(4) of the Road Traffic Act 1988 makes it clear that a specimen of blood is provided only if the accused consents to it being taken, and it is taken by a medical practitioner. Clearly therefore a specimen of blood taken without the accused's consent, or by someone other than a medical practitioner, cannot be admissible in evidence and cannot be used in any way or under any circumstances in proceedings under s 4 or 5 of the Road Traffic Act 1988, notwithstanding the terms of s 15(2) of the Road Traffic Offenders Act 1988. Also, s 9 of the Road Traffic Act 1988 provides specific protection for hospital patients, and it is submitted that any specimen taken in contravention of these provisions cannot be inadmissible. Accordingly, the terms of s 15(2) of the Road Traffic Offenders Act 1988 require some qualification.

5.3:2   Interpretation of section 15(2)

The only direct authority on this matter to date is to be found *obiter* in the judgment of Lord Fraser in *R v Fox* [1985] RTR 337, [1985] 1 WLR 1126. In that case the accused was the driver of a motor vehicle involved in an accident. No other vehicle was involved. The accused left the scene and went home. The police, who had no knowledge of his physical condition, went to his house and got no answer to their knock on the door, although they heard voices inside. The police therefore entered the premises and required the driver to give a specimen of breath (the roadside test), which he refused. He was then arrested and taken to a police station where he provided a breath specimen for analysis which exceeded the statutory limit.

It was held that under English law, the police officers were trespassing at the time they made the first requirement for a breath specimen, and when they purported to arrest the accused. (It should be noted that in Scotland this conclusion would not have been reached – see *Cairns v Keane* 1983 SCCR 277). In these circumstances it was held that neither the provision of a preliminary breath specimen, nor the arrest were necessary preconditions of the procedure for the provision of specimens under the equivalent of s 7 of the Road Traffic Act 1988, and that the accused could accordingly be convicted on the basis of these specimens. It was explained that although the police, who were acting in good faith, may have exceeded their common law powers in their alleged arrest of the accused, the evidence subsequently obtained of an offence committed prior to the arrest was admissible and not tainted by the illegality of the arrest itself.

In discussing the terms of the equivalent of s 15(2) of the Road Traffic Offenders Act 1988, that the proportion of alcohol in a specimen of breath, blood or urine shall 'in all cases' be taken into account (a matter which was not necessary for the decision), Lord Fraser said (at [1985] RTR 343): 'As at present advised, I do not think those words can make evidence admissible if it would not be admissible under the general law. I am inclined to read them as referring only to a specimen "provided pursuant to the provisions of this Act."' The effect therefore of the terms of s 15(2), it is submitted, is to allow any sample to be considered in evidence even although procedural requirements have not been followed, or some other illegal or improper act is associated with the procedure which does not however contravene the provisions of the Act. It is thought therefore that failure to observe the following provisions will not render the results of the analysis of the specimen inadmissible.

5.3:3 Circumstances where failure does not render a specimen inadmissible

1. Section 4(6) of the Road Traffic Act empowers a constable to arrest without warrant, a person whom he suspects of committing an offence under that section. If no arrest in fact takes place, it is clear that this has no bearing on the legality of the proceedings. The power of arrest is enabling only and does not have to be a prerequisite of the provision of a specimen (unlike earlier legislation). (A police constable has the right to enter any premises in the course of an investigation (*Cairns v Keane* 1983 SCCR 277)).

A constable must have 'reasonable cause' to suspect that a person is or has been committing an offence under s 4 in order to arrest a motorist. If it is established that the constable does not have reasonable cause for his suspicion, any power of arrest exercised in terms of this section will be invalid, but any subsequent specimen given by the accused will not thereby become inadmissible in evidence (see paragraphs 3.11 and 4.2:2).

2. Section 6(5) of the Road Traffic Act 1988, empowers a constable to arrest a person without warrant if, following a roadside breath test in terms of that section, he has reason to suspect that the accused's proportion of alcohol in his breath or blood exceeds the prescribed limit, or where the accused has failed to supply a breath specimen and the constable has reasonable cause to suspect that he has consumed alcohol. Again, a failure to arrest, or an improper arrest, will not invalidate the subsequent provision of a specimen for analysis, (unless the person arrested is at hospital as a patient). Reference may also be made to paragraphs 3.11 and 4.6.

3. Section 6 (the preliminary or roadside test). None of the provisions of this section are required to have been implemented before a specimen of breath, blood or urine is given in terms of s 7(1)(a) or (b). Again this is different from the requirements of earlier law. The principal purpose of this section is procedural only; in other words, a constable does not have to administer a breath test before requiring a specimen of breath, blood or urine. Even if a breath test is negative, it would appear to be still open to the constable to require a specimen for analysis. However, the provisions of s 6 are of course relevant in themselves if for any reason the outcome of the breath test procedure is to be used in any subsequent proceedings, eg if the driver fails to provide such a test contrary to s 6(4) (see paragraphs 4.5:1 and 4.5:2). Further, in certain circumstances, the evidence produced as a result of such a test may have evidential significance (*Gallagher v McKinnon* 1987 SLT 531, 1986 SCCR 704, 1987 CO Circulars A/2). In these latter cases, the other provisions of s 6 (including s 6(3)) will have to be observed if the requirement to provide a breath test, or the provision of the test and its result, have to be established in evidence.

5.3:4   Circumstances where failure will render a subsequent specimen inadmissible

On the other hand, it is submitted that the requirements of the following sections do have to be observed if the specimen is subsequently to be admissible in evidence.

1. Section 7 of the Road Traffic Act 1988. This section, which allows for the provision of specimens for analysis, contains within its terms a number of requirements which, it is submitted, must be observed before the specimen can be regarded as competent

evidence. For example, in terms of s 7(1) and (2) a breath specimen can only be given into an approved device at a police station. Section 7(3) details in specific terms the circumstances in which a blood or urine specimen is to be taken rather than a breath specimen. Section 7(4) stipulates *inter alia* that if a medical practitioner is of the opinion that for medical reasons a blood specimen should not be taken then the specimen shall be one of urine. Section 7(5) defines how a specimen of urine should be given. It is submitted that if any of these specific provisions within s 7 is not observed, then any specimen taken in terms of this section should not be admissible in evidence.

Section 7(7) requires that a constable must warn any person required to give a specimen in terms of this section that failure to provide such a specimen may result in prosecution. Again it is submitted that this requirement is mandatory, and failure to give the warning will invalidate any subsequent proceedings under s 7(6).

2. Section 8 of the Road Traffic Act 1988. The various requirements of this section as described therein clearly have to be observed before the specimens can be admitted into evidence.

3. Section 9 of the Road Traffic Act 1988. The provisions for the protection of hospital patients require to be observed and failure to do so will render any subsequent specimen inadmissible in evidence.

4. Section 11(4) of the Road Traffic Act 1988 and s 15(4) of the Road Traffic Offenders Act 1988. The requirement that a blood sample can only be taken with the accused's consent and by a medical practitioner is plainly a prerequisite of allowing that specimen to be admitted in evidence.

5. Section 15(5) of the Road Traffic Offenders Act 1988. The requirement to provide part of the specimen to the accused in terms of this section, if the accused so claims, must also, it is submitted, be observed before the results of the specimen can be admitted. It would appear that the motorist must expressly indicate that he wishes to take the divided specimen at the time it is offered to him (*Aitchison v Johnstone* 1987 SCCR 225). Reference should also be made to paragraph 5.7).

5.3:5 Circumstances where admissibility is a matter of discretion

If the evidence of a specimen in terms of the foregoing paragraphs would normally be admissible, it is submitted that there may still be a residual power to exclude the evidence if the court considered that the specimen had been obtained by fraud or deceit, or if the police had behaved oppressively to the motorist in obtaining the specimen. Reference should again be made to the opinion of Lord Fraser in *R v Fox* (see paragraph 5.3:2). Section 78(1) of the Police and Criminal Evidence Act 1984 gives courts in England a wide discretion to exclude evidence in any case which might cause unfairness. It is submitted that the same consideration applies in Scotland at common law. It should be underlined however that none of the matters in this and the previous two paragraphs have yet been authoritatively settled in Scotland; however, reference might usefully be made to *Douglas v Stevenson* 1986 SCCR 519, 1986 CO Circulars A/57; *Woodburn v McLeod* 1986 SLT 325, 1986 SCCR 107, 1986 CO Circulars A/4; and *Green v Lockhart* 1986 SLT 11, 1985 SCCR 257, 1985 CO Circulars A/25.

5.4   LEVEL OF ALCOHOL HIGHER THAN READING

The way in which s 15(2) is phrased indicates that it is open to the Crown to attempt to prove that the proportion of alcohol in an accused's breath, blood or urine was, at the time he was driving or in charge of his vehicle, higher than that provided in the specimen. The assumption provided in the sub-section is that the level of alcohol in the accused's body at the time of the alleged offence is to be not less than the proportion indicated in the specimens taken. In other words, the Crown is not precluded from proving that the proportion of alcohol in the accused's breath, blood or urine at the time of the alleged offence was greater than shown in the subsequently taken specimen. It is therefore possible for the Crown to secure a conviction even although the levels demonstrated to be present in the specimen were lower than the legal limit. By adopting the same procedures as described in paragraphs 3.8, 3.15:1 and 3.16:1, it may be possible for the court to embark upon a calculation based upon the time which has elapsed between the time of the alleged offence and the time the specimen was taken, and the rate at which alcohol metabolises in the human body, and thereafter conclude beyond reasonable doubt that at the material time, the accused was driving with more than the permitted level of alcohol.

5.5   THE STATUTORY DEFENCE (S 15(3))

5.5:1   Section 15(3)

Section 15(3) of the Road Traffic Offenders Act 1988 provides as follows:

If the proceedings are for an offence under section 5 of the Act or, where the accused is alleged to have been unfit through drink, for an offence under section 4 of that Act, that assumption shall not be made if the accused proves–

(a) that he consumed alcohol after he had ceased to drive, attempt to drive or be in charge of a motor vehicle on a road or other public place and before he provided the specimen, and

(b) that had he not done so the proportion of alcohol in his breath, blood or urine would not have exceeded the prescribed limit and, if the proceedings are for an offence under section 4 of that Act, would not have been such as to impair his ability to drive properly.

The Act referred to is the Road Traffic Act 1988, and the assumption referred to is that contained in s 15(2) of the Road Traffic Offenders Act 1988.

5.5:2   Onus and standard of proof

The onus is on the accused to establish this defence. The standard of proof which is required is on the balance of probabilities (*Neish v Stevenson* 1969 SLT 229 (overruling *Thaw v Segar* 1962 SLT (Sh Ct) 63). However, if the circumstances are such that the evidence casts a reasonable doubt on the prosecution case, the accused will be entitled to the benefit of such doubt. In practice, however, this situation is unlikely to occur; the evidence of post-incident drinking has by its nature to be clearly distinguished from what was consumed prior to the driver ceasing to drive, attempt to drive or be in charge of his vehicle, and in most cases it will be for the accused to remove any doubt about the quantity of alcohol consumed before and after the material time. The accused will have to establish each part of his defence. Accordingly, he will in normal circumstances require to establish when it was that he stopped driving, attempting to drive or be in charge of the vehicle. He will then require to establish the amount of alcohol which he has consumed after that time. Thereafter, the accused will require to show that but for the consumption of the alcohol, he as an individual would have provided a specimen at the time he ceased to drive, attempt to drive or be in charge which would have been lower than the maximum permitted level prescribed in s 12(2). The technical steps in the defence case are usually spoken to in practice by the evidence of an expert analyst.

This subject is more fully discussed in paragraphs 3.8, 3.16 and 3.16:1.

5.6   TAKING OF BLOOD SPECIMENS: S 15(4)

Section 15(4) of the Road Traffic Offenders Act 1988 provides as follows:

> A specimen of blood shall be disregarded unless it was taken from the accused with his consent by a medical practitioner.

(See also s 11(4) of the Road Traffic Act 1988).

Failure to observe the provisions of s 15(4) will make the evidence of the blood specimen and any analysis thereof inadmissible in evidence, notwithstanding the terms of s 15(2). Accordingly, if the specimen is not taken by a medical practitioner, or if it is taken without the accused's consent, the specimen will not be allowed in evidence. (See paragraphs 5.3:2 *et seq.*)

5.7   PART OF SPECIMEN TO BE SUPPLIED TO ACCUSED: S 15(5)

Section 15(5) of the Road Traffic Offenders Act 1988 provides as follows:

> Where, at the time a specimen of blood or urine was provided by the accused, he asked to be provided with such a specimen, evidence of the proportion of alcohol or any drug found in the specimen is not admissible on behalf of the prosecution unless–
> (a) the specimen in which the alcohol or drug was found is one of two parts into which the specimen provided by the accused was divided at the time it was provided, and
> (b) the other part was supplied to the accused.

This section repeats and replaces the terms of s 10(6) of the Road Traffic Act 1972 (as amended by s 25(3) and Schedule 8 of the Transport Act 1981, which, by virtue of SI 1983/576, came into force on 6 May 1983).

The intention of s 15(5) is to allow the accused the right to part of the specimen of blood or urine he has provided in terms of s 7(1)(b) of the Road Traffic Act 1988 in order to allow him to have it independently analysed. Failure to observe the terms of this sub-section will mean that the court cannot consider the results of any such analysis, notwithstanding the terms of s 15(2) of the Road Traffic Offenders Act 1988.

The purpose of this sub-section is achieved in practice by dividing the specimen of blood or urine into two and handing one of the two parts to the accused. It is submitted that, in particular, having regard to the terms of s 11(3) of the Road Traffic Act 1988, each of the two parts of the divided specimen must be sufficient to allow proper analysis to be carried out. In *Gallagher v McKinnon* 1987 SLT 531, 1986 SCCR 704, 1987 CO Circulars A/2, it was held that where the analysis of the specimen retained by the police differs from the analysis of the specimen handed to the accused, the court could look at extraneous evidence (but not the readings from the breath analyser device) in deciding which of the two results was accurate. Whether or not the accused has requested part of the specimen he has provided and such specimen has been given to him are questions of fact. It would appear from the terms of the sub-section that the motorist must take the initiative in asking for his part of the specimen (see also *Aitchison v Johnstone* 1987 SCCR 225).

The part of the specimen given to the accused must be capable of being analysed within a reasonable time. In *Ellis v Cruikshank* 1973 SCCR Supp 49, the specimen was found to be incapable of analysis some three months after its provision. It was held that any such specimen must be capable of analysis within a reasonable time at the point when it is delivered to the accused.

The supply of part of the specimen to the accused must be unconditional; where a police officer was only prepared to give the accused the specimen on condition that the motorist signed a receipt, this was held to invalidate the prosecution (*Smith v Skeen* 1974 SCCR Supp 64).

5.8 DOCUMENTARY EVIDENCE OF SPECIMENS (S 16)

5.8:1 Section 16

Section 16 of the Road Traffic Offenders Act 1988 reads in full as follows:

(1) Evidence of the proportion of alcohol or a drug in a specimen of breath, blood or urine may, subject to subsections (3) and (4) below and to section 15(5) of this Act, be given by the production of a document or documents purporting to be whichever of the following is appropriate, that is to say–

(a) a statement automatically produced by the device by which the proportion of alcohol in a specimen of breath was measured and a certificate signed by a constable (which may but need not be contained in the same document as the statement) that the statement relates to a specimen provided by the accused at the date and time shown in the statement, and

(b) a certificate signed by an authorised analyst as to the proportion of alcohol or any drug found in a specimen of blood or urine identified in the certificate.

(2) Subject to subsections (3) and (4) below, evidence that a specimen of blood was taken from the accused with his consent by a medical practitioner may be given by the production of a document purporting to certify that fact and to be signed by a medical practitioner.

(3) Subject to subsection (4) below–

(a) a document purporting to be such a statement or such a certificate (or both such a statement and such a certificate) as is mentioned in subsection (1)(a) above is admissible in evidence on behalf of the prosecution in pursuance of this section only if a copy of it either has been handed to the accused when the document was produced or has been served on him not later than seven days before the hearing, and

(b) any other document is so admissible only if a copy of it has been served on the accused not later than seven days before the hearing.

(4) A document purporting to be a certificate (or so much of a document as purports to be a certificate) is not so admissible if the accused, not later than three days before the hearing or within such further time as the court may in special circumstances allow, has served notice on the prosecutor requiring the attendance at the hearing of the person by whom the document purports to be signed.

(5) In Scotland–

(a) a document produced in evidence on behalf of the prosecution in pursuance of subsection (1) or (2) above and, where the person by whom the document was signed is called as a witness, the evidence of that person, shall be sufficient evidence of the facts stated in the document, and

(b) a written execution purporting to be signed by the person who handed to or served on the accused or the prosecutor a copy of the document or of the notice in terms of subsection (3) or (4) above, together with, where appropriate, a post office receipt for the registered or recorded delivery letter shall be sufficient evidence of the handing or service of such a copy or notice.

(6) A copy of a certificate required by this section to be served on the accused or a notice required by this section to be served on the prosecutor may be served personally or sent by registered post or recorded delivery service.

(7) In this section 'authorised analyst' means–

(a) any person possessing the qualifications prescribed by regulations made under section 76 of the Food Act 1984 or section 27 of the Food and Drugs (Scotland) Act 1956 as qualifying persons for appointment as public analysts under those Acts, and

(b) any other persons authorised by the Secretary of State to make analyses for the purposes of this section.

Section 16 replaces the provisions of s 10(3), (4), (5), (7), (8) and (9) of the Road Traffic Act 1972 (as amended by s 25(3) and Schedule 8 of the Transport Act 1981, which, by virtue of SI 1983/ 576, came into force on 6 May 1983). The section, in general terms, provides that the evidence of the proportion of alcohol in a breath test under s 7(1)(a) of the Road Traffic Act 1988 may be proved by a statement produced automatically by an authorised breath analyser device, and evidence of the amount of alcohol in a specimen of blood or urine provided in terms of s 7(1)(b) of that Act may be given by a certificate signed by a certified analyst. There has been a substantial number of cases dealing with the certificates automatically produced by the Camic Breath Analyser Device (the approved device currently in operation in Scotland) and these are reported in this chapter. The section also describes the proof of the taking of a blood specimen (s 16(2)), and the requirements of service in respect of the service of the certificates described in the section (s 16(3), (4), (5) and (6)). A definition of the term 'certified analyst' is also provided (s 16(7)).

5.8:2 Statement produced by a breath analyser device (s 16(1)(a))

Section 16(1)(a) of the Road Traffic Offenders Act 1988 reads as follows:

> Evidence of the proportion of alcohol or a drug in a specimen of breath, blood or urine may, subject to subsections (3) and (4) below and to section 15(5) of this Act, be given by the production of a document or documents purporting to be whichever of the following is appropriate, that is to say—
> (a) a statement automatically produced by the device by which the proportion of alcohol in a specimen of breath was measured and a certificate signed by a constable (which may but need not be contained in the same document as the statement) that the statement relates to a specimen provided by the accused at the date and time shown in the statement . . . .

5.8:3 Approved breath analyser device

By virtue of the Breath Analysis Devices (Approval) (Scotland) Order 1983, SI 1983/576 which came into force on 6 May 1983, two devices are approved by the Secretary of State for use in Scotland. These are the Camic Breath Analyser (S) and the Lion

Breath Analyser (Sc). The device commonly used in Scotland is the Camic Breath Analyser. However, an approved device is not currently available in every police station in Scotland; in particular a number of small and rural stations do not yet have one installed. In terms of s 7(3) of the Road Traffic Act 1988 only specimens of blood or urine can be required of motorists at police stations which do not have an approved device.

The prosecution are entitled to a presumption that the Camic Breath Analyser is an approved device within the meaning of the section (*Davidson v Aitchison* 1986 SLT 402, 1985 SCCR 415, 1986 CO Circulars A/31; *Valentine v Macphail* 1986 SLT 598, 1986 SCCR 321, 1986 CO Circulars A/24). It is unnecessary for the relevant Approval Order to be produced (*Lee v Smith* 1982 SLT 200, 1981 SCCR 267, 1981 CO Circulars A/29). Further, when the device has in practice done what it should have done if it was in proper working order, then it is to be presumed that the machine is in proper working order and has been correctly maintained (*Tudhope v McAllister* 1984 SLT 395, 1984 SCCR 182, 1984 CO Circulars A/15). The court is entitled to use its knowledge of how the device operates (see paragraph 5.8:4).

5.8:4   Operation of camic device

The Camic Breath Analyser device in general terms operates as follows. Firstly, the device must be in an operational condition and maintained in accordance with the manufacturer's directions. It should be operated only by a police officer who has been authorised to do so by the Chief Constable and who has been trained in the proper working of the device. The device has a visual display unit which at the outset of the test should indicate the time. The machine is then tested and must indicate that it is purged of alcohol. The accused is then instructed to give a first breath specimen into a mouth piece fitted to the machine. In particular, the accused in terms of s 11(3) of the Act must provide a specimen of breath in such a way that the specimen is sufficient to enable the test or analysis to be carried out and be provided in such a way as to enable the objective of the test or analysis to be satisfactorily achieved. In practice, the accused must supply a specimen of breath into the mouth piece until the red light shown on the machine changes to green. At that point the machine should be capable of producing on the visual display a reading which indicates the result of the analysis of the breath specimen which has just been provided. Thereafter, the machine should be satisfactorily purged of alcohol and the machine should indicate that this has been done. The accused is then invited to provide a second specimen of breath in circumstances similar to that provided in the first instance. When the breath specimen has been supplied, the machine should again indicate that it is working normally. Thereafter, the device automatically produces a statement indicating the results of the whole test. The statement also contains a form of certificate which is signed by one of the police officers who has witnessed the test. This document is known as a print-out and is considered to contain both a statement and a certificate which is described in s 16(3)(a) and s 16(5) and as such will be admissible in evidence so long as the other provisions of the Act are complied with. The evidence of the officer who signed the certificate is not essential if there is sufficient evidence from other officers of the conduct of the test and its result (*Donoghue v Allan* 1985 SCCR 93, 1985 CO Circulars A/4).

Judicial knowledge extends to the operation of the Camic Breath Analyser and the fact that it produces an automatic print-out, and the prosecution do not have to prove that the print-out and its contents qualify as including both a statement and a certificate as above described (*Annan v Mitchell* 1984 SCCR 32; *Aitchison v Matheson* 1984 SCCR 83).

It is open to the defence to establish any failure to comply with the manufacturer's instructions, and to argue that such failure should lead to acquittal (*Allan v Miller* 1986 SLT 3, 1985 SCCR 227, 1985 CO Circulars A/15). These instructions are given in Appendix C.

5.8:5   Informalities in print-out

There has been a number of cases concerned with informalities connected with the documents automatically produced by the breath analyser devices. The subsection does not indicate any particular formality in respect of the information produced by the machine in the statement or certificate; all that is required is that the statement and certificate should evidence the information required by the Act (*Jones v McPhail* 1984 SLT 396, 1984 SCCR 168, 1984 CO Circulars A/14; see also *Aitchison v Matheson supra*). Further, apparent defects in the statements are curable by parole evidence from a police officer present at the time the test was taken (*Aitchison v Matheson (supra)*). For example, when the statement did not indicate the name of the driver, or when the certificate was not signed by the constable supervising the taking of the specimen, the Crown may produce verbal evidence to show that the statement and certificate relate to the accused and the test which he has taken

(*NcNamee v Tudhope* 1985 SLT 322, 1984 SCCR 423, 1984 CO Circulars A/32; *Allan v Miller* 1986 SLT 3, 1985 SCCR 227, 1985 CO Circulars A/15; *Tudhope v Craig* 1985 SCCR 214, 1985 CO Circulars A/18). However, it must be emphasised that there requires to be evidence that the print-out relates to the accused (*O'Brien v Ferguson* 1987 SLT 96, 1986 SCCR 155).

On the other hand, when the statement gives information which is patently incorrect, then the prosecution may not be able to rely on the evidential presumptions created by this sub-section. Nonetheless, it may still be open for the prosecution to establish the results of the test by other evidence, such as testimony from police officers present at the time of what readings were produced on the visual display when the test was taken (*Smith v MacDonald*; *Smith v Davie* 1984 SLT 398, 1984 SCCR 190, 1984 CO Circulars A/13; see also *McLeary v Douglas* 1978 JC 57, 1978 SLT 140, 1978 CO Circulars A/1; *Gunn v Brown* 1987 SLT 94, 1986 SCCR 179, CO Circulars A/28).

If the informalities or defects in the print-out are so fundamental as to indicate that the machine's analytical function is unreliable, the police may turn to the alternative procedure of requiring a specimen of blood or urine.

5.8:6   Defects in print-out: reliability of device

In terms of s 7(3)(b) of the Road Traffic Act 1988, the provision of a specimen of breath for analysis must be made into a reliable device (see paragraph 4.11:4). If the device is not reliable, then the alternative requirement of a blood or urine specimen must be made. The device may be properly considered unreliable if for some technical reason it is not working or functioning properly. However, in terms of the reported cases, the circumstances in which the reliability or otherwise of the device has been considered usually relate to the information contained within the statement or print-out automatically produced by the device.

As indicated in the foregoing paragraph (5.8:5) certain informalities or apparent defects may be cured by parole evidence. However, certain defects may be so fundamental that they must be regarded as indicating that the machine is unreliable. The primary or best evidence that the machine is unreliable comes from the police officers who administered the test, and although it is probably good practice to produce the print-out in evidence where the alternative procedure is employed, it is not necessary to do so (*Houston v McLeod* 1986 SCCR 219; 1988 CO Circulars A/27). In *Tudhope v Quinn* 1984 SCCR 255, it was held that what the Crown had to prove was that the analytic or measuring function of the device was unreliable if the primary requirement of a breath specimen was to be set aside and a blood or urine specimen used instead. In *Gilligan v Tudhope* 1986 SLT 299, 1985 SCCR 434, 1986 CO Circulars A/1, the device produced a print-out which gave nonsensical times and dates for the test, but there appeared to be nothing wrong with the analytical function of the machine. It was held that in these circumstances, the machine was not unreliable, and that the alternative procedure of the provision of a sample of blood or urine was not open. Presumably the defects described in this case could have been cured by parole evidence from the police officers who administered the test. In *Ross v Allan* 1986 SLT 349, 1986 SCCR 100, 1986 CO Circulars A/2, the device gave a reading of 75 microgrammes in 100 millilitres of breath in respect of the first specimen of breath, and a reading of zero for the second. It was held that these readings clearly showed that the analytical function of the machine was not operating properly, that the device should therefore be regarded as unreliable, and that the Crown did not have to provide expert evidence on the question of the unreliability of the machine. This case was followed in *Lunney v Cardle* 1988 SLT 440, 1988 SCCR 104, 1988 CO Circulars A/14, where the two readings were 14 and 92 microgrammes respectively. The motorist was smelling of drink and subsequently gave a blood specimen. In the Appeal Court, the Lord Justice-Clerk (Ross) and Lord Hunter reserved their opinion on whether the test of the reliability of the machine was subjective to the police officers who administered the test, or whether it was objective, and whether the result of the subsequent breath specimen could be used in determining if the device had been properly described as unreliable. Lord McDonald concluded both that the test was subjective, and that the blood specimen could be so used. However, the *ratio decidendi* in both cases was that the disparity of the two readings shown in the print-out of itself justified the conclusion that the machine was unreliable. On the other hand, in the cases of *Aitchison v Meldrum* 1984 SLT 437, 1984 SCCR 241, 1984 CO Circulars A/17, and *Tudhope v Craig* 1985 SCCR 214, 1985 CO Circulars A/18, relatively minor defects in the operation of the machine, evidenced in the print-out, were held not to invalidate the results contained in the print-outs. In *Currie v MacDougall* 1988 SLT 632, 1988 SCCR 266, it was decided that a Camic device which was not regularly maintained and was used as a training device was properly regarded as unreliable. However, the Crown will normally have to show that if a device is regarded as unreliable that there is no other available and reliable device within the police station (*Houston v*

McLeod (*supra*)). Where the device was mistakenly thought to be not working properly and a blood sample was subsequently given, it was held that the original breath analysis was still competent evidence (*Hodgkins v Carmichael* 1989 SLT 514, 1989 SCCR 69 1989 CO Circulars A/5).

In summary, if the Crown seek to rely on the fact that the machine is unreliable in requiring the alternative procedure of a blood or urine specimen, it must be demonstrated from the print-out that the analytical function of the device is not operating correctly or satisfactorily. If there are other defects in the print-out which do not relate to the analytical function of the device, such defects may be curable by parole evidence. However, it should be noted that if the print-out is defective it may not be admissible in evidence (*Smith v Macdonald; Smith v Davie* 1984 SLT 398, 1984 SCCR 190, 1984 CO Circulars A/13) the Crown will have to rely on the visual testimony of the officers who conducted the test.

5.8:7   Analyst's certificate (s 16(1)(b))

Under this part of the sub-section, evidence of the proportion of alcohol in a specimen of blood or urine may, subject again to the provisions of s 16(3) to (6), be given by a document purporting to be 'a certificate signed by an authorised analyst as to the proportion of alcohol or any drug found in a specimen of blood or urine identified in the certificate.'

An 'authorised analyst' is defined in s 16(7).

As before, the prosecution have to prove that the specimen was taken from the accused and transmitted to the analyst (*O'Brien v Ferguson* 1987 SLT 96, 1986 SCCR 155). However, the fact that the specimen has been sent for analysis may be inferred (*McLeary v Douglas* 1978 JC 57, 1978 SLT 140, 1978 CO Circulars A/1; *Tudhope v Corrigall* 1982 SCCR 558, 1982 CO Circulars A/47); and, distinguishing *O'Brien v Ferguson* (*supra*), parole evidence may be used to link the specimen taken and the specimen analysed where there is a discrepancy in the certificates (*MacKinnon v Westwater* 1987 SCCR 730).

In a case where an analyst was cited to give evidence and had no recollection of the particular analysis in question but refreshed his memory from a register of print-outs which were possibly still extant but which were not produced, it was held that the analyst's evidence was competent and did not breach the best evidence rule (*McLeod v Fraser* 1987 SLT 142, 1986 SCCR 271, 1986 CO Circulars A/27).

In a case decided under earlier legislation (s 3(8) of the Road

Safety Act 1967), it was held that the certificate was intended to vouch the analyst's conclusion and not the providence of the specimen; accordingly factual errors in the certificate did not make the analyst's conclusions contained therein inadmissible (*Lawrie v Stevenson* 1968 JC 71, 1968 SLT 342).

5.8:8   Taking of blood specimens (s 16(2))

Section 16(2) of the Road Traffic Offenders Act 1988 provides as follows:

> Subject to subsections (3) and (4) below, evidence that a specimen of blood was taken from the accused with his consent by a medical practitioner may be given by the production of a document purporting to certify that fact and to be signed by a medical practitioner.

Sub-sections (3) and (4) are concerned with the requirements of service of certificates. What constitutes a 'medical practitioner' is discussed in paragraph 4.11:6. Section 16(5) of the Act also applies for the purposes of this sub-section.

Section 11(4) of the Road Traffic Act 1988 also provides that a person only provides a specimen of blood if, and only if he consents to its being taken by a medical practitioner, and it is so taken.

Accordingly, failure to observe the provisions of s 16(2) will be fatal to any prosecution based on a specimen of blood, notwithstanding the terms of s 15(2) of the Road Traffic Offenders Act 1988. If the specimen is not taken by a medical practitioner, or if the specimen is taken without the accused's consent, the specimen will not be allowed in evidence and evidence of the analysis of the specimen will be inadmissible.

Reference should be made to paragraphs 5.3:2 *et seq*.

5.8:9   Service of statement or certificate (s 16(3))

Section 16(3) of the Road Traffic Offenders Act 1988 reads as follows:

> Subject to subsection (4) below–
> (a) a document purporting to be such a statement or such a certificate (or both such a statement and such a certificate as is mentioned in subsection (1)(a) above is admissible in evidence on behalf of the prosecution in pursuance of this section only if a copy of it either has been handed to the accused when the document was produced or has been served on him not later than seven days before the hearing, and
> (b) any other document is so admissible only if a copy of it has been served on the accused not later than seven days before the hearing.

This sub-section has to be read along with the following sub-section (s 16(4)); and also along with s 16(5) and (6).

Section 16(3) provides for the requirements of service in respect of both kinds of certificate described in s 16(1). In particular, s 16(3)(a) refers to the statement and certificate comprised in the print-out automatically produced by the breath analysis device. Service of this statement and certificate can be effected on the accused at the time the device produces the print-out. It is submitted that this means that the document or documents must be given to the accused in the course of the procedure involved in the taking of the specimen, and that, for example, handing the document to the accused after he has left the police station does not comply with the requirement of service. Alternatively, in accordance with the second part of s 16(3)(a), where the accused has not been handed a copy of the document at the time it was produced, service of the document must be made on him not later than seven days before the trial diet. By virtue of s 16(3)(b), the requirement of service is satisfied in the case of an analyst's certificate (in terms of s 16(1)(b) of the Act), or a doctor's certificate (in terms of s 16(2) of the Act), by service of such certificates on the accused not later than seven days before the trial diet.

(All reference to 'days' in this and the following sub-section means clear and full days (*McMillan v HM Advocate* 1983 SLT 24, 1982 SCCR 309, 1982 CO Circulars A/19)).

If service of documents or certificates is not effected by either of the methods described in s 16(3), then the documents or certificates are inadmissible in evidence, and the prosecution cannot rely on the evidence contained within the documents or certificates to secure a conviction (*McLeary v Douglas* 1978 JC 57, 1978 SLT 140, 1978 CO Circular A/1). However, in the event that the certificate and statement automatically produced by a breath analyser device are not handed to the accused at the time and were not subsequently served on the accused, and thus became inadmissible in evidence, it is still open to the Crown to secure a conviction on the basis of parole evidence from the police officers who administered the test of the readings they observed on the visual display unit of the breath analyser device (*Gunn v Brown* 1987 SLT 94, 1986 SCCR 179, 1986 CO Circulars A/28).

Even if the accused declines to take the copy of the print-out at the time when it is produced by the breath analyser device, in terms of the first part of the sub-section, then service of the copy must still be made in terms of the second part of the sub-section (*Annan v Crawford* 1984 SCCR 382; *McDerment v O'Brien* SLT 485, 1985 SCCR 50, 1985 CO Circulars A/5). If service in terms of this sub-section has not been effected, objection to the production of the principal (which must be lodged) require to be taken before the close of the Crown case (*Skeen v Murphy* 1978 SLT (Notes) 2, 1977 CO Circulars A/24; *McLeary v Douglas* 1978 JC 57; 1978 SLT 140; 1978 CO Circulars A/1).

The fact that certificates were served with a complaint which was dropped and substituted by a fresh complaint which was not accompanied by further certificates does not invalidate the initial service of the certificates, which remain valid for the purposes of the second complaint (*Buonaccorsi v Tudhope* 1982 SLT 528, 1982 SCCR 249, 1982 CO Circulars A/27).

It is not necessary for the prosecution, in a case based on a blood or urine specimen, to produce the specimen on which the certificate is based (*Williamson v Aitchison* 1982 SLT 399, 1982 SCCR 102, 1982 CO Circulars A/8).

5.8:10 Certificate not admissible in evidence (s 16(4))

Section 16(4) of the Road Traffic Offenders Act 1988 provides:

A document purporting to be a certificate (or so much of a document as purports to be a certificate) is not so admissible if the accused, not later than three days before the hearing or within such further time as the court may in special circumstances allow, has served notice on the prosecutor requiring the attendance at the hearing of the person by whom the document purports to be signed.

This sub-section applies not only to the documents automatically produced by a breath analyser device in terms of s 16(1)(a) and s 16(3)(a), but also to certificates supplied by analysts or doctors in terms of s 16(1)(b) and s 16(2) respectively. If the defence wish to avoid the evidential consequences of s 16(3), then notice must be served on the Crown to this effect not later than three clear days before the trial diet. The court has the discretion to allow later intimation by the accused, but will normally only exercise this discretion on cause shown. The effect of such intimation by the accused is to require the attendance of the police officer who signs the certificate on the print-out to attend the trial diet to give evidence to the effect that he did so; or more commonly in practice, to require the presence of the authorised analyst who has examined the blood or urine specimen to speak to his findings, usually with a view to establishing one of the statutory defences.

If the accused wishes to challenge the contents of the print-out or the operation of the machine, he must do so by giving notice in terms of this sub-section; otherwise the print-out, its contents, and the operation of the device cannot be challenged (*Annan v Mitchell* 1984 SCCR 32).

5.8:11   Sufficiency of evidence (s 16(5))

Section 16(5) of the Road Traffic Offenders Act 1988 provides:

> (5) In Scotland–
> (a) a document produced in evidence on behalf of the prosecution in pursuance of subsection (1) or (2) above and, where the person by whom the document was signed is called as a witness, the evidence of that person, shall be sufficient evidence of the facts stated in the document, and
> (b) a written execution purporting to be signed by the person who handed to or served on the accused or the prosecutor a copy of the document or of the notice in terms of subsection (3) or (4) above, together with, where appropriate, a post office receipt for the registered or recorded delivery letter shall be sufficient evidence of the handing or service of such a copy or notice.

The effect of similar provisions under previous legislation was considered in *MacNeill v Perrie* 1978 CO Circulars A/13.

5.8:12   Definition

'*Purporting to be signed*' – see *Donlon v MacKinnon* 1981 SCCR 219, 1981 CO Circulars A/26.

5.8:13   Evidence

In *Donoghue v Allan* 1985 SCCR 93, 1985 CO Circulars A/4, the police officer who signed the certificate part of the print-out was not called as a witness, but it was held that this did not preclude a conviction if there was adequate other evidence vouching the document. In *McLeod v Fraser* 1987 SLT 142, 1986 SCCR 271, 1986 CO Circulars A/27, the analyst's certificate was not referred to in evidence (although it was a production) but the analyst himself gave evidence. It was held that notwithstanding the terms of this sub-section the analyst's testimony could be regarded as satisfying the best evidence rule.

The question of errors and defects in the certificates is discussed in paragraphs 5.8:5 and 5.8:6.

5.8:14   Methods of service (s 16(6))

Section 16(6) of the Road Traffic Offenders Act 1988 provides:

> A copy of a certificate required by this section to be served on the accused or a notice required by this section to be served on the prosecutor may be served personally or sent by registered post or recorded delivery service.

This sub-section prescribes the methods of service of the certificates, statements and notices referred to elsewhere in the section.

It is submitted that in Scotland, personal service means that the documents in question must be handed personally to the accused, or to the procurator fiscal or a member of his staff, although in England effective service was held to have taken place where the documents were given to the accused's agent (*Anderton v Kinnaird* [1986] RTR 11) and even, in one case, to the accused's counsel (*Penman v Parker* [1986] RTR 403). It is considered doubtful that these last two cases would be followed in Scotland; see *Geddes v Hamilton* 1986 SLT 536, 1986 SCCR 165, 1986 CO Circulars A/25.

5.8:15   Qualified analyst (s 16(7))

Section 16(7) of the Road Traffic Offenders Act 1988 provides:

> In this section 'authorised analyst' means–
> (a) any person possessing the qualifications prescribed by regulations made under section 76 of the Food Act 1984 or section 27 of the Food and Drugs (Scotland) Act 1956 as qualifying persons for appointment as public analysts under those Acts, and
> (b) any other person authorised by the Secretary of State to make analyses for the purposes of this section.

This sub-section provides the definition of the term 'authorised analyst' referred to in s 16(1)(b) (see paragraph 5.8:7).

Chapter Six

Miscellaneous; hospital patients; detention and interpretation

SECTIONS 9, 10 AND 11 OF THE ROAD TRAFFIC ACT 1988

6.1   Protection for Hospital Patients

6.1:1   Section 9
6.1:2   Definitions
6.1:3   General application

6.2   Power to detain persons affected by alcohol or drugs

6.2:1   Section 10

6.3   Interpretation (s 11)

6.1 PROTECTION FOR HOSPITAL PATIENTS

6.1:1 Section 9

Section 9 of the Road Traffic Act 1988 provides:

(1) While a person is at hospital as a patient he shall not be required to provide a specimen of breath for a breath test or to provide a specimen for a laboratory test unless the medical practitioner in immediate charge of his case has been notified of the proposal to make the requirement; and–
   (a) if the requirement is then made, it shall be for the provision of a specimen at the hospital, but
   (b) if the medical practitioner objects on the ground specified in subsection (2) below, the requirement shall not be made.

(2) The ground on which the medical practitioner may object is that the requirement or the provision of a specimen or, in the case of a specimen of blood or urine, the warning required under section 7(7) of this Act, would be prejudicial to the proper care and treatment of the patient.

6.1:2 Definitions

'While a person is at hospital as a patient.' – This phrase is to be strictly construed, and does not, for example, include a person in an ambulance waiting to go to hospital. Such a person will not qualify for the protection conferred by this section (*Manz v Miln* 1977 JC 78, 1977 CO Circulars A/19; see also *MacNeill v England* 1971 SLT 103; and *Watt v MacNeill* 1980 SLT 178, 1980 CO Circulars A/12). The term 'hospital' is defined in s 11 (paragraph 6.3:1).

'Provision of a specimen.' – The specimens referred to are a specimen of breath for a breath test in terms of s 6, or a specimen of blood or urine in terms of s 7(1) (b). The section does not refer to a specimen of breath for analysis in terms of s 7(1)(a) which can only be required at a police station (s 7(2)).

'Medical practitioner' – see paragraph 4.11:6.

6.1:3 General application

It should be noted that the constable must seek out the medical practitioner's opinion before he can require a specimen of a person who is in hospital as a patient. In particular, it is clear that in terms of sub-section (2), the constable must obtain the medical practitioners' opinion not only as to whether the patient can provide a sample of breath into the breathalyser or a specimen or blood or urine, but as a quite separate issue, whether the requirement or request for a specimen, or the warning which must be given in terms of s 7(7) to the effect that a failure to provide a blood or urine specimen may render the driver liable to prosecution, would be prejudicial to the proper care and treatment of the patient.

Failure to observe the requirements imposed by this section will render the specimen inadmissible (paragraphs 5.3:2 *et seq*). It has not been decided whether a requirement made by a police officer in the face of an objection by the medical practitioner in charge, will constitute a reasonable excuse for failing to provide a specimen in terms of s 8(7), but this point is probably academic. By virtue of s 15(4) of the Road Traffic Offenders Act 1988, and s 11(4) of the Road Traffic Act 1988, any specimen of blood has to be taken by a medical practitioner with the accused's consent.

6.2　POWER TO DETAIN PERSONS AFFECTED BY ALCOHOL OR DRUGS

6.2:1　Section 10

Section 10 of the Road Traffic Act 1988 provides:

(1) Subject to subsections (2) and (3) below, a person required to provide a specimen of breath, blood or urine may afterwards be detained at a police station until it appears to the constable that, were the person then driving or attempting to drive a motor vehicle on a road, he would not be committing an offence under section 4 or 5 of this Act.

(2) A person shall not be detained in pursuance of this section if it appears to a constable that there is no likelihood of his driving or attempting to drive a motor vehicle whilst his ability to drive properly is impaired or whilst the proportion of alcohol in his breath or urine exceeds the prescribed limit.

(3) A constable must consult a medical practitioner on any question arising under this section whether a person's ability to drive properly is or might be impaired through drugs and must act on the medical practitioner's advice.

This section in effect allows a police officer to detain any motorist who has been required to provide a specimen of breath, blood or urine at the police station until he is satisfied either that, in his opinion, the level of alcohol in the accused's body is such that were he to drive he would no longer be committing an offence or that there is no likelihood of him driving. The decision in these matters is left entirely to the constable in question, and there is no sanction provided by the section in respect of any abuse of power in respect thereof other than by making a complaint in the normal way. However, if the accused's condition arises from the consumption of drugs, the constable is required to seek out a medical practitioner's advice on the question of whether the accused's ability to drive is impaired and having done so the constable must act on the advice given.

6.3　INTERPRETATION

Section 11 of the Road Traffic Act 1988 provides:

(1) The following provisions apply for the interpretation of sections 4 to 10 of this Act.

(2) In those sections–

'breath test' means a preliminary test for the purpose of obtaining, by means of a device of a type approved by the Secretary of State, an indication whether the proportion of alcohol in a person's breath or blood is likely to exceed the prescribed limit,

'drug' includes any intoxicant other than alcohol,

'fail' includes refuse,

'hospital' means an institution which provides medical or surgical treatment for in-patients or out-patients,

'the prescribed limit' means, as the case may require–
(a) 35 microgrammes of alcohol in 100 millilitres of breath,
(b) 80 milligrammes of alcohol in 100 millilitres of blood, or
(c) 107 milligrammes of alcohol in 100 millilitres of urine, or such other proportions as may be prescribed by regulations made by the Secretary of State.

(3) A person does not provide a specimen of breath for a breath test or for analysis unless the specimen–
(a) is sufficient to enable the test or the analysis to be carried out, and
(b) is provided in such a way as to enable the objective of the test or analysis to be satisfactorily achieved.

The effect of the interpretation section has been referred to *passim* in the preceding chapters on sections 4–10 of the Road Traffic Act 1988 and ss 15 and 16 of the Road Traffic Offenders Act 1988, and the section is reproduced here for convenience.

Chapter Seven

Other road traffic offences

7.1 GENERAL: HIGHWAY CODE

In addition to the offences covered by ss 1–11 of the Road Traffic Act 1988 and described in the preceding chapters, there are a very large number of further offences, directions and regulations contained in the extensive legislative instruments concerned with road traffic. The Highway Code does not create offences as such; rather it contains a series of directions for the guidance of persons using roads. Although in terms of s 38(1) of the Road Traffic Act 1988, the Highway Code continues to have effect, a failure *per se* on the part of anyone using the road to observe the provisions of the code does not make that person guilty of a criminal offence. Section 38(7) of the Act provides:

A failure on the part of a person to observe a provision of the Highway Code shall not of itself render that person liable to criminal proceedings of any kind but any such failure may in any proceedings (whether civil or criminal, and including proceedings for an offence under the Traffic Acts, the Public Passenger Vehicles Act 1981 or sections 18 to 23 of the Transport Act 1985) be relied upon by any party to the proceedings as tending to establish or negative any liability which is in question in those proceedings.

Accordingly, the provisions of the Highway Code may provide useful guidance in determining whether a civil wrong, or an offence in terms of any of the principal acts described has or has not been committed (*McCrone v Normand* 1989 SLT 332). The Secretary of State has the responsibility for issuing the Highway Code and has the power to revise it from time to time as the need arises, although in terms of s 38(5) of the Act he is obliged to consult such representative organisations as he thinks fit. Further, the Secretary of State and local authorities have powers and responsibilities to furnish road safety training and information, in terms of ss 39 and 40. The Highway Code is published by Her Majesty's Stationery Office; some of the most relevant provisions are reproduced in Appendix A. There follows a description of some of the principal traffic offences contained in the legislation, although it must be remembered that there are a very large number of other provisions which do not often feature in practice. The penalties for offences under the Road Traffic Act 1988 are contained in Schedule 2 of the Road Traffic Offenders Act 1988, which also includes penalties in respect of other offences such as those described in the Road Traffic Regulation Act 1984 and contraventions of the Construction and Use regulations in terms of s 42 of the Road Traffic Act 1988. Penalties in respect of offences under other Acts and regulations are normally found within the body of such legislation.

7.2   RACES AND TRIALS

7.2:1   Section 12

Section 12 of the Road Traffic Act 1988 provides:

(1) A person who promotes or takes part in a race or trial of speed between motor vehicles on a public way is guilty of an offence.

(2) In this section 'public way' means, in England and Wales, a public highway and, in Scotland, a public road.

7.2:2 Definitions

'Motor vehicle': see paragraph 1.2:1.

'Public road': see paragraphs 1.8:1 and 3.3:5.

7.2:3 General application

For an offence to be committed under this section, it is not necessary that the race or trial of speed should have been pre-arranged. In *Ferrari v McNaughton* 1979 SLT (Notes) 62, 1979 CO Circulars A/13 the evidence indicated that two vehicles engaged upon a race or trial of speed quite spontaneously. In these circumstances, the Appeal Court held that a contravention of s 12 had occurred. No definition exists within the legislation of what constitutes a race or trial of speed and whether such an event has taken place will depend on the facts and circumstances in each case.

Competitions or trials may be permitted to take place on the road, provided that they are properly authorised and conducted in accordance with the relevant regulations (Road Traffic Act 1988, s 13).

Similar provisions regulating cycle racing on public roads are found in s 31.

7.3 SEATBELTS AND PROTECTIVE HEADGEAR

Section 14 of the Road Traffic Act 1988 makes provision for seat belts to be worn by adults driving or riding in motor vehicles. The relevant regulations, which provide detailed descriptions of the vehicles to which this requirement applies, exemptions and technical descriptions relating to the seatbelts to be used, are the Motor Vehicles (Wearing of Seat Belts) Regulations 1982, SI 1982/1203 and regulations 46, 47 and 48 of the Road Vehicles (Construction and Use) Regulations 1986, SI 1986/1078, as amended by SI 1987/1133. The exemptions to this requirement chiefly apply to those driving a vehicle constructed or adapted for the delivery or collection of goods or mail to consumers or addresses for the purpose of making local rounds or collections; drivers performing a manoeuvre, including reversing; the holder of a certificate in the prescribed form signed by a medical practitioner that it is inadvisable on medical grounds for the driver to wear a seatbelt; a constable or similar person protecting or escorting another person; firemen, and taxi drivers. The foregoing provisions do not apply to children under fourteen years of age; s 15 of the Road Traffic Act 1988 and the Motor Vehicles (Wearing of Seatbelts by Children) 1982, SI 1982/1342 impose limited restrictions on the carrying of such children in motor vehicles without seat belts. Section 15(3) provides for children under fourteen to wear seat belts while in the rear of a vehicle; the regulations implementing this requirement have not yet been issued.

Protective headgear for motor cyclists is governed by ss 16, 17 and 18 of the Road Traffic Act 1988, and the Motor Cycles (Protective Helmets) Regulations 1980, SI 1980/1279 (as amended by SI 1986/472).

7.4   TRAFFIC DIRECTIONS; CONSTABLE'S DIRECTIONS (S 35)

7.4:1   General

By virtue of s 35(1) of the Road Traffic Act 1988, where a constable is engaged in the regulation of traffic in a road, a person who, while driving or propelling a vehicle, neglects or refuses to stop the vehicle or makes it proceed in or keep to a particular line of traffic when directed to do so by the constable in the execution of his duty shall be guilty of an offence. Section 35(2) gives similar powers to a constable to enable a traffic survey to be carried out.

Whether an offence under this section has taken place is a matter of fact. A police officer does not have to be specially authorised to regulate traffic; however the Crown must show that the officer was acting in the execution of his duty. The section however does not specify that the constable must be in uniform. It is important to note that in terms of s 21(3) of the Road Traffic Offenders Act 1988, the Crown can secure a conviction under this section on the evidence of only one witness (see also *Sutherland v Aitchison* 1970 SLT (Notes) 48).

It would appear to be a possible defence to a charge of this kind that the constable was acting capriciously (*Beard v Wood* [1980] RTR 454, [1980] Crim LR 384). In *Keane v McSkimming* 1983 SCCR 220, it was observed that it was sufficient for the prosecution to show that the signal given by the police officer was obvious; it is not necessary for a conviction that it is established in evidence that the driver in fact saw the signal. However, it is also clear from this case that the fact that the driver did not see the signal may in appropriate circumstances be a good defence to the charge.

7.4:2 Traffic signs (s 36)

It is an offence in terms of s 36 of the Road Traffic Act 1988 for a person driving or propelling a vehicle not to comply with a traffic sign of the prescribed size, colour and type or as otherwise authorised by the provisions of the Road Traffic Regulation Act 1984. The sign must indicate a statutory prohibition, restriction or requirement, and must also be properly established in terms of the legislation (s 35(2)). However, any traffic sign placed at or near a road is presumed to be properly authorised and lawfully placed unless the contrary is proved. At the same time, any traffic sign must conform exactly to the description of that sign given in the appropriate regulations (*Davies v Heatley* [1971] RTR 145). In *Skeen v Smith* 1979 SLT 295, 1979 CO Circulars A/19, a sign displayed on a pole at a road junction was erected properly, but the corresponding 'stop' sign marked on the road was not entirely clear. It was held that this did not entitle the driver to ignore the sign on the pole.

Part V of the Road Traffic Regulation Act 1984 gives general provisions as to traffic signs, and allows the Secretary of State to delegate the responsibility for placing such signs to the local authority. The principal regulations are the Traffic Signs Regulations 1981, SI 1981/859, as amended.

As in s 35, in terms of s 21(3) of the Road Traffic Offenders Act 1988, a conviction for an offence under s 36 may follow from the evidence of one witness only (see also *Sutherland v Aitchison* 1970 SLT (Notes) 48).

7.4:3 Directions to pedestrians (s 37)

A pedestrian proceeding across or along a carriageway in contravention of a direction to stop given by a constable engaged in regulating traffic in the execution of his duty, is guilty of an offence (s 37 of the Road Traffic Act 1988). The constable must be in uniform. Unlike the two preceding sections, s 21(3) of the Road Traffic Offenders Act 1988 does not apply to this offence, and the prosecution must offer full corroborative evidence to secure a conviction.

A constable may also require a person committing an offence under s 37 to give his name and address, and if that person refuses to do so, his refusal constitutes a further offence (Road Traffic Act 1988, s 169).

For possible defences to a change under s 37, reference should be made to paragraph 7.4:1.

7.5   POWERS OF POLICE OFFICERS TO STOP VEHICLES AND REQUIRE INFORMATION (S 163)

7.5:1   General

By virtue of s 163 of the Road Traffic Act 1988, a person driving a motor vehicle on a road, or riding a cycle on a road, must stop on being required to do so by a police constable in uniform. Failure so to stop is an offence. It is sufficient for a conviction that the Crown proves that the policeman's signal was obvious; it does not have to be proved that the driver saw the signal (*Keane v McSkimming* 1983 SCCR 220). This offence is not one provable by the evidence of one witness only in terms of s 21 of the Road Traffic Offenders Act 1988; full corroborated evidence is required for conviction.

7.5:2   Duty to give information and documents (s 164)

By virtue of s 164 of the Road Traffic Act 1988, a police constable may require certain classes of person to produce their driving licence. The express purpose of this production of the licence is to enable the constable to ascertain the name and address of the holder of the licence, and its date and authority of issue. The classes of person of whom this requirement can be made are: a person driving a motor vehicle on a road; a person whom a constable has reasonable cause to believe was driving a motor vehicle on a road when it was involved in an accident or who has committed a motor vehicle offence; a person who is supervising a provisional licence holder, or who was supervising a provisional driver when an accident or a suspected offence occurred. If the driver is not able to produce his licence at the material time when he is required to do so, he can escape conviction in terms of sub-sections (7) and (8). Sub-section (7) arises when a driver has previously surrendered his licence to a police officer or other authorised person in terms of the fixed penalty procedure and s 56 of the Road Traffic Offenders Act 1988. Sub-section (8) covers the normal situation where a driver does not have his licence with him at the time the requirement was made. In those circumstances, the driver can escape conviction if (a) he produces his licence personally within seven days at a nominated police station, or (b) if he produces it at the police station as soon as reasonably practicable, or if he proves that it was not reasonably practicable for him to produce it to the police station before the day on which proceedings were commenced by the service of the complaint. In association with the requirement to produce a licence at a nominated police station, the police officer will normally issue a standard form (HORT 1) to the driver.

It should be noted that in certain circumstances the officer may seize a licence produced to him (sub-sections (3), (5)).

7.5:3 Duty to give name and address and certain documents (s 165)

By virtue of s 165 of the Road Traffic Act 1988, broadly the same categories of person as are described in s 164 (apart from the drivers of invalid carriages) may also be required by a constable to give their name and address, and the name and address of the owner of the vehicle. In addition holders of a full licence may be required to produce certain documents relevant to the vehicle for examination, namely the insurance certificate, the MOT certificate, and any relevant goods vehicle test certificate. There may be further duties to provide information in terms of s 171 (see paragraph 7.5:9). Again, it is a defence to a charge under this section if the driver produces the document or any other required evidence to a nominated police station within seven days, or as soon as reasonably practicable, or if he proves that it was not reasonably practicable for him to have presented the necessary information to the police station before the day on which any complaint was served.

7.5:4 Duty to give name and address in reckless and careless driving (s 168)

By virtue of s 168 of the Road Traffic Act 1988, the driver of a vehicle who is alleged to have committed an offence under s 2 or 3 of the Act (reckless or careless driving) must give his name and address to any person (not just a police officer) having reasonable grounds for requiring that information. Failure so to give the name and address, or the giving of a false name and address, is an offence. What constitutes reasonable grounds for making the requirement is a matter of fact in each case. The same requirement can be made in a case of reckless or careless cycling in terms of ss 28 and 29 of the Act. Any person who fails to give his name and address or to produce his licence in these circumstances may be arrested without warrant (s 167). In a prosecution under s 167, evidence identifying a driver who claimed he did not know who was driving at the material time, is admissible (*Clarke v Allan* 1988 SLT 274; 1987 SCCR 333; 1987 CO Circulars A/8).

7.5:5 Duty on pedestrian to give name and address (s 169)

A constable may require a person who is committing an offence under s 37 of the Road Traffic Act 1988 (failure by a pedestrian to comply with a direction to stop given by a constable) to give his name and address, and failure to do so will constitute a further offence (s 169 of the Road Traffic Act 1988) (see paragraph 7.4:3).

7.5:6   Duty to give information as to identity of driver (s 172)

Section 172 of the Road Traffic Act 1988 requires the keeper or driver of a vehicle, or any other person, to give information to a duly authorised police officer as to the identity of the driver of the vehicle at any time the driver is alleged to have been guilty of most road traffic offences. The section is frequently used in the course of police investigations and reads in full as follows:

(1) This section applies–
(a) to any offence under the preceding provisions of this Act except–
    (i) an offence under Part V, or
    (ii) an offence under section 13, 16, 51(2), 61(4), 67(9), 68(4), 96 or 117,
and to an offence under section 178 of this Act,
(b) to any offence under sections 25, 26, 27 and 45 of the Road Traffic Offenders Act 1988, and
(c) to any offence against any other enactment relating to the use of vehicles on roads.

(2) Where the driver of a vehicle is alleged to be guilty of an offence to which this section applies–
(a) the person keeping the vehicle shall give such information as to the identity of the driver as he may be required to give by or on behalf of a chief officer of police, and
(b) any other person shall if required as stated above give any information which it is in his power to give and may lead to identification of the driver.
In this subsection references to the driver of a vehicle include references to the person riding a cycle.

(3) A person who fails to comply with the requirement of subsection (2)(a) above is guilty of an offence unless he shows to the satisfaction of the court that he did not know and could not with reasonable diligence have ascertained who the driver of the vehicle or, as the case may be, the rider of the cycle was.

(4) A person who fails to comply with the requirement of subsection (2)(b) above is guilty of an offence.

7.5:7   Definitions (s 172)

'*Keeper of the vehicle.*' This phrase is intended to refer to the person in whose custody the vehicle is, at the time of making the requirement. It is submitted that the keeper of any vehicle is not necessarily confined to the person who is the registered owner.

'*Any other person.*' This phrase includes the driver himself (*Foster v Farrell* 1963 SLT 182). Thus, where a police officer is investigating an alleged offence in terms of sub-section (1), he is entitled to ask the person who is said to have been driving at the material time to confirm whether or not he was driving at the time the alleged offence is said to have been committed.

'*By or on behalf of a chief officer of police.*' This phrase includes any police officer whom the Chief Constable of the area has authorised to make the requirement on his behalf. The Chief Constable may, but does not have to, make a specific authorisation to each individual officer; a general authorisation may be given to particular officers to exercise this power (*Gray v Farrell* 1969 SLT 250). A police officer who has not been duly authorised in terms of this section cannot ask the driver or any other person to confirm the driver's identity at the material time in terms of this section (*Foster v Farrell* (*supra*)).

7.5:8   General application (s 172)

It is a defence to an offence alleged under this section that the person required to provide the information can demonstrate to the satisfaction of the court that he did not know and could not have ascertained with reasonable diligence who was the driver of the vehicle at the material time (s 172(3)). In requiring information under this section, the police officer in making the requirement does not have to indicate that the person who was driving the vehicle at the material time is alleged to have been guilty of a particular offence (*McNaughton v Buchan* 1980 SLT (Notes) 100, 1980 CO Circular A/19; *McMahon v Cardle* 1988 SCCR 556, 1988 CO Circulars A/42; *Duncan v McGillivray* 1989 SLT 48, 1988 CO Circulars A/41). A statement made by a driver in response to a requirement in terms of this section is admissible in evidence in any subsequent prosecution (see *Foster v Farrell* (*supra*); *Gray v Farrell* (*supra*); and *Galt v Goodsir* 1982 JC 4, 1982 SLT 94, 1981 SCCR 225). The officer should explain that failure to answer is an offence (*Duncan v McGillivray* (*supra*)).

7.5:9   Duty of owner of vehicle to give insurance information (s 171)

The chief purpose of this section is to allow a police officer to require the owner of a vehicle to give such information as is necessary to determine whether a driver was driving without insurance on any occasion when the driver has been asked to produce a certificate of insurance under ss 165(1) or 170 of the Act.

7.6   DUTIES ON DRIVER IN CASE OF ACCIDENT (S 170)

7.6:1   General

Section 170 of the Road Traffic Act 1988 reads in full as follows:

(1) This section applies in a case where, owing to the presence of a motor vehicle on a road, an accident occurs by which—
 (a) personal injury is caused to a person other than the driver of that motor vehicle, or
 (b) damage is caused—
  (i) to a vehicle other than that motor vehicle or a trailer drawn by that motor vehicle, or
  (ii) to an animal other than an animal in or on that motor vehicle or a trailer drawn by that motor vehicle, or
  (iii) to any other property constructed on, fixed to, growing in or otherwise forming part of the land on which the road in question is situated or land adjacent to such land.

(2) The driver of a motor vehicle must stop and, if required to do so by any person having reasonable grounds for so requiring, give his name and address and also the name and address of the owner and the identification marks of the vehicle.

(3) If for any reason the driver of the motor vehicle does not give his name and address under sub-section (2) above, he must report the accident.

(4) A person who fails to comply with sub-section (2) or (3) above is guilty of an offence.

(5) If, in a case where this section applies by virtue of sub-section (1)(a) above, the driver of the vehicle does not at the time of the accident produce such a certificate of insurance or security, or other evidence, as is mentioned in s 165(2) of this Act—
 (a) to a constable, or
 (b) to some person who, having reasonable grounds for so doing, has required him to produce it,
the driver must report the accident and produce such a certificate or other evidence.
This sub-section does not apply to the driver of an invalid carriage.

(6) To comply with a duty under this section to report an accident or to produce such a certificate of insurance or security, or other evidence, as is mentioned in s 165(2)(a) of this Act, the driver—
 (a) must do so at a police station or to a constable, and

(b) must do so as soon as is reasonably practicable and, in any case, within twenty-four hours of the occurrence of the accident.

(7) A person who fails to comply with a duty under sub-section (5) above is guilty of an offence, but he shall not be convicted by reason only of a failure to produce a certificate or other evidence if, within five days after the occurrence of the accident, the certificate or other evidence is produced at a police station that was specified by him at the time when the accident was reported.

(8) In this section 'animal' means horse, cattle, ass, mule, sheep, pig, goat or dog.

7.6:2 Definitions (s 170)

'Motor vehicle' – see paragraph 1.2:1.

'A road' – see paragraphs 1.8:1 and 3.3:5.

'Accident' – see paragraph 1.9:1.

'Personal injury'. It is submitted that the meaning of this phrase is not confined to physical injury, but could include shock or even emotional distress.

'Stop'. The Act does not provide a definition of this word, nor a description of the period over which the duty to stop must be exercised. However it is clear that the driver must stop at, or as near as reasonably practicable, to the *locus* of the accident, and further that he must remain there for such time, as in the circumstances, gives persons entitled to have the particulars described in the section sufficient opportunity to require them of the driver personally (*Campbell v Copeland* 1972 JC 24; *Singh v McLeod* 1987 SLT 550, 1986 SCCR 656; 1987 CO Circulars A/5).

'Animal'. For the purposes of this section, animal means a horse, cattle, ass, mule, sheep, pig, goat or dog (s 170(8)). Accordingly, no duty to stop is imposed if damage is caused to fowl, deer, or any other wild or domestic animal.

7.6:3 General application (s 170)

The circumstances in which a duty under this section can arise are extremely wide. If an accident which is covered by any of the situations described in sub-sections 1(a) and (b) can be attributed in any way to the presence of a motor vehicle on a road, then the driver of that motor vehicle is under an immediate duty to stop. As indicated in the preceding paragraph, the driver must stop as near as is practicable to where the accident occurred. It will also be noted that the offending vehicle need not necessarily be being driven at the material time; if for example an accident happens as a result of a vehicle being dangerously parked, the duty to stop imposed upon the driver of that vehicle by this section will still arise. Even although the driver complies with all other parts of s 170 of the Act, a failure to stop at the material time will nonetheless contravene the provisions of the first part of s 170(2).

In addition to the duty imposed on a driver to stop following such an accident, in terms of the first part of s 170(2), the same section imposes an additional and quite separate duty on the driver in these circumstances to provide his name and address, and the name and address of the owner of the vehicle and the identifying marks of the vehicle, to any person who requires that information from him and who has reasonable grounds for making that requirement. Whether such a person has reasonable grounds for requiring this information will depend on the facts and circumstances of each case. The duty to furnish the required information is personal to the driver and may not be delegated (*Campbell v Copeland* 1972 JC 24). Again, an offence can be committed under this part of s 170(2) even where all other parts of s 170 are complied with by the offending driver. On the other hand, in the case of *Adair v Fleming* 1932 JC 51, 1932 SLT 263, it was held that where a vehicle had collided with another vehicle and the driver of the offending vehicle had given his name and address to the driver of the other vehicle, the driver of the offending vehicle was not, in the circumstances, thereafter under a duty to report the accident to the police in terms of s 170(3).

If the circumstances of an incident of driving are such that a driver had, or should have had reasonable cause to suppose that he might have been involved in an accident, then he has a duty in terms of this section to stop and satisfy himself about what had happened. In *Sutherland v Aitchison* 1975 JC 1, a driver on a single track road mounted the verge in order to pass a vehicle coming in the opposite direction. As he did so he heard a noise which he thought might have been his exhaust hitting a stone, but which was in fact a collision between the two vehicles. It was held that in these circumstances the driver, having heard some noise, was under a duty to stop and see if he had been involved in an accident. Accordingly, a driver would appear to have a duty to satisfy himself that he has not been involved in an accident, if the circumstances suggest that he might have been. Section 170(2) does not qualify in any way the time limits within which the duty conferred by the section must be discharged and accordingly it is submitted that the duty to stop or to furnish information if properly required to do so, must be discharged as soon as reasonably practicable after the duty has arisen.

Section 170(3) and (6) makes provision for an offence which is quite separate and distinct from the offence described in s 170(2). It is therefore possible, and not unusual, for a driver to contravene both sub-sections. The duty incumbent upon a driver in terms of s 170(3) and (6) arises in particular if he has failed in any way to discharge his duties under s 170(2). Thus, if a driver has failed to stop at an accident, or has declined to give his name and address to someone having reasonable grounds to require this information, or has not given his name and address because there was no-one at the scene of the accident, or no-one who had reasonable grounds for requiring the information, then he must discharge the obligation described in s 170(6). It should be emphasised that a driver does not have any kind of discretion to report the matter to the police within the twenty-four hours following the accident. Rather, he is under an absolute duty to report the matter to the police as soon as reasonably practicable, and in any event within the period of twenty-four hours. On the other hand, however, a driver who fulfils all of the duties incumbent on him in terms of s 170(2) is under no duty to report an accident to the police in terms of s 170(3) and (6) (*Adair v Fleming (supra)*).

In *Wood v McLean* 1947 JC 18, 1947 SLT 22, it was held that it was sufficient for a conviction under an earlier version of the offence described in s 170(3) and (6) for the prosecution to show firstly that the driver's name and address were not given to anyone at the locus of the accident, and secondly that the accident was not duly reported to the police. It was also suggested in that case that if the accused sought out a person with an interest in the matter and reported the incident within twenty-four hours, this might provide a defence. However, it is submitted that such a defence could only be successfully pled in the most exceptional of circumstances.

Any direct link between the presence of the vehicle on the road and the accident which occurs as a result, such as a passenger falling off the platform of a bus, imposes the duties described in s 170 (*Quelch v Phipps* [1955] 2 QB 107).

Where the accident involves personal injury in terms of s 170(1)(a), the driver must produce a certificate of insurance at the time of the accident, to a constable or to a person who has reasonable grounds for requiring him to produce it. If he does not, he must report the accident to the police as soon as reasonably practicable and in any event within twenty-four hours, and produce the certificate of insurance within five days (s 170(5), (6) and (7)).

7.6:4   Accident inquiries

The Secretary of State may direct that inquiry be made into the cause of any accident which arises out of the presence of a vehicle on a road (Road Traffic Act 1988, s 181). The inquiry may be public. Such an inquiry, which normally takes place if the accident involves the death of a person who was at the material time in the course of his employment, has the power to inspect any vehicle in connection with that inquiry, but any report made to or by the Secretary of State following such inquiry may not be used in any subsequent legal proceedings.

7.7   TAKING AND DRIVING AWAY (S 178)

7.7:1   Section 178

Section 178 of the Road Traffic Act 1988 provides:

(1) A person who in Scotland—
(a) takes and drives away a motor vehicle without having either the consent of the owner of the vehicle or other lawful authority, or
(b) knowing that a motor vehicle has been so taken, drives it or allows himself to be carried in or on it without such consent or authority,
is subject to subsection (2) below, guilty of an offence.

(2) If—
(a) the jury, on proceedings under this section on indictment, or
(b) the court, on summary proceedings under this section,
is satisfied that the accused acted in the reasonable belief that he had lawful authority, or in the reasonable belief that the owner would, in the circumstances of the case, have given consent if he had been asked for it, the accused shall not be liable to be convicted of the offence.

(3) A constable may arrest without warrant a person reasonably suspected by him of having committed or of attempting to commit an offence under this section.

In terms of s 23 of the Road Traffic Offenders Act 1988, if an accused on indictment is charged with stealing a car, a jury is entitled to bring an alternative verdict under this section.

7.7:2   Definitions (s 178)

'*Drives*' – see paragraphs 1.7:1 and 3.3:2.

'*Motor vehicle*' – see paragraph 1.2:1.

7.7:3 General application (s 178)

The offence described in this section was originally created to deal with the offence of joy-riding, which occurs when a vehicle is taken without the permission of its rightful owner for the purposes of a single trip or for a short period, and where the taker of the vehicle does not necessarily have the intention of depriving the owner of his property on a permanent basis. Such cases may cover a variety of situations in practice, and formerly were charged simply as theft. However, because it could be argued in such cases that the intention permanently to deprive the owner of his property (a necessary ingredient of a common law charge of theft) might well be absent, it was considered appropriate to provide a special statutory offence. It is competent to charge an accused with the alternative of a common law charge of theft and an offence in terms of s 178.

For a conviction under s 178(1)(a), the prosecution must prove that the accused both took and drove away the vehicle, and that he did so without the owner's permission. In particular, if the owner's permission is only given for a particular journey, but the driver then embarks on a wholly unauthorised journey, an offence may be committed under this section (*Barclay v Douglas* 1983 SCCR 224).

For a conviction under s 178(1)(b), the prosecution must show that the accused knew that the vehicle had been stolen (see eg *Ashcroft's Curator Bonis v Stewart* 1988 SLT 163).

7.7:4 Penalties

The penalties under s 178 are found in Schedule 2, Part 1 of the Road Traffic Offenders Act 1988. Part 2 of the same schedule provides for discretionary disqualification, obligatory endorsement, and eight penalty points on the accused's licence in a common law charge of stealing or attempting to steal a motor vehicle. For these consequences however, it is necessary for the Crown to have served on the accused the appropriate notice of penalties.

7.8 SPEED LIMITS

7.8:1 General

By virtue of the Road Traffic Regulation Act 1984 ss 81(1) and 89, it is an offence for anyone to drive a motor vehicle on a restricted road at a speed in excess of 30 mph. A restricted road is defined in s 82 of the Act, and is in effect a road provided with a system of street lighting furnished by means of lamps placed not more than 200 yards apart. Speed limits on roads other than restricted roads are provided for in s 84 of the Act, and the responsibility for erecting the necessary speed restriction signs are dealt with under s 85. The detailed description of the signs themselves are found in the Traffic Signs (Speed Limits) Regulations and General Directions 1969, SI 1969/1487. Failure by the relevant authority to observe these directions in any material respect may preclude a driver being found guilty of a speeding offence (*Smith v Rankin* 1977 SLT (Notes) 12).

Further speed limits may be imposed by the Secretary of State on a temporary basis, and failure to observe these limits is also an offence (s 88). Regulations made under this section, and at present continued indefinitely, are the 70 miles per hour, 60 miles per hour, and 50 miles per hour (Temporary Speed Limit) (Continuation) Order 1978, SI 1978/1548.

Finally, it is an offence for any person to drive a motor vehicle of any class on a road at a speed greater than the maximum speed specified for a vehicle of that class. The various speeds specified for various classes of vehicles are set out in Schedule 6 to the Road Traffic Regulation Act 1984.

7.8:2 Evidence

In the prosecution of any person for a speeding offence, evidence of the measurement of speed by a device designed or adapted for measuring by radar the speed of vehicles is inadmissible unless the device is approved by the Secretary of State (Road Traffic Offenders Act 1988, s 20). The evidence produced by such devices will normally be sufficient for conviction (*Farrell v Simpson* 1959 SLT (Sh Ct) 23).

There are two main radar systems approved and in use in Scotland for the detection of speeding offences. The first is the Muniquip hand-held gun; the second is the radar trap where a vehicle is timed between two radar beams. In both cases the prosecution must be prepared to show if necessary that the equipment has been tested and is working properly. The same is true of the Vascar equipment which is also in use, and which is not a radar device but a machine fitted to a police vehicle to record the time which an observed vehicle takes to cover a known distance and thus arrives at its speed.

In *Westwater v Milton* 1980 SLT (Sh Ct) 63, it was held that a driver was not prejudiced and could properly be convicted when an inexperienced police officer failed to keep the offending speed on the visual display of the Muniquip gun for inspection.

In *Morrison v M'Cowan* 1939 SLT 422 the distance covered in a speeding charge was held to be calculated with sufficient accuracy by a measuring device and a Ordnance Survey map. Convictions for speeding can theoretically be secured by hand-held stop watches and other observations. In *Morrison v M'Cowan* 1939 JC 45, 1939 SLT 422, a speeding offence was proved by the time taken for a particular journey as measured on a map; See also *Gillespie v Macmillan* 1957 JC 31, 1957 SLT 283; *Houston v Leslie* 1958 JC 8 1958 SLT 109; *Farrell v Simpson* 1959 SLT (Sh Ct) 23. Significantly, these are all now somewhat elderly authorities, and it is extremely unlikely that such procedures are in current use.

Exemption from speed restrictions is given to fire, ambulance and police vehicles if complying with the speed limits would be likely to hinder the purposes for which the vehicle was being used at the time (Road Traffic Regulation Act 1984, s 87).

7.9   PARKING

7.9:1   General

The local roads authority (see the Roads (Scotland) Act 1984, s 151) has the power to provide off-street parking, and parking on roads without payment, in terms of s 32 *et seq* of the Road Traffic Regulation Act 1984. Parking may also be authorised on the road for payment of a charge, and by the provision of parking meters (ss 45–49). Section 52 deals with offences relating to interference with parking devices and the incorrect display of tickets. Excess parking charges are the responsibility of the owner of the vehicle (s 107; but see also ss 108–111). The power to provide parking places extends to the provision, on roads, or elsewhere, of stands and racks for bicycles (s 63). The Secretary of State has power to make regulations in respect of the removal of vehicles illegally, obstructively or dangerously parked, or abandoned, or broken down (ss 99, 101, 102 and 104; see also Refuse Disposal (Amenity) Act 1978, s 2). A police officer has the power in general terms to fix an immobilisation device to a vehicle illegally parked (s 104–106); however the necessary regulations have not been made introducing this power to Scotland.

The power to exempt vehicles with Disabled Persons badges from parking restrictions are found in the Local Authorities' Traffic Orders (Exemptions for Disabled Persons) (Scotland)

Regulations 1982 (SI 1982/1740); see also s 21 of the Chronically Sick and Disabled Persons Act 1970).

The local roads authority may also make such orders as it considers expedient for the regulation of traffic (Road Traffic Regulation Act, s 1 *et seq.*) However, once such an order is made, it only becomes effective when the authority has erected the appropriate signs (Local Authorities Traffic Orders (Procedure) (Scotland) Regulations 1969, SI 1969/487). (*MacLeod v Hamilton* 1965 SLT 305; *Macmillan v Gibson* 1966 SLT (Sh Ct) 84). Such signs (eg 'No Waiting' signs) may be made subject to exemptions (eg for loading).

7.9:2 Statutory provisions

Section 19 of the Road Traffic Act 1988 provides specifically that a heavy commercial vehicle (which is described in s 20; see paragraph 1.6:4), cannot be parked wholly or partly on the verge of a road, on any land situated between two carriageways, or on a footway. Exemption is provided in cases where the driver proves that the parking was done with the permission of a uniformed police officer, or took place in an emergency, or that it was engaged in loading or unloading in circumstances described in the section.

Additional provisions were supplied to s 19 by Schedule 2, Part II of the Road Traffic (Consequential Provisions) Act 1988, presumably because they were for some reason omitted from the principal Act. A new s 19(3A) allows the Secretary of State to make regulations providing for exceptions to the general prohibition found in s 19; and a new s 19A makes it an offence for a person to park a vehicle, other than a heavy commercial vehicle, on the verge of an urban road, between two carriageways of an urban road, or on a footway in an urban road, all under the same exceptions as are found in s 19.

It is also an offence (again subject to certain exceptions) to drive or park a motor vehicle on a cycle track (Road Traffic Act 1988, s 21). An offence which occurs more often in practice, however, is found in s 22 of the same Act, which prohibits a person in charge of a vehicle from causing or permitting that vehicle to remain at rest on a road in such a position, or in such a condition, or in such circumstances as to be likely to cause danger to other persons using the road. The word 'vehicle' is not qualified in any way in the section (eg by the word 'motor') and no exemptions or defences are indicated.

Regulation 101 of the Road Vehicles (Construction and Use)

Regulations 1986 imposes general restrictions, subject to certain exceptions, on parking on roads during the hours of darkness.

7.10 PEDESTRIAN CROSSINGS

The local roads authority has the power to establish, alter or remove pedestrian crossings on any roads within their area (s 23(1) of the Road Traffic Regulation Act 1984 as amended by the Roads (Scotland) Act 1984, Sch 9). Any pedestrian crossings on trunk roads are the responsibility of the Secretary of State (s 24 as similarly amended). The purpose of pedestrian crossings is to afford precedence in certain circumstances to pedestrians using a road over other road users. Two kinds of pedestrian crossings are described in the Act; the power to make regulations in respect of such crossings is contained in s 25.

The first kind of pedestrian crossing is the uncontrolled or 'Zebra' crossing. The 'Zebra' Pedestrian Crossing Regulations 1971, SI 1971/1524, provides in detail for the physical characteristics and markings for such crossings, including road markings, stud and globes, and in particular provides an absolute right of precedence in the circumstances therein described to pedestrians within the limits of such crossings. The regulations also provide for prohibitions against the waiting of vehicles and pedestrians on a crossing and against vehicles overtaking within the area of a crossing. Cases involving this kind of crossings as reported are *McKerrell v Robertson* 1956 SLT 50, 1956 SLT 290, and *Wishart v McDonald* 1962 SLT (Sh Ct) 29, (1962) 78 Sh Ct Rep 3.

The second form of crossing is the controlled or 'Pelican' type. Such crossings are governed by traffic lights, operated by push buttons, which follow the normal sequence, except that in the process of reverting from red to green the flashing amber light is displayed which allows a vehicle to proceed over the crossing unless a pedestrian is at that time engaged in using the crossing. When the red light is showing, vehicles must not cross the area of the crossing used by pedestrians, whether pedestrians are present or not. The 'Pelican' Pedestrian Crossing Regulations and General Directions 1987, SI 1987/16, as amended, govern the construction and use of such crossings.

7.11 SCHOOL CROSSINGS AND PLAYGROUNDS

In terms of s 26 of the Road Traffic Regulation Act 1984, local authorities are empowered to make arrangements for the patrolling of school crossings. The principal responsibility for providing such crossings lies with the regional or islands council; in practice the crossings are often implemented on their behalf by the appropriate district council. A properly appointed school crossing patrol is entitled to require vehicles to stop at places where children are crossing a road on or from their way to school. It is an offence for any person driving a vehicle to fail to comply with such a requirement (Road Traffic Regulation Act 1984, s 28). Sections 29 and 31 allow a local roads authority to make orders prohibiting the use of traffic on roads which are to be used as playgrounds.

7.12   CONSTRUCTION AND USE (S 41)

7.12:1   General

There are a very large number of provisions, normally introduced by statutory instrument, which regulate the construction, maintenance, use, weight and equipment of motor vehicles and trailers on the roads. A considerable number of these statutory provisions reflect the terms of the European Economic Communities' directives and regulations. A detailed examination of these regulations is outwith the scope of this book; many of the regulations specify what the statutory requirements are in very considerable detail. It is therefore proposed to deal with this subject in broad outline. Section 41 of the Road Traffic Act, and in particular sub-sections (2)–(4), indicates the general headings under which the various regulations are issued. Section 41(1)–(4) reads as follows:

(1) The Secretary of State may make regulations generally as to the use of motor vehicles and trailers on roads, their construction and equipment and the conditions under which they may be so used.

Sub-sections (2) to (4) below do not affect the generality of this subsection.

(2) In particular, the regulations may make provision with respect to any of the following matters—
  (a) the width, height and length of motor vehicles and trailers and the load carried by them, the diameter of wheels, and the width, nature and condition of tyres, of motor vehicles and trailers,
  (b) the emission or consumption of smoke, fumes or vapour and the emission of sparks, ashes and grit,
  (c) noise,
  (d) the maximum weight unladen of heavy locomotives and heavy motor cars, and the maximum weight laden of motor vehicles and

trailers, and the maximum weight to be transmitted to the road or any specified area of the road by a motor vehicle or trailer of any class or by any part or parts of such a vehicle or trailer in contact with the road, and the conditions under which the weights may be required to be tested,

(e) the particulars to be marked on motor vehicles and trailers,

(f) the towing of or drawing of vehicles by motor vehicles,

(g) the number and nature of brakes, and for securing that brakes, silencers and steering gear are efficient and kept in proper working order,

(h) lighting equipment and reflectors,

(j) the testing and inspection, by persons authorised by or under the regulations, of the brakes, silencers, steering gear, tyres, lighting equipment and reflectors of motor vehicles and trailers on any premises where they are (if the owner of the premises consents),

(k) the appliances to be fitted for—

 (i) signalling the approach of a motor vehicle, or

 (ii) enabling the driver of a motor vehicle to become aware of the approach of another vehicle from the rear, or

 (iii) intimating any intended change of speed or direction of a motor vehicle,

 and the use of any such appliance, and for securing that any such appliance is efficient and kept in proper working order,

(l) for prohibiting the use of appliances fitted to motor vehicles for signalling their approach, being appliances for signalling by sound, at any times, or on or in any roads or localities, specified in the regulations.

(3) The Secretary of State may, as respects goods vehicles, make regulations under this section—

(a) prescribing other descriptions of weight which are not to be exceeded in the case of such vehicles,

(b) providing for the marking on such vehicles of weights of any description or other particulars by means of plates (of any material) fixed to them,

(c) providing for the circumstances in which any particulars which are to be marked on such vehicles are to be so marked,

(d) providing that weights of any description or other particulars which are to be marked on particular goods vehicles may be determined in accordance with regulations under s 49 of this Act.

(4) Regulations under this section with respect to lighting equipment and reflectors—

(a) may require that lamps be kept lit at such times and in such circumstances as may be specified in the regulations, and

(b) may extend, in like manner as to motor vehicles and trailers, to vehicles of any description used on roads, whether or not they are mechanically propelled.

7.12:2 Construction and use offences (ss 42–44)

Section 42(1) of the Road Traffic Act 1988 makes any failure to comply with regulations created by virtue of s 41 an offence. Section 42(2) provides defences which may be available in charges of overloading or excess weight, and these are discussed in paragraph 7.12:7. The penalties for such offences under s 42(1) are set out in Schedule 2, Part I of the Road Traffic Offenders Act 1988. Section 43 provides for temporary exemption from the regulations, and s 44 for authorisation of use on roads of special vehicles which do not comply with s 41 regulations.

7.12:3 Statutory instruments

The principal secondary legislation dealing with s 41 offences is the Road Vehicles (Construction and Use) Regulations 1986, SI 1986/1078. These regulations apply to both wheeled vehicles and track-laying vehicles. The definition section of these regulations (reg 3) is particularly comprehensive. Also of importance are the Road Vehicles Lighting Regulations 1984, SI 1984/812. In addition there are a huge number of regulations dealing with a variety of subjects and all of these are subject to a continuous stream of amendments. In practical terms, the only method of keeping up to date with the details of this secondary legislation is by recourse to one of the specialist road traffic 'encyclopedias' which are issued regularly on a loose-leaf system, and which seek to present the current state of all aspects of road traffic legislation.

7.12:4 Type approval schemes

Certain of the construction and use requirements have, however, been superseded by type approval schemes. It is part of the European Economic Communities' overall plan to harmonise road traffic law, and eventually it is hoped that a universal and comprehensive series of schemes covering the manufacture of vehicles and parts will be introduced. In terms of such schemes, the manufacturer of a vehicle or of a vehicle part produces to the Secretary of State a type vehicle or part for inspection. If approval is given, the manufacturer is provided with a type approval certificate and is then enabled to produce vehicles or parts, of identical construction, as long as he issues certificates indicating that these further vehicles or parts conform exactly with the approval certificate. These are known as certificates of conformity. This scheme has been introduced to avoid the necessity of all vehicles and parts being individually inspected at the instance of the government. At present, some of these provisions are optional and some dealing mainly with certain kinds of passenger vehicles are obligatory. Reference to these schemes is made in ss 54–65 of the Road Traffic Act 1988; the principal regulations are the Motor Vehicles (Type Approval) (Great Britain) Regulations 1984, SI 1984/981, and the Motor Vehicles (Type Approval and Approval Marks) (Fees) Regulations 1984 , SI 1984/1404.

7.12:5 Maximum lengths

The Road Vehicles (Construction and Use) Regulations 1986, regulation 7 provides that subject to certain exceptions, the overall length of certain vehicles or combination of vehicles, including articulated vehicles and trailers must not exceed prescribed overall maximum lengths. Regulation 8 gives certain prescribed overall width dimensions which must not be exceeded principally in commercial vehicles. Regulation 9 provides for certain maximum heights in the case of buses (4.57 metres) and articulated lorries. Regulation 10 provides further requirements in respect of the height of vehicles and in particular the indications required in respect of special vehicles and overall travelling height. The maximum overhang permitted and the exceptions to the general provisions are provided in regulation 11. Regulation 12 provides details of the minimum ground clearance in respect of various vehicles. Regulations 13 and 14 apply to the turning circles, and connecting sections and direction–holding of articulated buses first used on or after 1 April 1982.

Detailed definitions of overall length, overall width, and overhang, together with definition of the various classes of vehicle are provided in the definition section (reg 3). Two cases in which these matters have been considered are *Guest Scottish Carriers Limited v Trend* [1967] 3 All ER 52; *Hawkins v Russett* [1983] RTR 406.

7.12:6 Weight

The regulations governing the weight of various vehicles are of particular importance. As has been indicated above, in terms of s 41(2)(d) and (e) of the Road Traffic Act 1988, the Secretary of State has the power to make regulations in respect of the maximum laden and unladen weight of vehicles, and the maximum weight to be transmitted to the road by any vehicle, the conditions under which such weights may be required to be tested, and the particulars to be marked on vehicles and trailers.

The Road Traffic Act 1988, s 190 provides the method of calculating the unladen weight of vehicles and trailers; for cases on this section see *McCowan v Stewart* 1936 JC 36, 1936 SLT 370; *Blaikie v Morrison* 1957 JC 46, 1957 SLT 290. Regulation 23 of the 1986 Regulations provides that certain multi-wheel vehicles must have a compensating arrangement to ensure that under the most adverse conditions every wheel will remain in contact with the road and will not be subject to abnormal variations of load.

There are detailed and technical provisions in respect of the maximum permitted laden weights of various kinds of vehicles. These are of particular significance to heavy commercial vehicles. The restrictions apply not only to the total laden weights, but also, as a separate matter, to the weight transmitted to the road by one or more wheels and axles. It is therefore possible for a vehicle to commit an overloading offence in respect of the maximum permitted wheel or axle weight even where the total permitted laden weight is not exceeded. The provisions are set out in tabulated form in regulations 75 to 80 of the Road Vehicles (Construction and Use) Regulations 1988, and are to be read with the definition section (reg 3). In any prosecution of a vehicle or trailer for overloading, the prosecution must adduce evidence that the weighbridge is accurate (*Grierson v Clark* 1958 JC 22, 1958 SLT 112). Section 17 of the Road Traffic Offenders Act 1988 affords a presumption that the plated weight is the weight of the vehicle. Regulations 81–82 and 83–90 provide restrictions on the use of vehicles carrying wide or long loads or appliances, and on the number of trailers to be drawn by particular vehicles, the distance between motor vehicles and trailers, provisions in respect of unbraked trailers, the use of bridging plates between motor vehicles and trailers, requirements on leaving trailers at rest, and on passengers in trailers. Regulation 91 makes provision in certain circumstances for attendants on trailers and other vehicles.

7.12:7   Weight offences: defences

In prosecutions in respect of offences under s 42(1) of the Road Traffic Act 1988 where it is alleged that any of the weight regulations described in the preceding paragraph have been contravened, s 42(2) provides two statutory defences. First, it is a defence if the vehicle is being used on the road at a time when it was proceeding to a weighbridge which was the nearest available one to the place where the loading of the vehicle was completed for the purpose of being weighed or was proceeding from a weighbridge after being weighed to the nearest point at which it was reasonably practicable to reduce the weight to the relevant limit without causing an obstruction on any road. However, this defence is to be strictly applied; courts have in practice been reluctant to sustain such a defence if the vehicle has diverted in any way from what, in the circumstances, can be reasonably described as a direct route between the loading point and the weighbridge. Further, it would not appear to be a sustainable defence to argue that there was no such weighbridge available or open.

Secondly, in cases where the limit of weight has not been exceeded by more than five per cent (and only in such cases), it is a defence to prove that the load was not exceeded at the time the loading of the vehicle was originally completed, and since that time no person has made any addition to the load. This second statutory defence is designed to cater for the situation where a load can be shown to have increased in weight since the start of its journey. This can happen, for example, where a load such as timber increases in weight through the absorption of snow or rain water. Again however, the courts have tended to impose a strict construction on such defences. Apart from the two defences allowed by statute, overloading of any sort is an absolute offence. In particular, any consequence or effect brought about by the circumstances or condition of a particular road are irrelevant in computing the laden weight on a particular vehicle.

If it appears to an authorised police officer or other authorised official that a vehicle is overloaded, the further use of that vehicle on the road may be prohibited. Alternatively, the vehicle may be used subject to such directions as the authorised official thinks fit (Road Traffic Act 1988, ss 70–73; see also ss 78–79).

7.12:8 Plated weights and other plated particulars

The Secretary of State is empowered to make regulations providing for the marking of certain particulars, including weight, applicable to certain classes of goods vehicles (Road Traffic Act 1988, s 41(3)). The terms used are 'plated particulars' and 'plated weight', and these are defined in s 41(7). These details must be shown on a plate which is securely attached to the vehicle in a conspicuous and readily accessible position (Road Vehicles (Construction and Use) Regulations 1986, reg 66). This latter regulation also contains a table which gives general descriptions of various classes of vehicles, including trailers, to which the legislation applies, and also lists the kinds of vehicles exempted from the requirements. Schedule 8 to the Regulations provides in detail what particulars must be shown on the plate. Part III of Schedule 8 makes general provisions in respect of power to weight ratios and also determines the relevant weights to be shown on plates in accordance with regulation 66. The plated weight of any particular vehicle therefore is the weight which must be stamped on the plate of the particular vehicle in terms of regulation 66 and Schedule 8. It should be noted that the plated weight (or where appropriate the train weight) is not necessarily the same as the design weight. In terms of the Road Traffic Act 1988, s 41(6), the Secretary of State has to make sure that the plated weight or train weight of any vehicle is fixed having regard to the design weight of that vehicle, and does not exceed that weight. The power to weight ratio is calculated in accordance with regulation 45. Further, every goods vehicle to which the Testing and Plating Regulations apply, must have a Ministry Plate (regulation 70 and Schedule 10 and 10A, introduced by amendment regulations 1987, SI 1987/676).

Plates which must be attached to motor cycles are covered in regulation 69 and Schedule 9.

The phrases 'design weight' and 'train weight' are defined in regulation 3.

Tests of the satisfactory condition of goods vehicles and the determination of plated weights, and the requirement of obligatory goods vehicle test certificates are dealt with in ss 45–53 and s 64 of the Road Traffic Act 1988.

As indicated in paragraph 7.12:6, the maximum permitted laden weights of various classes of vehicles are furnished in detail in regulations 75–80, which should be consulted in detail in respect of any particular case. Reference should also be made to Schedule 11 which gives measurements in respect of these regulations.

7.12:9 Brakes

The detailed technical regulations concerning brakes are extensive and complex. The principal provisions in respect of brakes are contained in regulations 15 and 16 of the Road Vehicles (Construction and Use) Regulations 1986. These regulations refer in turn to Community Directive 79/489, which amends Council Directive 71/320 on the approximation of braking devices, and Community Directive 85/647.

Regulation 17, however, provides that every motor vehicle which is equipped with a braking system which embodies a vacuum or pressure reservoir is to be equipped with a device readily visible to the driver which is capable of indicating any pending failure of, or deficiency in, the vacuum or pressure system. The section contains certain limited exceptions to this requirement. In *Hamilton v MacKenzie* 1968 SLT 166, 1968 SLT (Notes) 36 it was held that there had been a breach of this requirement when the warning device, although installed, was found to be not working properly.

Regulation 18 provides that every part of every braking system and the means of operating thereof must be maintained in good and sufficient working order and be properly adjusted.

In general terms most vehicles require to have bridging systems, namely a service braking system (which is the principal means by which a vehicle is brought to a halt) and a secondary or parking brake system. Both brake systems require to be maintained to certain levels of efficiency, which are expressed in terms of a percentage of a total braking efficiency of which the brakes should be capable. The phrase 'braking efficiency' is defined in the definition regulation 3. Regulation 18 contains a table which describes the efficiencies of the respective braking systems which are required for various kinds of vehicle. This section provides an absolute offence and for example both a driver and his employers may be found guilty of using a vehicle with inadequately maintained brakes (*James & Son Limited v Smee; Green v Burnett* [1955] 1 QB 78). As the regulation contains an absolute offence, it is therefore not a defence to a charge under these regulations that a regular system of inspection was enforced by the owners of the vehicle (*Hawkins v Holmes* [1974] RTR 436).

In *Watson v Muir* 1938 JC 181, 1939 SLT 14 it was held that although it was desirable that the owner or user of any vehicle should be present while the braking system of any vehicle was being tested, such attendance was not essential and evidence of any such examination conducted in the absence of the owner or user was admissible in evidence.

7.12:10 Wheels and tyres

Tyres are also subject to detailed provisions and requirements in terms of regulation 24 of the Road Vehicles (Construction and Use) Regulations 1986, which gives a full description of the classes of vehicles and the types of tyres which must be used. The phrases 'pneumatic tyre', 're-cut pneumatic tyre' and 'resilient tyre' are all defined in the definition section (regulation 3). Regulation 25 makes provision for tyre loads and speed ratings in such a way as to ensure that the tyres are able to bear the maximum axle weight. The prohibition against the mixing of different kinds of pneumatic tyres on the same vehicle is provided in regulation 26. The regulation contains the necessary additional definitions of the different kinds of tyre involved. Regulation 27 provides for the condition and maintenance of tyres and in particular contains the detailed provisions which can form the basis of a prosecution for driving with a worn or defective tyre.

In these circumstances it is an offence to use or cause or permit to be used a vehicle on the road with such defects. The customary definitions apply and in particular it is plain that using includes parking the vehicle on a public road and is not confined to the vehicle being in motion.

Further, if the vehicle in question is the subject of a hire agreement, then the person who is 'using' the vehicle at the material time is the hirer and not the hire firm; see *Farrell v Moggach* 1976 SLT (Sh Ct) 8; *Mackay Brothers & Co v Gibb* 1969 JC 26, 1969 SLT 216.

7.12:11   Vision and glass

The regulations also provide that each motor vehicle is to be designed and constructed so that the driver has at all time a full view of the road ahead (reg 30). All glass or other transparent material fitted to a motor vehicle is to be maintained in such a condition that it does not obscure vision of the driver while the vehicle is being driven on a road (reg 30(3)). There is also provision as to the kind of glass which must be fitted to certain vehicles in certain circumstances and in particular regulations 31 and 32 make provision for the fitting of safety glass.

Regulation 33 provides comprehensive details on the provision of mirrors to vehicles, and regulation 34 provides for windscreen wipers and washers.

7.12:12   Instruments and equipment

Regulation 35 provides that every vehicle shall be fitted with a speedometer capable of indicating speed in both miles per hour and kilometres per hour and regulation 36 provides that speedometers should be properly maintained at all material times. Further, regulation 37 provides that every vehicle subject to the included exceptions shall be fitted with a horn which is not a reversing alarm or a two tone horn. Apart from such instruments designed to inform members of the public that goods are on a vehicle for sale, it is a specific condition that the sound omitted by any horn other than a reversing alarm or two tone horn shall be continuous in uniform and not strident. Exceptions are granted to motor vehicles used for fire brigade, ambulance or police purposes and other vehicles in the public or social service. Regulation 39 covers the construction and maintenance of petrol tanks.

Regulation 36A (introduced by the Road Vehicles (Construction and Use) (Amendment) Regulations 1988, SI 1988/271 provides that every coach first used on or after 1 April 1974 must have a speed limiter, set to restrict the speed of the vehicles to 70 mph; however this provision is not yet in force.

7.12:13 Protective systems

Seatbelt anchorage points and seatbelts are the subject of regulations 46–47, and their maintenance is governed by regulation 48; the requirements in respect of their use are described in paragraph 7.3:1. Certain vehicles must have rear under-run protection and side-guards; see regulations 49–52.

Every vehicle propelled by an external combustion engine must be fitted with an exhaust system including a silencer and the exhaust gases from the engine are not allowed to escape into the atmosphere without first passing through the silencer. All exhaust systems and silencers must be properly maintained and certain noise limits are applied to various vehicles (see regulations 55–59). Regulation 61 covers the emission of smoke vapour, gases and oily substances from vehicles and regulation 60 requires that all vehicles should comply with the EEC regulations on radio interference suppression.

7.12:14 Control of noise

In terms of regulation 97, no motor vehicle is to be used on a road in such a manner as to cause excessive noises which could have been avoided by the exercise of reasonable care on the part of the driver. There is further a general duty in terms of regulation 98 to stop the engine when a vehicle is stationary apart from the necessities of traffic. The use of audible warning instruments is regulated in detail by regulation 99.

7.12:15 Avoidance of danger

The regulations make a number of provisions in respect of the safe use of vehicle. Regulation 100(1) requires that every motor vehicle and trailer drawn thereby and all parts and accessories of such vehicles and trailers shall at all times be in such condition, and the number of any passengers carried by such vehicles or trailers shall be such, that the weight, distribution and adjustment of the load of such a vehicle or trailer shall at all times provide that no danger is caused or is likely to be caused to any person in or on the vehicle or trailer or on the road. It should be noted that this is different from the restrictions on overloading. Regulation 100(2) requires that the load carried by a vehicle or trailer shall at all times be so secured and be in such a position that neither danger nor nuisance is likely to be caused to any person or property by reason of the load or any part of it falling or being blown from the vehicle or by reason of any other movement of the load or part thereof in relation to the vehicle. Regulation 100(3) provides that no motor vehicle or trailer shall be used for any purpose for which it is so unsuitable as to cause or be likely to cause danger or nuisance to any person in or on the vehicle or trailer or on a road. These provisions are designed to secure the proper conduct of a vehicle on the road and in particular to avoid items falling from a vehicle onto the road. However, it should be noted that it is not necessary for part of the load actually to fall on a road or off a lorry, for an offence to be committed under this section. In particular, in terms of regulation 100(2), it is possible for an accused person to be convicted in circumstances where he was not aware of the defects in the load which caused the contravention of the sub-section (*MacNeill v Wilson* 1981 SLT (Notes) 109; 1981 SCCR 80; 1981 CO Circulars A/19; see also *Wells v Guild* 1988 SCCR 438). Regulation 100(1) therefore requires: that the condition of the vehicle shall be at all times safe; that the number of passengers carried by a vehicle is, at all times, not excessive; and that weight distribution and packing of the load is at all times safe. Regulation 100(2) contains an offence of unlawful loading in circumstances where the load has been secured but there is still danger or nuisance or both to the public. Regulation 100(3) is restricted to offences related to the use of vehicle for a purpose for which it is unsuitable.

Regulation 101 makes specific provision for the parking of motor vehicles in darkness and regulation 103 prohibits any person in charge of a motor vehicle or trailer to cause or permit the vehicle to stand on a road so as to cause any unnecessary obstruction. Accordingly, where the accused parked his car in a bus bay for five minutes but the prosecution did not establish that any bus was in fact obstructed, then an offence was not committed under this regulation (*Brown v Cardle* 1983 SLT 218; 1982 SCCR 495, 1982 CO Circulars A/41). The Crown must also show that the obstruction was unnecessary (*McDonald v Annan* 1979 CO Circulars A/22). Regulation 104 makes it an offence to drive or cause or permit any other person to drive a motor vehicle on a road if proper control of the vehicle and a full view of the road and traffic ahead is not available to the driver. Regulation 105 makes it an offence to open a door of a vehicle on a road so as to injure or endanger any person; this regulation is sometimes used as the foundation of prosecutions particularly where a person in a parked vehicle has opened a door so that it comes into contact with a passing vehicle. Regulation 106 requires that no person shall drive or cause or permit a motor vehicle to be driven backwards on a road further than is necessary.

7.12:16 Lighting

There are again numerous and complex provisions dealing with the lighting requirements of vehicles. These are contained not in the Road Vehicles (Construction and Use) Regulations 1986 but in the Road Vehicles Lighting Regulations 1984, SI 1984/812. In general terms it is an offence to use, or to cause or to permit to be used on a road, any specified vehicle unless that vehicle is equipped with the prescribed lamps, reflectors, rear markings and devices.

Regulation 11 gives detailed provision for the colour of lights to be shown by lamps and reflectors, and regulation 12 qualifies the movement of such items. Regulation 13 provides that lamps must show a steady light except in the case of a direction indicator, warning beacons or special warning lamps and the like.

Regulations 15A and 22A (introduced by the Road Vehicles Lighting (Amendment) Regulations 1987, SI 1987/1315) require slow moving vehicles such as agricultural tractors and trailers to carry warning beacons. Regulation 16 and Schedule 1 indicate the obligatory lamps, reflectors, rear markings and devices which must be shown by various kinds of vehicles. Optional lamps and other devices must conform with the provisions in regulation 17. It should be noted that such lights as are regarded as obligatory in terms of the regulations must be carried at all times and it is an offence to fail to have such obligatory lamps, reflectors, rear markings or devices even where they are not at the time required.

In *Johnston v Cruickshank* 1963 JC 5, 1962 SLT 409, it was held that where a tractor unit draws a trailer, the motor vehicle for the purposes of these regulations is the driving unit and not the whole vehicle.

Certain exemptions are granted to these general requirements by virtue of regulations 4–9.

In terms of regulations 18 and 19 provision is made for the lighting of projecting trailers and vehicles carrying overhanging or projecting loads or equipment and additional side marker lamps.

All such lamps and reflectors, rear markings and devices must be properly maintained and kept clean and in good working order (regulation 20) and there are requirements about the use of front and rear position lamps, rear registration plate lamps and side marker lamps (reg 21). There are restrictions about the use of headlamps and front fog lamps (regulation 22). In general, a vehicle must be used with dipped beam headlamps during the hours of darkness, except on a road restricted for the purposes of s 71 of the Road Traffic Regulation Act 1967 by virtue of a system of street lighting when it is lit; and in seriously reduced visibility. There are also specific restrictions on the use of headlamps and front and rear fog lamps, reversing lamps, hazard warning signal devices and warning beacons and work lamps provided in regulation 23.

7.13   TESTING AND INSPECTION

In terms of reg 74 of the Road Vehicles (Construction and Use) Regulations 1986, various persons, including a police constable in uniform and duly authorised inspectors are entitled to test and inspect the brakes, silencer steering gear and tyres of any vehicle on any premises where that vehicle is located. The conditions of requiring such a test are: that any person empowered in terms of the regulation must produce his authorisation if required to do so; that the premises can only be entered upon with the consent of the owner and that no test can be carried out unless the owner of the vehicle consents thereto and forty-eight hours notice of the proposed test is given. Regulation 24 of the Road Vehicles Lighting Regulations 1984 extends this power of testing and inspection to lighting equipment and reflectors.

Section 67 of the Road Traffic Act 1988 also empowers an authorised examiner (which includes a properly appointed police officer) to test the condition of a vehicle on the road. The motorist has the right to ask for a deferment of such a test (s 67(6)), but can be convicted of an offence revealed by the examination even although he has not had the opportunity to elect for such a deferment (*Brown v McIndoe* 1963 SLT 233). Section 68 gives the power to inspect goods vehicles to secure proper maintenance, and s 77 to test the condition of used vehicles in sales rooms. In *Watson v Muir* 1938 JC 181, 1939 SLT 14, it was held that although it was desirable that the owner or user of any vehicle should be present at any test it is not essential.

By virtue of s 75 it is an offence to sell a vehicle in an unroadworthy condition; s 76 makes it an offence to fit or supply defective or unsuitable vehicle parts.

Other officials entitled to carry out these various tests and inspections are referred to in chapter 9.

Chapter Eight

Licences, disqualification, endorsement and fixed penalties

8.16   **Car tax**

8.17   **Test certificates (MOT Certificates)**

8.1   DRIVERS' LICENCES

8.1:1   General

Section 87 of the Road Traffic Act 1988 provides:

(1) It is an offence for a person to drive on a road a motor vehicle of any class if he is not the holder of a licence authorising him to drive a motor vehicle of that class.

(2) It is an offence for a person to cause or permit another person to drive on a road a motor vehicle of any class if that other person is not the holder of a licence authorising him to drive a motor vehicle of that class.

Certain limited exceptions to this absolute requirement are provided in s 88. Licences are issued at the instance of the Secretary of State through the Drivers Vehicle Licensing Centre (DVLC) Swansea, which is responsible for keeping details of all licences, including disqualifications and endorsements thereon.

Prescribed classes of drivers who are normally resident outside the United Kingdom may drive on licences already held by them for a period of one year (Motor Vehicles (International Circulation) Order 1975, SI 1975/1208).

Conditions under which driving licences are issued are found in the Motor Vehicles (Driving Licences) Regulations 1987, SI 1987/1378; see also *Ogilvie v O'Donnell* 1983 SCCR 257. Changes of name and address must be intimated (s 99(4)).

In a charge of driving without a licence in terms of this section, once the Crown has shown *prima facie* that a driver has no licence, the responsibility for proving that he has a licence rests on the accused (*Milne v Whaley* 1975 SLT (Notes) 75).

Sections 97 and 98 of the Road Traffic Act 1988 cover the granting and form of licences; s 100 allows an appeal to the sheriff against a refusal to grant a licence, but a further appeal to the Sheriff Principal is incompetent (*Hopkin v Ayr Local Taxation Office* 1964 SLT (Sh Ct) 60).

8.1:2   Definitions and penalties

'*Drives*' – see paragraph 1.7:1.

'*Road*' – see paragraph 1.8:1.

'*Motor vehicle*' – see paragraphs 1.2:1 *et seq.*

'*Causing or permitting*' – see paragraph 1.10:3.

Penalties for such an offence are found in Schedule 2, Part I of the Road Traffic Offenders Act 1988, and normally involve discretionary disqualification and obligatory endorsement. If disqualification is not ordered two penalty points must be endorsed on the licence.

8.1:3   Test of competence to drive

A driving licence will not be issued unless a test of competence to drive has been passed (Road Traffic Act 1988, s 89). The nature of the test is found in the Motor Vehicles (Driving Licences) Regulations 1987, SI 1987/1378, regulations 20 and 21, in addition to what is required in s 89 itself. Section 90 allows for a review that the test was properly conducted in accordance with the regulations by way of application to the sheriff. However, such an appeal is not intended to be a review of the test; to succeed the appellant must demonstrate that the test was not conducted properly, and that there has been for example, malice or oppression or unfair conduct in the way in which the test was conducted (*Corrigan v Fox* 1966 SLT (Sh Ct) 79). A further appeal to the Sheriff Principal is incompetent (*Hopkin v Ayr Local Taxation Officer* 1964 SLT (Sh Ct) 60).

8.1:4   Physical fitness

An applicant for a driving licence must furnish a declaration as to whether he is suffering from any relevant or prospective disability which may make his driving a source of danger to the public (s 92). Certain prescribed disabilities are given in the Motor Vehicles (Driving Licences) Regulations 1987, SI 1987/1378, regulation 24. A licence may be revoked if the Secretary of State is at any time satisfied on inquiry that the licence holder is suffering from a relevant or prospective disability (s 93). This section may be invoked in practice where a court becomes aware during a road traffic prosecution that a driver may be suffering from such a disability, and intimates this to the Secretary of State in terms of s 22 of the Road Traffic Offenders Act 1988. Section 22 provides that the court must notify the Secretary of State of these disabilities if they become evident irrespective of the outcome of the prosecution. If a licence holder becomes aware that he is suffering from a relevant or prospective disability during the currency of his licence, he must likewise intimate this (s 94); and he must also intimate the refusal by any authorised insurer to provide him with statutory insurance cover on health grounds (s 95). It is an offence to drive with defective eyesight (s 96).

8.1:5 Duration and form of licences

The earliest ages at which persons may hold licences are specified in s 101 (see paragraph 8.2:1). Thereafter, full driving licences are issued and in normal course remain valid until the holder's seventieth birthday, after which they have to be renewed at three year intervals (s 99).

Section 98 requires that the licence should indicate the classes of vehicle that the driver is entitled to drive and any restrictions on the driving of such vehicles. Classes of vehicles are detailed in Schedule 3 of the Motor Vehicles (Driving Licences) Regulations 1987, SI 1987/1378. Special conditions attaching to the grant of heavy goods vehicles licences and public service vehicles licences and dealt with in chapter 9.

8.1:6 Provisional licences

Provisional licences are granted for the purpose of enabling the applicant to pass a test of competence to drive (s 97(2)). This section, and regulations 8–11 of the Motor Vehicles (Driving Licences) Regulations 1987 (*supra*) provide for the conditions and duration of such licences.

8.1:7 Driving instruction

No instruction in the driving of motor vehicles for payment can be undertaken by any person who is not on the register of approved instructors, and who is not licensed to undertake such instruction. Driving instruction is dealt with in Part V of the Road Traffic Act 1988. The relevant regulations are the Motor Cars (Driving Instruction) Regulations 1977, SI 1977/1043. The Road Traffic Offenders Act 1988, s 18, provides that a certificate from the Registrar relating to the status of any person on the register is sufficient proof of the facts stated therein.

8.2   DISQUALIFICATION BY REASON OF AGE

8.2:1   General

Section 101(1) of the Road Traffic Act 1988 provides:

A person is disqualified for holding or obtaining a licence to drive a motor vehicle of a class specified in the following Table if he is under the age specified in relation to it in the second column of the Table.

TABLE

Class of motor vehicle	Age (in years)
1. Invalid carriage	16
2. Motor cycle	16
3. Small passenger vehicle or small goods vehicle	17
4. Agricultural tractor	17
5. Medium-sized goods vehicle	18
6. Other motor vehicles	21

However, some important qualifications have been made to these general rules by the Motor Vehicles (Driving Licences) Regulations 1987, SI 1987/1378, regulation 4. In particular, in item 2, the age is to be read as 17 except in the case of mopeds and other minor classes of excepted vehicles. For this purpose mopeds are defined in regulation 3.

Section 32 of the Act disqualifies persons under fourteen years of age from driving an electrically assisted pedal cycle.

8.2:2   Obtaining licence or driving while disqualified

Section 103 of the Road Traffic Act 1988 provides:

(1) If a person disqualified for holding or obtaining a licence—
    (a) obtains a licence while he is so disqualified, or
    (b) while he is so disqualified drives on a road a motor vehicle or, if the disqualification is limited to the driving of a motor vehicle of a particular class, a motor vehicle of that class,
he is guilty of an offence.

(2) A licence obtained by any person who is disqualified is of no effect.

(3) A constable in uniform may arrest without warrant any person driving or attempting to drive a motor vehicle on a road whom he has reasonable cause to suspect of being disqualified.

This is an absolute offence and there can be no room for a

defence of mistake or ignorance. It will be noted that a licence only entitles the holder to drive vehicles of categories specified in the licence. Failure to observe these categories will result in an offence under this section (*Ogilvie v O'Donnell* 1983 SCCR 257). Duplication of licences is prohibited (s 102).

8.2:3 Definitions and penalties

'*Drives*' – see paragraph 1.7:1.

'*Road*' – see paragraph 1.8:1.

'*Motor Vehicle*' – see paragraph 1.2:1.

The penalties for this offence are found in Schedule 2, Part I of the Road Traffic Offenders Act 1988, and normally involve discretionary disqualification and obligatory endorsement. If disqualification is not imposed, two penalty points are endorsed on the licence where the offender was disqualified as under age, and six points where the offender was disqualified by order of court. Proceedings may be summary or on indictment; the maximum prison sentences are six months and twelve months respectively.

8.3 EVIDENCE

In order to obtain a conviction under s 103, the prosecution must adduce sufficient evidence that the accused has been disqualified (*Herron v Nelson* 1976 SLT (Sh Ct) 42; *Andrews v McLeod* 1982 SLT 456, 1982 SCCR 254, 1982 CO Circulars A/16). If the prosecution attempt to prove the disqualification by reference to a schedule of previous convictions in any form, and that schedule reveals that the accused has previous convictions other than that which imposed the period of disqualification, any subsequent conviction under this section will be quashed (*Herron v Nelson (supra)*; *Mitchell v Dean* 1979 SLT (Notes) 12; *Boustead v McLeod* 1979 JC 70, 1979 SLT (Notes) 48; *Robertson v Aitchison* 1981 SLT (Notes) 127 1981 SCCR 149). However, reference should also be made to *Moffat v Smith* 1983 SCCR 392, 1983 CO Circulars A/25, and *Johnston v Allan* 1983 SCCR 400, 1983 CO Circulars A/35.

In terms of s 19 of the Road Traffic Offenders Act 1988, in any proceedings for an offence under s 103(1)(b) of the Act (driving while disqualified) a conviction or extract conviction of which a copy has been served on the accused not less than fourteen days before his trial, which purports to be signed by the clerk of court, and which shows that the person named in it is disqualified, is to be sufficient evidence of the application of that disqualification to the accused, unless the accused serves notice on the prosecutor, not less than six days before his trial, that he denies that the conviction applies to him.

A person who is charged under this section with driving while disqualified by virtue of age, is regarded as being in a special capacity in terms of the Criminal Procedure (Scotland) Act 1975, s 312(x), that is to say, that the fact that he is so disqualified is to be held as admitted unless this is challenged by a preliminary objection before his plea is recorded (*Smith v Allan* 1985 SLT 565, 1985 SCCR 190, 1986 CO Circulars A/8).

8.4　DISQUALIFICATION FOLLOWING OFFENCE

8.4:1　General

Apart from considerations of disability or age described earlier in this chapter, disqualification of a driver by removal of his licence usually occurs as a consequence of penalties imposed for road traffic offences. In general terms, disqualification may follow in three sets of circumstances; firstly, when the legislation provides that disqualification is obligatory following a particular offence (Road Traffic Offenders Act 1988, s 34(1)); secondly, when the legislation provides that disqualification is discretionary following a particular offence and the court elects to exercise its discretion in favour of disqualification (s 34(2)); and thirdly, where the offence committed involves the application of what is known as the totting up procedure (s 35). Whether a particular offence carries obligatory or discretionary disqualification is noted in Schedule 2, Part I of the Road Traffic Offenders Act 1988.

8.4:2　Consequences of disqualification

In every case where disqualification is obligatory or discretionary, and in every case where penalty points are to be imposed, details of the convictions, and where appropriate the number of penalty points, must be endorsed on the accused's licence (Road Traffic Offenders Act 1988, s 44).

Following disqualification (either obligatory or discretionary), the court may order the driver to give details of his date of birth and other information (Road Traffic Offenders Act 1988, s 25); and on conviction of an offence involving obligatory endorsement, the court must order the licence to be produced (s 27). Where the licence is produced, the court may take into account any existing endorsements (s 31). Where the licence is not produced, a document purporting to be information from the Secretary of State's records (known as a DVLC print-out) may likewise be considered, provided the accused admits the accuracy of the record as it applies to him (s 32). Reference should also be made to paragraphs 8.8:1 *et seq*.

Where a person fails to comply with a court order to produce his licence to the court in terms of s 27, a police constable may require the production of the licence and seize it (Road Traffic Act 1988, s 164(5)).

8.4:3 Duration of disqualification

By virtue of s 37(1) of the Road Traffic Offenders Act 1988, any period of disqualification commences from the moment it is imposed by the court; there is no provision for back-dating or post-dating such an order.

In cases of obligatory or discretionary disqualification not involving the application of the totting-up procedure, a period of disqualification may not be imposed on a consecutive basis (*Williamson v McMillan* 1962 SLT 63). Any period of disqualification must be for a fixed term; however, in appropriate circumstances a driver may be banned for life.

Where a person is convicted of an offence involving obligatory disqualification, the minimum period of disqualification is twelve months, unless the court considers that special reasons exist for restricting the period of disqualification, or for not imposing disqualification at all (s 34(1)). There are two exceptions to this rule. Firstly, where a driver is convicted of causing death by reckless driving (s 1 of the Road Traffic Act 1988) the minimum period of disqualification is two years (s 34(4)). Secondly, where a driver is convicted, within ten years, of a second offence involving (i) s 4(1) of the Road Traffic Act 1988 (driving or attempting to drive while unfit through drink or drugs), (ii) s 5(1)(a) (driving or attempting to drive with excess alcohol), or (iii) s 7(6) (failing to provide a specimen where that offence, because it relates to a specimen for analysis rather than for the roadside breathalyser test, involves obligatory disqualification) then the second offence carries a minimum period of disqualification of three years (s 34(3)). It is clear that any of these qualifying offences, if repeated or committed in addition to either of the other qualifying offences mentioned, causes the three year minimum period to be introduced; the rule is not restricted to cases where two similar offences under any one of the nominated offences, occur within the prescribed period. However, it should be noted that neither an offence under s 5(1)(b) of the Road Traffic Act 1988 (being in charge of a vehicle with excess alcohol) nor an offence under s 6(4) (failure to provide a road-side test) is included in the list of offences which trigger the three year minimum period. The ten year period mentioned in s 34(3) is calculated from the date of the commission of the first offence.

Where conviction follows an offence involving discretionary disqualification, there is no minimum period; the disqualification is for such period as the court thinks fit (s 34(2)).

In cases under the totting-up procedure, the minimum period, in the absence of special reasons, is six months unless there is one, or more, periods of disqualification within the preceding three years when the minimum periods of disqualification are one and two years respectively (s 35).

If disqualification is suspended pending an appeal in terms of s 38, the period of suspension is not included in calculating the period of disqualification (s 43).

8.4:4   Notice of penalties

Disqualification is a penalty, and accordingly must be intimated as such in the notice of penalties served on an accused in respect of a summary complaint. In *Coogans v MacDonald* 1954 JC 98, 1954 SLT 279, the notice of penalties served with a summary complaint did not include a reference to disqualification as a consequence of the offence. It was held that in these circumstances any disqualification subsequently imposed by the court was incompetent. However, in *Campbell v McLeod* 1975 SLT (Notes) 6, where the notice of penalties erroneously indicated that the minimum period of disqualification was twelve months, but where in the circumstances the minimum period of disqualification provided by the statute for the offence in the circumstances was three years, it was held on appeal that the driver could not complain that the notice of penalties was incompetent and a disqualification period of three years was confirmed. The Crown will normally be allowed to amend the notice of penalties if the accused is not prejudiced thereby (*Slater v Jessop* 1988 CO Circulars A/43; reference should also be made to *Donnachie v Smith* 1989 SCCR 144). Where disqualification is a consequence of conviction, the notice of penalties should indicate that disqualification may be avoided if there are special reasons for allowing this (*Kempsell v MacDonald* 1956 SLT 114). However, if the notice of penalties does not specifically mention that the totting-up procedure will operate, this does not preclude the court from applying that procedure (*Urry v Gibb* 1979 SLT (Notes) 19, 1978 CO Circulars A/41).

8.5 OBLIGATORY DISQUALIFICATION

8.5:1 General

By virtue of s 34 and Schedule 2, Part I of the Road Traffic Offenders Act 1988, certain offences carry obligatory disqualification. These are contraventions of: s 1 of the Road Traffic Act 1988 (causing death by reckless driving); s 2 (reckless driving) if committed within three years of a previous conviction for an offence under s 1 or 2; s 4(1) (driving or attempting to drive while unfit through drink or drugs); s 5(1)(a) (driving or attempting to drive with excess alcohol in breath, blood or urine); s 7 (failing to provide specimen for analysis or laboratory test where the specimen was required to ascertain the ability to drive or the proportion of alcohol at the time the accused was driving or attempting to drive); and s 12 (motor racing and speed trials on public roads). Culpable homicide by the driver of a motor vehicle also attracts compulsory disqualification (Schedule 2, Part II). In all of these instances, disqualification can only be avoided if the offending motorist successfully pleads that there are special reasons for him not being disqualified.

Disqualification is also obligatory in certain circumstances where the motorist has been guilty of repeated offences within a three year period (the totting-up procedure: see paragraph 8.8). Such disqualification may also be avoided on specific grounds provided by statute (see paragraph 8.10:4).

8.5:2 Special reasons: general

A court may only refrain from disqualifying a driver for the minimum period as described in paragraph 8.4:3 for the offences referred to in paragraph 8.5:1, where it is is satisfied that special reasons exist for not imposing such disqualification, or for reducing the period of disqualification to one shorter than the minimum period specified above. In *Kempsell v MacDonald* 1956 SLT 114, the Appeal Court indicated that where disqualification was a possible consequence of a road traffic offence, the notice of penalties should indicate that disqualification may be avoided if there are special reasons for so doing. In that case, the Appeal

Court remitted the case back to the sheriff to see whether such special reasons existed.

Special reasons can be defined as mitigating or extenuating circumstances relating to the offence itself, which do not amount to a defence to the charge which causes the obligatory disqualification, but which may justify the court in imposing either no disqualification at all or alternatively a lesser period than the minimum prescribed. A principal consideration in deciding whether such reasons qualify as being special or not is that they must relate to the nature of the offence itself and cannot under any circumstances refer to the personal circumstances of the driver (*Adair v Munn* 1940 JC 69, 1940 SLT 414). A further essential condition is that special reasons must as a prime consideration be governed by the overall interests of public safety (*Adair v Munn* (*supra*); *Fairlie v Hill* 1944 JC 53, 1944 SLT 224; *Carnegie v Clark* 1947 JC 74, 1947 SLT 218). Accordingly, special reasons are a question of law and are not purely a matter of discretion for the court.

8.5:3   Not special reasons

As indicated above considerations other than those which apply to the offence itself cannot under any circumstances constitute special reasons. Secondly, the major consideration to be taken into account is the question of danger or risk or potential danger or risk to the public safety. The courts have explored various circumstances and concluded that in the following situations, special reasons were not established.

A. *Triviality of offence*

The comparative triviality of an offence cannot justify a court considering that special reasons exist for not imposing disqualification, if the legislation provides for obligatory disqualification. For example, if a particular driver has exceeded the statutory alcohol limits in terms of s 5(1)(a) of the Road Traffic Act 1988 by a small margin, this cannot justify a claim that special reasons exist for imposing anything less than the statutory minimum period of disqualification (*Herron v Sharif* 1974 SLT (Notes) 63).

B. *Personal hardship*

As indicated above, special reasons must relate to the quality and nature of the offence and not the circumstances of the offender.

Thus in cases involving obligatory disqualification, even exceptional hardship will not justify the court in mitigating or refraining from disqualification. In *Carnegie v Clark* 1947 JC 74, 1947 SLT 218, it was held that where disqualification might result in a medical student being expelled from university, this did not entitle the court not to disqualify the driver.

In *Adair v Munn* 1940 JC 69, 1940 SLT 414; and *Muir v McPherson* 1953 SLT 307, it was made clear that loss of livelihood and consequent hardship following therefrom to the driver' family could not amount to special reasons. Even a disabled driver who requires his licence to remain mobile cannot argue that his condition amounts to special reasons for not disqualifying (*Copeland v Pollock* 1976 CO Circulars 1428).

C. Previous character

It has long been established that the fact that a driver has a clean driving record for a long number of years cannot amount to special reasons (*Muir v Sutherland* 1940 JC 66, 1940 SLT 403).

D. Ability of driver to meet consequences

In a case where the accused was convicted of driving without insurance, the fact that he was financially able to meet any claims made against him arising out of his driving did not justify the court in finding special reasons for not disqualifying (*Robertson v McGinn* 1955 JC 57).

E. Consequences to public interest

The fact that a period of disqualification may have particularly serious consequences for the public interest where the driver has significant public duties to perform which he cannot do without his licence, again does not amount in normal circumstances to special reasons for refraining from disqualification. In *Murray v Macmillan* 1942 JC 10, a driver was not disqualified in circumstances which related to his war time duties; but in the subsequent cases of *McFadyean v Burton* 1954 JC 18, 1953 SLT 301, and *Robertson v McGinn* 1955 JC 57, it was made very clear that *Murray* was an exceptional case and not to be followed.

F. Special reasons unrelated to the offence

In *MacDonald v MacKenzie* 1975 SLT 190, a motorist agreed to give a blood sample from his arm; this was found to be impossible and he declined to give any further samples. The court held that in these circumstances, special reasons did not exist.

In *Smith v Peaston* 1977 JC 81, 1977 CO Circulars A/22, a vehicle was stopped by police officers purportedly acting under the equivalent of s 163 of the Road Traffic Act 1988. On the subsequent conviction of the driver for a drink driving offence it was held that an allegation that the police officers had no justification for exercising these powers, even if correct, would not amount to special reasons for not imposing disqualification.

In cases under s 7(6) of the Road Traffic Act 1988 (refusal to provide specimen for analysis), it is well recognised that the special reasons must relate to the refusal, and not to other circumstances which might amount to special reasons in another situation. In *Smith v Nixon* 1985 SLT 192, 1984 SCCR 373, 1984 CO Circulars A/30, an accused was driving in an emergency, ie specifically to join his mountain rescue team which had been called out in circumstances where the lives of others might be in danger. While it is possible in certain circumstances that such a consideration might amount to special reasons for not disqualifying if the accused had been convicted of a drink/driving offence, it was held that special reasons had not been established in respect of the refusal to provide a specimen. Similarly in *Lamb v Heywood* 1988 SLT 728, 1988 SCCR 42, the fact that the appellant was intent only on moving his car a minimal distance did not constitute special reasons in respect of a refusal to provide a specimen for analysis.

In *Tudhope v O'Kane* 1986 SCCR 538, a refusal to provide a specimen because the accused was a teetotaller was held, exceptionally, to amount to special reasons. However, it is not a special reason where the accused maintains that he had only taken alcohol after driving had ceased (*Emms v Lockhart* 1988 SLT 222; 1987 SCCR 622, 1988 CO Circulars A/5).

G. *Shortness of distance*

The fact that a motorist has embarked only on a short journey will not in normal circumstances amount to special reasons (*Skeen v Irvine* 1980 CO Circulars A/31; *Lambs v Heywood* 1988 SLT 728, 1988 SCCR 42). However, in view of the fact that one of the cardinal considerations is the interest of public safety, a minimal distance driven may be relevant in certain situations (see paragraph 8.4:4:B). In England, a journey of very short duration is a matter which may be taken into account (see paragraph 8.5:4:H).

H. Impairment of ability to drive

A claim, even if established in evidence, that the accused driver's ability to drive was not impaired, for example, in terms of s 4(1) of the Road Traffic Act 1988, will not, it is submitted, establish that there are special reasons for not disqualifying in a charge under s 5(1)(a).

I. Medical condition

In *Scott v Hamilton* 1988 SCCR 262, a lady motorist pled guilty to failing to provide a specimen for analysis, but claimed that she had been suffering from pre-menstrual tension and was not amenable to reason. It was held that this was not a special reason for not disqualifying.

8.5:4 Circumstances which may justify special reasons

As indicated above, the case of *Adair v Munn* 1940 JC 69, 1940 SLT 414, is authority for the view that special reasons are a question of law and not of discretion, and that prime consideration must be given to the interest of public safety. The courts have held that special reasons may exist in the following circumstances.

A. Medical emergency

Where a driver is compelled to drive by an unforeseen medical emergency and circumstances where he assured he would not have otherwise driven, special reasons may exist (*Copeland v Sweeney* 1977 SLT (Sh Ct) 28; *Graham v Annan* 1980 SLT 28; *Watson v Hamilton* 1988 SLT 316, 1988 SCCR 13). However, failure to use another reasonably available method of undertaking the journey will exclude the establishment of special reasons (*Copeland v Sweeney (supra)*).

B. Other emergencies

In *Ortewell v Allan* 1984 SCCR 208, a disqualified driver pushed a broken down car off a busy main road and then got into the driving seat and was pushed or free-wheeled into a car park where it collided with another vehicle. In these circumstances, the Appeal Court held that there were grounds for restricting the period of disqualification.

C. Laced drinks

Where a driver consumes alcohol unknown to himself because his drink has been interfered with, by the addition of an alcoholic beverage by a third party, special reasons for not disqualifying may exist. It is submitted that, because of the nature of such a defence, the greatest care must be taken in presenting accurate and reliable evidence in support of the submission that there are special reasons. In *Skinner v Ayton* 1977 SLT (Sh Ct) 48, it was held that special reasons could only be found in these circumstances if the accused establishes in evidence that his drink was in fact laced, that he did not know or have reasonable cause to suspect that this had happened, and that the alcohol level in the accused's blood would not have exceeded the legal limit but for the lacing of the drink. It is submitted that in presenting an argument that special reasons exist in these circumstances, the same overall approach should be taken as in the case of post-accident drinking defences (see paragraphs 3.8 and 3.16:1). In particular, it is submitted that in establishing that the alcohol level in the accused's blood would not have exceeded the legal limit but for the fact that further alcohol had been introduced unknown to him into his system, evidence (by an analyst or suitably qualified doctor) relating to the effect that such addition of alcohol would have had on his system should normally be adduced where possible.

D. Driving when instructed by police

In *Farrell v Moir* 1974 SLT (Sh Ct) 89, a driver was ordered to drive his vehicle by a police officer in order that it should cease being an obstruction to other traffic. In these circumstances, because it was demonstrated that the driver would not otherwise have been driving but for the direction of the police officer, it was held that there were special reasons for not imposing a period of disqualification.

E. Triviality of offence

In *Smith v Henderson* 1950 JC 48, 1950 SLT 182, the Appeal Court approved of a failure to endorse a driver's licence where the offence was very trivial. This case was effectively overruled by *Tudhope v Birbeck* 1979 SLT (Notes) 47, 1979 CO Circulars A/18. Further, the supposed triviality of an offence is no longer relevant because the penalty point system currently in operation takes account of the relative gravity of respective offences. It is plainly the intention of the legislature that offences must be visited with the sentences within the parameters provided by the penalty point system and accordingly the relative triviality of the offence will not under any circumstances justify a failure to endorse or disqualify.

F. Reasons unconnected with offence

Where a driver refused to give a specimen for analysis on the ground that he was a teetotaller, this was held to amount to a special reason (*Tudhope v O'Kane* 1986 SCCR 538). This is perhaps a somewhat exceptional case.

G. Public interest

As indicated earlier, in *Murray v McMillan* 1942 JC 10, it was held that where very special and significant damage might be caused to the public interest by the disqualification of an offender (as in the case of a doctor who had to carry out essential tasks during the time of war), special reasons for not disqualifying were established. However, it has been repeatedly said in other cases (for example in *Fairlie v Hill* 1944 JC 53, 1944 SLT 224; *McFadyean v Burton* 1954 JC 18; 1953 SLT 301; *Robertson v McGinn* 1955 JC 57) that such a situation was entirely remarkable and it is extremely unlikely that it would be followed in any circumstances.

H. General directions in English cases

In England the Appeal Court in the case of *Chatters v Burke* [1986] RTR 396, DC, laid down a number of considerations which should be looked at in coming to the conclusion that special reasons exist. These matters are as follows: firstly, how far the vehicle was driven; secondly, in what manner it was driven; thirdly, the state of the vehicle; fourthly, whether it was the intention of the driver to go further; fifthly, an assessment of the conditions of the road and traffic travelling at the time; sixthly whether there was a possibility of danger of the driver coming into contact with other road users or pedestrians; and finally, the reasons for the driving of the vehicle. The Appeal Court made it clear that the sixth of these considerations was by far the most important.

8.5 PROCEDURE IN SPECIAL REASON SUBMISSIONS

8.5:1 General

It is for the accused to raise the question of special reasons at the time of sentence. The court is not entitled to conclude that special reasons exist for not imposing disqualification from the submissions made to him without the matter having been specifically argued by the accused. Reference should be made to *McLeod v Scoular* 1974 JC 28, 1974 SLT (Notes) 44; *Tudhope v Birbeck* 1979

SLT (Notes) 47, 1979 CO Circulars A/9; and *McNab v Feeney* 1980
SLT (Notes) 52, 1980 CO Circulars A/1. The facts relied on may
have become sufficiently clear from the evidence if the matter has
gone to trial. If however the accused pleads guilty the appropriate
procedure is for the accused or his solicitor to indicate at the time of
pleading guilty, that the plea is qualified by the submission that
special reasons exist for not imposing disqualification. It is considered good practice for the defence agent to indicate this intention
in advance of the date of sentence to the procurator fiscal in order to
allow the fiscal suitable opportunity for considering the nature of the
special reasons. If on hearing the nature of the special reasons at the
time of sentence, the procurator fiscal requires further time to
examine the reasons so adduced, the court will normally grant a
continuation for that purpose. It should be emphasised that if a form
of motion is not made at the time of sentence to the effect that special
reasons exist for not disqualifying, the accused will not be permitted
to raise the question of special reasons thereafter unless the circumstances are exceptional (*Hynd v Clark* 1954 SLT 85; distinguishing
Trotter v Burnett 1947 JC 151).

It is proper practice for evidence to be led in support of the
special reasons that are to be established rather than simply to rely
on *ex parte* statements by the accused's solicitor. However, it is
open for the prosecutor to accept *ex parte* statements as correct in
appropriate circumstances (*McLeod v Scoular* 1974 JC 28, 1974
SLT (Notes) 74). If the Crown do not accept what is said by the
accused, then the onus of proof is on the accused and the standard
of proof that must be reached is the balance of probabilities (*Farrell
v Moir* 1974 SLT (Sh Ct) 89, *Skinner v Ayton* 1977 SLT (Sh Ct) 48;
see also *Irvine v Pollock* 1952 JC 51, 1952 SLT 185 and
MacFadyean v Burton 1954 JC 18, 1953 SLT 301).

In particular, in *McLeod v Scoular* 1974 JC 28, 1974 SLT (Notes)
44, the High Court laid down the rules relating to the onus and
standard of proof and the procedure to be followed in cases where
special reasons are argued. Firstly, the prosecutor may agree that
what is said by the accused is true in which case the court may deal
with the submissions in the absence of evidence. It is of course
always open to the court to continue the case for further information if required. Secondly, if the accused has been found guilty
following a trial, the court may be satisfied from the evidence heard
as to whether special reasons have been established or not without
further enquiry. Thirdly, where the Crown disputes the statement
by the defence, the court should order a further hearing to allow
the defence to lead evidence in support of its case and the opportunity of leading evidence to contradict the defence case. This

procedure should also be adopted in cases where the procurator fiscal can neither admit nor deny what is said by the accused. The proper procedure in all circumstances where special reasons are to be put forward is that the accused or his solicitor should at the time of tendering the plea of guilty when sentence is to be imposed intimate that special reasons are to be advanced and give a general outline of the facts on which these reasons are to be based. Thereafter, the procurator fiscal should be asked whether he is in a position to accept what is said or whether he either denies the accused version of events or is in a position neither to confirm or deny that version. If the procurator fiscal is in a position to confirm the submissions made by the defence, the matter can then be dealt with. However, in all other circumstances, it is submitted that the proper course is to defer sentence for the purpose of fixing a hearing on the special reasons.

If the accused does not appear personally and is not represented by a solicitor, but pleads guilty by letter, the responsibility still remains on the accused to raise the question of special reasons. If he does not do so in the course of his letter, then the mandatary period of disqualification or endorsement, as appropriate, must be imposed. However, the Appeal Court has made it clear that where an accused pleads guilty by letter, the court should normally continue the matter to allow for the personal appearance of the accused. If therefore the accused states in his letter that special reasons do or might exist for not imposing disqualification, then in general terms the same procedure should be followed as in the preceding paragraph. In other words, if the procurator fiscal is in a position to agree expressly with what is said in the letter for the purposes of considering special reasons, it may be possible for the court to dispose of the case on that basis. However, in all other circumstances, a continuation should be granted in order to allow a hearing to be fixed on the question of special reasons and the accused given an opportunity to attend. Fuller details about the procedure to be adopted in this situation were given in the case of *Keane v Perrie* 1983 SLT 63, 1982 SCCR 377, 1982 CO Circulars A/30.

8.7 DISCRETIONARY DISQUALIFICATION

Discretionary disqualification is available in a significant number of offences, which are detailed in the tables forming Parts I and II of Schedule 2 to the Road Traffic Offenders Act 1988. Discretionary disqualification is always a matter for the court. The court must take into account all facts and circumstances which are relevant in reaching its decision. However, that accused should always be given an opportunity of leading before the court any reasons why he should not be disqualified in such cases (*MacDonald v McGillivray* 1986 SCCR 28).

8.8   DISQUALIFICATION FOR REPEATED OFFENCES

In addition to offences which carry obligatory or discretionary disqualification, disqualification will also follow in certain circumstances where a driver has been guilty of repeated offences within a three year period, by virtue of s 35 of the Road Traffic Offenders Act 1988. Generally, in addition to other penalties, a number of offences under the legislation carry penalty points which on conviction are endorsed on the licence by the court or DVLC Swansea. In the event of a motorist acquiring twelve or more such points within a three year period, the court must order disqualification for special minimum periods, unless there are grounds for not doing so.

In respect of some offences, a set number of penalty points must be endorsed on the driver's licence; in respect of others, the court must select a number of penalty points from a range provided. The offences to which penalty points relate are found in the Road Traffic Regulation Act 1984 (c 27) and the Road Traffic Act 1988. The penalty points themselves are detailed against the appropriate offences in Schedule 2, Parts I and II of the Road Traffic Offenders Act 1988. However, disqualification under the totting-up procedure cannot be imposed consecutively on other periods of disqualification given at the same time (*Middleton v Tudhope* 1986 SCCR 241, 1986 CO Circulars A/41).

The general purpose of what has become known as the totting-up procedure is to penalise by disqualification, drivers who repeatedly commit relatively minor offences, as opposed to the imposition of obligatory disqualification for the more serious offences.

8.9   NOTICE OF PENALTIES

The notice of penalties served on an accused in association with any complaint involving charges which carry penalty points, must indicate that penalty points and endorsements will follow unless there are mitigating circumstances (*Tudhope v Eadie* 1984 SLT 178, 1983 SCCR 464, 1984 CO Circulars A/2); see also *Miller v*

Allan; England v Allan 1984 SLT 280, 1984 SCCR 28, 1984 CO
Circulars 1984 A/3).
For amendment of penalty notices, see *Johnston v MacDougall*
1989 CO Circulars A/6.

8.10 TOTTING-UP AND PENALTY POINTS:
STATUTORY PROVISIONS

8.10:1 General

Section 28 of the Road Traffic Offenders Act 1988 provides:

(1) Where a person is convicted of an offence involving obligatory or
discretionary disqualification, the number of penalty points to be
attributed to the offence, subject to subsection (2) below, is—
  (a) in the case of an offence under a provision of the Traffic Acts
    specified in column 1 of Part I of Schedule 2 to this Act or an offence
    specified in column 1 of Part II of that Schedule, the number shown
    against the provision or offence in the last column or, where a range
    of numbers is so shown, a number falling within the range, and
  (b) in the case of an offence committed by aiding, abetting, counselling
    or procuring, inciting to the commission of, an offence involving
    obligatory disqualification, ten penalty points.

(2) Where a person is convicted of two or more such offences, the
number of penalty points to be attributed to those of them that were
committed on the same occasion is the number or highest number that
would be attributed on a conviction of one of them.

(3) The Secretary of State may by order made by statutory
instrument—
  (a) alter the number of penalty points shown in subsection (1)(b) above
    or against a provision or offence specified in that Schedule or, where
    a range of numbers is shown, alter that range, and
  (b) provide for different numbers to be so shown in respect of the same
    offence committed in different circumstances;
but no such order shall be made unless a draft of it has been laid before
Parliament and approved by resolution of each House of Parliament.

Where a range of penalty points is available, the procedure that the
court must adopt is to consider what number of points within the
specified range is appropriate to the particular offence, having
regard to all the circumstances of the offence and the offender
(*Briggs v Guild* 1987 SCCR 141).
    In the event of the accused person being convicted of two or
more offences which carry penalty points, the proper procedure for
the court is to consider the appropriate number of points to be
imposed in respect of each offence, and order that the higher or

highest of these numbers is to be the number of penalty points to be endorsed on the licence. It is submitted that the section does not require that the court must impose the highest possible number of penalty points provided by Schedule 2, where there are multiple changes involving penalty points.

For example, an accused may face charges under s 3 of the Road Traffic Act 1988 (careless driving) which carries 3–9 points, and a charge under s 6 (failing to provide a breathalyser specimen) which in the event of non-disqualification carries 4 points. If the court considers that the appropriate number of points on the careless driving charge is 3, then the mandatory 4 points which go with the second charge, being a higher number of points, is what the court should order to be endorsed on the licence. If the court considers that six penalty points are appropriate for the careless driving charge, six points rather than four will be endorsed.

8.10:2   Statutory provisions (s 29)

Section 29 of the Road Traffic Offenders Act 1988 provides:

(1) Where a person is convicted of an offence involving obligatory or discretionary disqualification, the penalty points to be taken into account on that occasion are (subject to subsection (2) below)—
  (a) any that are to be attributed to the offence or offences of which he is convicted, and
  (b) any that were on a previous occasion ordered to be endorsed on any licence held by him, unless the offender has since that occasion and before the conviction been disqualified under s 34 or 35 of this Act.

(2) If any of the offences was committed more than three years before another, the penalty points in respect of that offence shall not be added to those in respect of the other.

The critical starting date in the calculation of the number of penalty points on a licence is the date of the commission of the offences, rather than the date of the conviction. Any penalty points imposed on a licence outwith the three year period from the date of commission of the starting offence to the date of commission (not the date of conviction) of the offence or offences currently under consideration fall to be disregarded. However, this means that any penalty points endorsed on a licence following a conviction which is prior in time to the offences being considered, where the commission of the offence relative thereto is after the date of the commission of the offence under consideration, have also to be taken into account. In other words, penalty points for any offences committed after, but dealt with before, the current offence are included in the calculation. The section also makes it clear that any period of disqualification imposed under s 34 or s 35 of the Act (for offences involving obligatory or discretionary disqualification), has the effect of cancelling out all penalty points within the three year period prior to the disqualification.

8.10:3 Statutory provisions: production of licence

In terms of s 27 of the Road Traffic Offenders Act 1988, where a person who is the holder of a licence is convicted of an offence involving obligatory endorsement (which includes all offences involving obligatory or discretionary disqualification) the court must require the licence to be produced to it before it can make any order involving such endorsement. Conversely, s 7 imposes a duty on every accused prosecuted for an offence involving obligatory disqualification to produce his licence for the hearing; see also paragraph 8.4:2.

Section 31 then provides:

(1) Where a person is convicted of an offence involving obligatory endorsement and his licence is produced to the court—
  (a) any existing endorsement on his licence is prima facie evidence of the matters endorsed, and
  (b) the court may, in determining what order to make in pursuance of the conviction, take those matters into consideration.

(2) This section has effect notwithstanding anything in ss 311(5) and 357(1) of the Criminal Procedure (Scotland) Act 1975 (requirements as to notices of penalties and previous convictions).

This section is self-explanatory but must be read along with the terms of s 29, which for totting-up purposes, restricts consideration of such previous endorsements to the preceding three years.

Where the licence is not available for production to the court, (for example where it is lost or destroyed, or has been sent to DVLC Swansea for alteration) then it is open to the court to consider a DVLC print-out (normally produced by the prosecution), if the accused agrees that the particulars therein are accurate and relate to himself (see also *McCallum v Scott* 1987 SLT 49). The terms of s 32 are as follows:

(1) Subsections (2) or (5) below apply where a person is convicted in Scotland of an offence involving obligatory endorsement but his licence is not produced to the court.

(2) The court may, in determining what order to make in pursuance of the conviction, take into consideration (subject to subsection (3) below)—

(a) particulars of any previous conviction or disqualification pertaining to him, and

(b) any penalty points ordered to be endorsed on any licence held by him which are to be taken into account under s 29 of this Act,

which are specified in a document purporting to be a note of information contained in the records maintained by the Secretary of State in connection with his functions under Part III of the Road Traffic Act 1988.

(3) If the prosecutor lays before the court such a document as is mentioned in subsection (2) above, the court or the clerk of court must ask the accused if he admits the accuracy of the particulars relating to him contained in the document.

(4) Where the accused admits the accuracy of any particulars, the prosecutor need not adduce evidence in proof of those particulars, and the admission must be entered in the record of the proceedings.

(5) Where the accused does not admit the accuracy of any particulars the prosecutor must, unless he withdraws those particulars, adduce evidence in proof of them, either then or at any other diet.

(6) This section has effect notwithstanding anything in sections 311(5) and 357(1) of the Criminal Procedure (Scotland) Act 1975 (requirements as to notices of penalties and previous convictions).

Again this section is self-explanatory; it is submitted that the procedure for establishing the accuracy of the particulars contained in the print-out should be strictly observed. If no licence or print-out is property before the court, the Crown must serve a schedule of previous convictions (*Anderson v Allan* 1985 SCCR 262).

The DVLC code used in noting convictions on licences is given in Appendix D.

8.10:4   Statutory provisions (s 35): mitigating circumstances

Section 35 of the Road Traffic Offenders Act 1988 provides:

(1) Where—

(a) a person is convicted of an offence involving obligatory or discretionary disqualification, and

(b) the penalty points to be taken into account on that occasion number twelve or more,

the court must order him to be disqualified for not less than the minimum period unless the court is satisfied, having regard to all the circumstances, that there are grounds for mitigating the normal consequences of the conviction and thinks fit to order him to be disqualified for a shorter period or not to order him to be disqualified.

(2) The minimum period referred to in subsection (1) above is—
(a) six months if no previous disqualification imposed on the offender is to be taken into account, and
(b) one year if one, and two years if more than one, such disqualification is to be taken into account;

and a previous disqualification imposed on an offender is to be taken into account if it was imposed within the three years immediately preceding the commission of the latest offence in respect of which penalty points are taken into account under s 29 of this Act.

(3) Where an offender is convicted on the same occasion of more than one offence involving obligatory or discretionary disqualification—
(a) not more than one disqualification shall be imposed on him under subsection (1) above,
(b) in determining the period of the disqualification the court must take into account all the offences, and
(c) for the purposes of any appeal any disqualification imposed under subsection (1) above shall be treated as an order made on the conviction of each of the offences.

(4) No account is to be taken under subsection (1) above of any of the following circumstances—
(a) any circumstances that are alleged to make the offence or any of the offences not a serious one,
(b) hardship, other than exceptional hardship, or
(c) any circumstances which, within the three years immediately preceding the conviction, have been taken into account under that subsection in ordering the offender to be disqualified for a shorter period or not ordering him to be disqualified.

(5) References in this section to disqualification do not include a disqualification imposed under section 26 of this Act or section 44 of the Powers of Criminal Courts Act 1973 (disqualification by Crown Court where vehicle used for commission of offence).

(6) In relation to Scotland, references in this section to the court include the district court.

(7) This section is subject to section 48 of this Act.

It is clear from the terms of s 35(1) that it does not matter on how many occasions during the three year period that endorsement has taken place. Once 12 penalty points have been accumulated on a driver's licence within that period, then the totting up procedure automatically comes into effect. It is therefore possible that the procedure will operate following a second endorsement. Immediately 12 points are accumulated on a licence then the court has no option but to impose the minimum period of disqualification as described in sub-section (2), unless there are mitigating circumstances.

Section 35(2) provides certain minimum periods of disqualification; six months in the ordinary case, and one year and two years where one or two previous disqualifications respectively, have to be considered. A previous disqualification is to be considered if it was within the three year period preceding the commission (not the conviction) of the latest offence for which penalty points are to be taken into account.

Section 35(3) deals with the situation where more than one offence involving obligatory or discretionary disqualification is dealt with on the same occasion. It may be that the offences were committed on different dates; the important consideration in this sub-section is that such offences are dealt with on the same occasion. The sub-section provides that only one period of disqualification under the totting-up procedure is to be imposed in such circumstances. However, the court is entitled to take into account all the offences in determining the length of that period of disqualification. It will also be noted that while s 35(2) provides certain minimum periods of disqualification in certain circumstances, no upper ceiling is given.

Section 35(4) imposes significant qualification on what may be adduced as mitigating circumstances in an effort to avoid disqualification under s 35(1). However, it is clear that the standard required to establish mitigating circumstances is not so exacting or high as that which applies in the establishment of special reasons for avoiding obligatory disqualification. In particular, the circumstances which can be considered in determining whether or not mitigating circumstances exist, are not confined to the nature of the offence as in the case of special reasons. Both the circumstances of the offence and of the offender may be relevantly considered. Accordingly, the court can take into account such matters as the fact that the accused has a previously unblemished personal character.

Although in general terms the discretion open to the court in considering mitigating circumstances is far wider than is the case in special reasons, s 35(4)(a) emphasises that the triviality of the particular offence for which the accused has been convicted is not a mitigating circumstance (however, see *North v Tudhope* 1985 SCCR 161 at 163). Nor is the court entitled to take into account that there is a significant period between the current offence and the earlier offences which contributed to the accumulation of twelve penalty points (see *Smith v Baker* 1979 SLT (Notes) 19; *Macnab v Smith* 1977 CO Circulars A/30). However, as a matter to be weighted into the balance, it is possible for the accused to submit that consideration should be given to the relative triviality of the other offences which go to make up the twelve points.

Section 35(4)(b) makes it clear that any hardship caused by the disqualification must be exceptional to qualify as mitigating circumstances. A series of authorities in the Appeal Court has made it clear that the loss of employment by itself following disqualification, does not necessarily mean exceptional hardship has been caused. These authorities – *Scott v Scott* 1983 SCCR 458, *Stephens v Gibb* 1984 SCCR 195, *Pender v Keane* 1984 SCCR 325 and *North v Tudhope* 1985 SCCR 161 – were all summarised in the case of *Allan v Barclay* 1986 SCCR 111, 1986 CO Circulars A/14, in which the Appeal Court said that the fact that the accused was likely to lose his employment is not in itself exceptional hardship, but that such exceptional hardship may well be established where the loss of employment can be associated with other consequences which involve what was called 'reflected hardship' of a serious kind on the accused's business, his immediate family or his long term future prospects.

Section 35(4)(c) provides that an accused person can argue that a particular set of mitigating circumstances exist and so avoid totting-up disqualification only once within any three year period. If an accused successfully argues that he should not be disqualified for given reasons under the totting-up procedure, then he is disallowed from presenting similar arguments for a similar purpose in any court in the United Kingdom within three years of the conviction following which he avoided disqualification. It would seem to be open for an accused to argue that exceptional hardship or other mitigating circumstances exist for quite separate reasons on a second occasion.

8.10:5 Procedure in mitigating circumstances submissions

The procedure in dealing with pleas of guilty to offences which do not involve obligatory or discretionary disqualification but which do involve disqualification under the totting-up procedure is broadly the same as in the case of letter pleas and special reasons cases (see paragraph 8.6:1). It should be emphasised that if the accused is to be disqualified, then it is proper practice for him to be given every opportunity to put forward reasons why he should not be disqualified. The Appeal Court has made it clear that it regards it as a 'sensible practice' for the accused to be required to appear personally if disqualification is a possibility (*Stephens v Gibb* 1984 SCCR 195 and *MacDonald v McGillivray* 1986 SCCR 28).

8.10:6 Procedural consequences

If a period of disqualification (either obligatory or under the totting-up procedure) is avoided because of special reasons or mitigating circumstances, the court must give the reasons for its decision in open court, and cause these reasons to be entered on the record of proceedings (s 47(1)). If the court does not order disqualification, the appropriate number of penalty points must be endorsed on the licence (s 44). Where endorsement is ordered the court may, and where disqualification is ordered it must, send the licence to DVLC, Swansea (s 47(2)).

Following the expiry of a period of disqualification, a person may not drive until he has applied for and received the return of his licence (*Stewart v Paterson* 1959, SLT (Sh Ct) 66).

8.11 REQUIREMENT TO RESIT A DRIVING TEST (S 36)

8.11:1 General

Section 36 of the Road Traffic Offenders Act 1988 provides:

(1) Where a person is convicted of an offence involving obligatory or discretionary disqualification, the court may order him to be disqualified until he passes the test of competence to drive prescribed by virtue of section 89(3) of the Road Traffic Act 1988.

(2) That power is exercisable by the court whether or not the person convicted has previously passed that test and whether or not the court makes an order under section 34 or 35 of this Act.

Accordingly, the court is given the power in terms of this section to order any driver who is disqualified to resit a driving test once the period of disqualification has expired. It is clear that this power should not be exercised to provide an additional punishment to the sentences imposed on a driver in a particular case. Such an order can only be imposed where the circumstances of the offence, and/or a driver's previous convictions for road traffic offences indicate that it is in the public interest that the driver's ability and skill should be checked before that driver is allowed to resume driving following his period of disqualification (see *Sweeney v Cardle* 1982 SLT 312, 1982 SCCR 10, 1982 CO Circulars A/9). In particular, a token period of disqualification should not be imposed where the purpose of so doing is simply to make the driver resit a driving test (*McLean v Annan* 1986 SCCR 52); nor should such a requirement be made automatically in cases where a long period of disqualification is imposed (*Sweeney v Cardle supra*).

Section 37(1) allows a driver in these circumstances to obtain a provisional licence in order to pass his test (see also *Stewart v Paterson* 1959 SLT (Sh Ct) 66).

8.11:2 Appeal against disqualification

Section 38(2) of the Road Traffic Offenders Act 1988 provides:

> A person disqualified by an order of a court in Scotland may appeal against the order in the same manner as against a sentence.

The form of such an appeal is therefore the same as in an appeal against sentence. The appellant may apply for an interim suspension of the disqualification to the court which made the order (s 39(2)), or which failing, to the High Court of Justiciary (s 41). In the latter case, the application may be to a single judge. Any period of interim suspension is not included in the period of disqualification (s 43).

8.11:3 Removal of disqualification

Section 42 of the Road Traffic Offenders Act 1988 provides:

> (1) Subject to the provisions of this section, a person who by an order of a court is disqualified may apply to the court by which the order was made to remove the disqualification.
>
> (2) On any such application the court may, as it thinks proper having regard to—
> (a) the character of the person disqualified and his conduct subsequent to the order,
> (b) the nature of the offence, and
> (c) any other circumstances of the case,
> either by order remove the disqualification as from such date as may be specified in the order or refuse the application.
>
> (3) No application shall be made under subsection (1) above for the removal of the disqualification before the expiration of whichever is relevant of the following periods from the date of the order by which the disqualification was imposed, that is—
> (a) two years, if the disqualification is for less than four years,
> (b) one half of the period of disqualification, if it is for less than ten years but not less than four years,
> (c) five years in any other case;
> and in determining the expiration of the period after which under this subsection a person may apply for the removal of a disqualification, any time after the conviction during which the disqualification was suspended or he was not disqualified shall be disregarded.

(4) Where an application under subsection (1) above is refused, a further application under that subsection shall not be entertained if made within three months after the date of the refusal.

(5) If under this section a court orders a disqualification to be removed, the court—
  (a) must cause particulars of the order to be endorsed on the licence, if any, previously held by the applicant, and
  (b) may in any case order the applicant to pay the whole or any part of the costs of the application.

(6) The preceding provisions of this section shall not apply where the disqualification was imposed by order under section 36(1) of this Act.

This section is self-explanatory. Apart from the restrictions in sub-sections (3) and (4), there is no limit on the number of such applications that may be made during the period of disqualification. It is clear from the terms of the section that the application is to be made to the court where the disqualification was imposed. If an accused person has received periods of disqualification in more than one court, it follows that an order in one court lifting the disqualification imposed there will not in any way affect the disqualifications imposed in other courts. The section affords no power to reduce the disqualification; an application must either by refused or granted *simpliciter*.

8.11:4   Removal of disqualification: procedure

Whether the application is made in the sheriff court or the High Court of Justiciary, it is presented in the form of a petition. Although there is no specific provision governing the procedures to be observed, it is submitted that it is normal and proper practice for the applicant to serve a copy of the petition on the procurator fiscal or the Crown Agent, depending on whether the application is in the sheriff court or the High Court of Justiciary. Service should be made in sufficient time to allow the Crown to instruct their own report (normally from a local police officer) on the merits of the petition. A separate petition is required for each indictment or complaint in respect of which disqualification was imposed. In terms of the section it is suggested that the court should have regard to the character of the person disqualified and his conduct subsequent to the order, the nature of the offence committed which caused the disqualification, and any other circumstances of the case.

In presenting the application to the court, it is submitted that the applicant should be prepared to lead evidence in support of his application rather than rely on *ex parte* statements. However, if the circumstances are sufficiently clear, and the police report is favourable, and if in addition the Crown do not dispute the salient facts put up by the petitioner, there appears to be no bar to such an application proceeding entirely on the basis of statements made by the accused or his solicitor. However, such applications should be presented with considerable care. It is normal for such applications to be granted only where the applicant can demonstrate clearly that his behaviour since the commission of the offence is such as to indicate that it is unlikely that he will commit such offences again. In addition, pressing reasons must be adduced to demonstrate why the appellant should have his licence restored. These can include the avoidance of hardship, for example by indicating that the restoration of the licence will allow the applicant to resume employment, or by demonstrating that the lack of a licence causes the applicant serious personal difficulty or hardship to his family. Any such claims however, should be properly vouched and supported where appropriate by evidence. It is also normal for such applicants to provide testimonials of good conduct which will satisfy the court that the applicant can safely have his licence restored to him.

There is no appeal from the decision of the court to which the application is made (*McLeod v Levitt* 1969 JC 16, 1969 SLT 286).

8.12 ENDORSEMENT OF LICENCES

8.12:1 General

Section 44 of the Road Traffic Offenders Act 1988 provides:

(1) Where a person is convicted of an offence involving obligatory endorsement, the court must order there to be endorsed on any licence held by him particulars of the conviction and also—
  (a) if the court orders him to be disqualified, particulars of the disqualification, or
  (b) if the court does not order him to be disqualified—
    (i) particulars of the offence, including the date when it was committed, and
    (ii) the penalty points to be attributed to the offence.

(2) Where the court does not order the person convicted to be disqualified, it need not make an order under subsection (1) above if for special reasons it thinks fit not to do so.

(3) In relation to Scotland, references in this section to the court include the district court.

(4) This section is subject to section 48 of this Act.

Endorsement is not a penalty as such, rather it is a direction that certain matters must be marked or noted on the accused's licence. These matters are details of any period of disqualification, or if no disqualification is imposed, details of the offence and the number of penalty points attributed by the court thereto. Details of offences which require endorsement, and the number of penalty points for such offences are found in Schedule 2 of the Act.

These details are normally endorsed on the licence by DVLC Swansea. Where disqualification is ordered, the court must send the licence with the details of the disqualification to DVLC; where endorsement is ordered, the court may (and usually does) do likewise (s 47(2)). However, endorsement of the licence may be endorsed by the clerk of court if for any reason the licence is not to be sent to Swansea. In practice, details of the date of the offence, the date of conviction, the nature of the offence, and the disposal including penalty points and disqualification period are physically marked on the licence. The nature of the offence is indicated by a code, which is reproduced as Appendix D at the end of this book. Any endorsements on a licence are *prima facie* evidence of the matters so endorsed (s 31). The effect of endorsement and the periods for which various endorsements remain live are described in s 45. Reference should also be made to paragraph 8.11:3.

8.12:2   Special reasons for not endorsing licence

Section 44(2) (*supra*) allows a court to refrain from endorsing a licence if there are special reasons for doing so. As in the case of special reasons for not disqualifying, a special reason for not endorsing is a matter of law, and not at large for the discretion of the court (*Muir v Sutherland* 1940 JC 66, 1940 SLT 403). Triviality of the offence is not a ground for not endorsing (*Tudhope v Birbeck* 1979 SLT (Notes) 47, 1979 CO Circulars A/9, not following *Smith v Henderson* 1950 JC 48, 1950 SLT 182), particularly since the introduction of the penalty points system. In addition, *Stephens v Gibb* 1984 SCCR 195, and *Holden v MacPhail* 1986 SCCR 486, make it clear that endorsement should normally follow on the appropriate conviction. It is for the accused to raise the question of special reasons (*McLeod v Scoular* 1974 JC 28, 1974 SLT (Notes) 44).

McNab v Feeney 1980 SLT (Notes) 52, 1980 CO Circulars A/1, describes the procedure to be followed after conviction or where a plea of guilty is tendered by the accused or his agent; *Keane v Perrie* 1983 SLT 63, 1982 SCCR 377, 1982 CO Circulars A/30, indicates the procedure following a letter plea of guilty. The court may not refrain from endorsement unless special reasons are spoken to by or on behalf of the accused at the time. If the court finds that special reasons exist for not endorsing the licence, these reasons must be given in open court and marked on the record (complaint) by the clerk of court (s 47(1); see also *MacNab v MacPherson* 1978 JC 21; 1977 CO Circulars A/30).

8.12:3 Notice of penalties

The notice of penalties which accompanies the service of the complaint on an accused must indicate that endorsement of licence and penalty points will follow conviction (*Tudhope v Eadie* 1984 SLT 178, 1983 SCCR 464, 1984 CO Circulars A/2; *Miller v Allan*; *England v Allan* 1984 SLT 280; 1984 SCCR 28, 1984 CO Circulars A/3).

8.12:4 Connected offences

Where a number of offences occur at the same time, the prosecution of these may be separated, some being processed under the normal procedure of service of a complaint, others by the procedure of fixed penalty. The fixed penalty procedure covers offences to which a fixed number of penalty points applies. If in dealing with such a case, the court becomes aware that a connected offence is to be, or has been considered by the fixed penalty procedure, the number of penalty points that will apply or has been applied must be deducted from the penalty points to be imposed by the court (Road Traffic Offenders Act 1988, ss 28 and 30).

8.12:5 Exemption from disqualification and endorsement construction and use

Where a person is convicted of an offence under s 42(1) of the Road Traffic Act 1988 (which relates to contraventions of the construction and use regulations), the court must not order him to be disqualified or order his licence to be endorsed with or without penalty points if he proves that he did not know, and had no reasonable cause to suspect that the facts of the case were such that the offence would be committed (s 48). It is submitted that the standard of proof required to discharge the burden of establishing this defence by an accused is on the balance of probabilities.

8.12:6   Offender escaping endorsement by deception

Where a person is convicted of an offence involving a deception which might have had a bearing on disqualification, the court dealing with the deception offence has the same powers of disqualification as the deceived court, and must take into account any orders actually imposed by that court (Road Traffic Offenders Act 1988, s 49).

8.13   FIXED PENALTIES AND CONDITIONAL OFFERS

In order to reduce the volume of road traffic cases going through the courts, a system of fixed penalties has been introduced which allows for the avoidance of prosecution by an offender by payment of a fixed penalty in respect of certain minor traffic offences. It is a feature of the general system that a number of these offences involve endorsement and penalty points being imposed on a licence without any order of court. As far as Scotland is concerned, the general fixed penalty system includes the procurator fiscal's conditional offer.

For the purposes of the working of the system offences are divided into those which are endorsable (generally moving traffic offences) and those which are not (generally stationary offences). In England, endorsable offences are dealt with under ss 54–61 of the Road Traffic Offenders Act 1988, but these sections (apart from s 60 which deals with court procedure in Scotland) do not apply to Scotland, such offences being dealt with by the procurator fiscal's conditional offer system.

The statutory provision for the system of conditional offers is found in ss 75–77 of the Act. Put briefly, where it appears that certain sorts of offences have been committed, the fiscal may make a conditional offer to the alleged offender to the effect that on payment of a fixed penalty any liability to conviction will be discharged. Where the offence involves obligatory endorsement, the alleged offender must deliver his licence to the relevant clerk of court, who endorses the particulars of the conviction or the licence. The fixed penalty must be paid within twenty-eight days (s 75(7)). If the licence holder may be subject to disqualification, the conditional offer procedure is not available (s 75(4) and (5)). If the alleged offender declines the offer, prosecution for the offence will normally follow.

The offences in respect of which conditional offers may be made are listed in Schedule 3 of the Road Traffic Offenders Act 1988.

Where an offence does not involve obligatory endorsement, the notice of penalty may be fixed to the offending vehicle, rather than given at the time to the motorist (s 62). The subsequent procedure is described in ss 63–65. Briefly, the police then serve a 'notice to owner' in terms of s 63(2). The owner can either pay the fixed penalty, or, if he does not, a prosecution will then be initiated by the service of a complaint. Alternatively, the motorist may deny that he was the driver of the vehicle at the material time, and provide a statutory statement of ownership, together with a signed request by the person purporting to be the driver to request a hearing (or in other words inviting a prosecution). It would seem that if the driver does not sign the statutory statement, the registered keeper will become liable for what is known as a registered fine, which amounts to one and a half times the fixed penalty. If the fixed penalty is ignored, it is, after the response period has expired, registered with the clerk of a court of summary jurisdiction (in effect the local District court) for the area in which the defaulter appears to reside as a fine amounting to one and a half times the fixed penalty. The clerk of court is then required to notify the defaulter of the registration. At this stage the defaulter can have the registration made invalid if he makes a statutory declaration within 21 days to the effect that either (a) he did not know of the fixed penalty until he received the notice of registration, or (b) that he was not the owner of the vehicle at the time of the alleged offence and that he has a reasonable excuse for failing to comply with the notice, or (c) that he gave notice requesting a hearing. It is not clear how a reasonable excuse is to be determined, nor in what form the statutory declaration is to proceed. It is however to be conclusively presumed that a person on whom the notice of fixed penalty was served was the driver of the vehicle at the material time, unless it is shown that the vehicle was in the possession of some other person without the consent of the accused (s 64(5) and (6)). Fixed penalty notices under s 62 may be fixed to vehicles by traffic wardens as well as by police officers (s 86). Particular provision is made for hired vehicles by s 66.

The intended consequence of the present fixed penalty system is to put the onus on any accused motorist who wishes to dispute any charge to take the necessary statutory action, and failure to do so will mean that either the fixed penalty must be paid or, failing such payment, an increased fine is registered against the motorist, subject to the safeguards described above.

8.14 INSURANCE

8.14:1 Section 143

Section 143 of the Road Traffic Act 1988 provides:

(1) Subject to the provisions of this Part of this Act—

(a) a person must not use a motor vehicle on a road unless there is in force in relation to the use of the vehicle by that person such a policy of insurance or such a security in respect of third party risks as complies with the requirements of this Part of this Act, and

(b) a person must not cause or permit any other person to use a motor vehicle on a road unless there is in force in relation to the use of the vehicle by that other person such a policy of insurance or such a security in respect of third party risks as complies with the requirements of this Part of this Act.

(2) If a person acts in contravention of subsection (1) above he is guilty of an offence.

(3) A person charged with using a motor vehicle in contravention of this section shall not be convicted if he proves—

(a) that the vehicle did not belong to him and was not in his possession under a contract of hiring or of loan,

(b) that he was using the vehicle in the course of his employment, and

(c) that he neither knew nor had reason to believe that there was not in force in relation to the vehicle such a policy of insurance or security as is mentioned in subsection (1) above.

(4) This Part of this Act does not apply to invalid carriages.

8.14:2 Definitions

'Motor Vehicle' – see paragraph 1.2:1.

'Road' – see paragraph 1.8:1.

'Policy of Insurance' – the requirements in respect of a policy of insurance are provided by s 145. A policy of insurance includes a cover note (s 161(1)).

'Causing or permitting' – see paragraph 1.10:3.

8.14:3 Insurance: general

From the terms of s 143, it is clear that the principle which underlies the requirement of compulsory insurance is that cover must be provided in respect of the use to which the vehicle is to be put, rather than in respect of the person who is using the vehicle. It therefore follows that anyone charged with a contravention of the section does not necessarily have to be the owner of the vehicle, and that a corporate body may competently be charged with such an offence. Whether insurance cover is effective in respect of any particular use is a matter of fact and law to be understood from the facts and circumstances of each case; the question to be determined is whether the material use is legally covered by the insurance contract (*Agnew v Robertson* 1956 SLT (Sh Ct) 90).

The insurance contract normally stipulates the conditions under which insurance cover is to be effective. If these conditions are not observed in any material respect, the contract may be avoided and an offence will result. For example, most contracts of insurance require that the user of any vehicle is properly licensed. Accordingly, if a person drives a vehicle of a class not covered by his licence, he will in normal circumstances automatically be also guilty of an offence under this section.

No policy of insurance is valid or effective for this part of the Act unless and until a certificate of insurance is delivered by the insurer to the person by whom the policy is effected (s 147(1)). Even if all the other requirements of drawing up a policy of insurance have been satisfied, it is an offence for a vehicle to be used on the road before the certificate of insurance is delivered. Once the certificate has been delivered, the fact that the person to whom it has been delivered subsequently becomes bankrupt, or the company to which it is delivered is wound up or goes into receivership does not affect claims by third parties (s 153; see also Third Parties (Rights Against Insurers) Act 1930). If a contract of insurance is avoidable, the contract remains valid until it is in fact avoided (*Goodbarne v Buck* [1940] 1 KB 771).

As an offence is constituted under s 143(1) by use of a vehicle on a road without being covered by insurance, prosecutions are not confined to instances where the vehicle is being driven at the material time. The section is also contravened if a vehicle is parked on a public road and is not covered; and this will apply even in cases where the vehicle cannot physically be moved (*Simpson v McDonald* 1960 SLT (Notes) 83). Similarly, a vehicle being towed is in use and must be insured (*Robb v McKechnie* 1936 JC 25, 1936 SLT 300).

8.14:4 Onus of proof

It has been held in both Scotland and England that the onus of proof that a particular use is covered by an appropriate policy of insurance rests on the person charged with using the vehicle at the material time, on the principle that whether insurance for such use at the material time was in force or not is a matter which should be within the user's knowledge (*Philcox v Carberry* [1960] Crim LR 563; *Milne v Whalley* 1975 SLT (Notes) 75). It is of course open to any accused person in these circumstances to show that he was not using the vehicle at the material time.

Section 143(3) of the Act provides a statutory defence to persons who are driving a vehicle which they do not own and have not hired or leased, who are using the vehicle in the course of their employment, and who neither knew or had reason to believe that no policy of insurance was in force at the material time.

Section 143(1) does not apply to invalid carriages. Further exemptions are granted in s 144, and in terms of s 183 the requirement for insurance does not apply to vehicles and persons who are at the material time in the service of the Crown. However, on the principle that it is the use of the vehicle that is important, there must be insurance cover in respect of any private use of Crown vehicles (*Salt v McKnight* 1947 JC 99, 1947 SLT 327).

8.14:5   Requirements of insurance policies

To comply with the requirements of the Act, an insurance policy must be issued by an authorised insurer (s 145(1)). The term 'authorised insurer' is defined in s 145(5) and it is a prerequisite of authorisation that the insurance company is a member of the Motor Insurers' Bureau (s 145(5) and (6).) The policy must insure specified persons or classes of persons in respect of any liability by the policy holder in respect of the death of, or bodily injury to, any person, or damage to property which may be caused by, or arise out of, the use of the vehicle on the road in Great Britain or in the states of the European Community (s 145(3) and (4)). This is generally known as third-party insurance, and is the minimum required; additional or comprehensive insurance is also offered by insurance companies (s 145(3)).

The policy must also insure against any liability for emergency treatment (s 145(3)(c)) in terms of ss 157–159; however, such payments must be made 'under or in consequence of' the policy (*Glasgow Royal Infirmary v Municipal Mutual Insurance* (1953) 69 Sh Ct Rep 297). The policy is not required to cover liability for death or bodily injury of any person employed by the insured in respect of that person's employment (s 145(4)).

There are restrictions on attempts by insurance companies to qualify the cover provided by a policy (s 148), and on private agreements to avoid liability (s 149); and special provision in respect of car-sharing agreements (s 150).

8.14:6 Motor insurers bureau

As indicated in the preceding paragraph, an authorised insurer must be a member of the Motor Insurers' Bureau. By s 151 (subject to the provisions of s 152), the insurers are required to satisfy any judgment against persons insured for third-party risks. Such risks must of course be *ex facie* of the policy (*Robb v McKenzie* 1936 JC 25, 1936 SLT 300). If such a judgment is not satisfied by the insurers, then the claim must be met by the Motor Insurers' Bureau, in terms of an agreement between the Bureau and the Ministry of Transport dated 17 June 1946. A further agreement dated 21 April 1969 extended the obligation to judgments obtained against untraced drivers. The texts of these agreements are published by Her Majesty's Stationery Office. The address of the Bureau is Aldermary House, 10–15 Queen Street, London. It should be stressed that notice of the commencement of any action against an uninsured driver must be given to the Bureau within 21 days, and it is advisable to give such notice in any case where it is thought that the judgment might be unsatisfied.

Notwithstanding the Bureau's obligations the principal responsibility for meeting any claim rests with the insured (*Corfield v Groves* [1950] 1 All ER 488), and the Bureau is not accountable for any unsatisfied judgment which proceeds on a liability which the Act does not require to be covered (*Lees v Motor Insurers' Bureau* [1952] 2 All ER 511).

8.15 VEHICLES EXCISE

8.15:1 General

Section 1(1) of the Vehicles (Excise) Act 1971 provides:

> Subject to the provisions of this Act, a duty of excise shall be charged in respect of every mechanically propelled vehicle used or kept on any public road in Great Britain and shall be paid upon a licence to be taken out be the person keeping the vehicle.

An excise duty is therefore charged on every mechanically propelled vehicle used or kept on the public roads and this duty is paid in respect of a licence which must be taken out by the keeper of the vehicle.

8.15:2 Definitions

'*Public road*' – see paragraph 1.8:1.

'*Mechanically propelled vehicle*' – see paragraph 1.2:1. The Act does not require any duty to be paid in respect of any vehicle which is not mechanically propelled. Section 185(1) of the Road Traffic Act 1988 provides a number of definitions of mechanically propelled vehicles, but this list of definitions is not exhaustive.

'*Used or kept*'. The section does not qualify the word 'used' in any way. Any kind of use will therefore require the vehicle to be licensed. Further, s 38(2) of the Vehicles Excise Act 1971 provides 'For the purposes of any provision of this Act in any subsequent enactment relating to the keeping of mechanically propelled vehicles on public roads, a person keeps such a vehicle on a public road if he causes it to be on such a road for any period, however short, when it is not in use there.' Accordingly, it is clear that, in terms of this Act, Parliament intended that any vehicle which is mechanically propelled and which is on a public road in any circumstances whatsoever, irrespective of the time or the nature of the use involved, must be covered by an excise licence; see also paragraph 8.15:5.

The duty charged in terms of s 1(2) is described in the Schedules to the Act.

8.15:3 Obtaining a licence

In terms of regulation 4 of the Road Vehicles (Registration and Licensing) Regulations 1971, SI 1971/450, the keeper of a mechanically propelled vehicle satisfies this statutory requirement by applying to the Secretary of State (through the Post Office) for an excise licence. In making such an application, the keeper must produce evidence of insurance or security (Motor Vehicles (Third-party Risks) Regulations 1972, SI 1972/1217, regulation 9); an appropriate test certificate where the vehicle is over three years old (Motor Vehicles (Production of Test Certificates) Regulations 1969, SI 1969/418); and, where appropriate at the first licensing of a vehicle subject to the type approval regulations, a suitable certificate or certificates in terms of the Motor Vehicles (Type Approval) Great Britain) Regulations 1984, SI 1984/981, regulation 14. In addition the appropriate level of duty requires to be paid.

Different classes and weights of vehicle attract different rates of duty, and these are described in the Schedules to the Act. As to what constitutes an agricultural vehicle; see *East Lothian County Council v Lambert* 1950 SLT (Sh Ct) 41 and *Hub of the Wheel*

Limited v Kyle 1970 SLT 241. The commencement and duration of licences and the rate of duty are provided by s 2 of the Vehicles (Excise) Act 1971.

8.15:4   Exemptions

There are certain exemptions from excise duty given principally to vehicles such as fire engines, ambulances, road rollers, vehicles connected wholly with the haulage of lifeboats, road construction vehicles concerned solely with the conveyance of road construction machinery, snow ploughs and gritters, and certain local authority works vehicles (s 4). Also exempt are certain invalid vehicles and National Health Service vehicles. In terms of s 5 of the Act exemption is granted in respect of any vehicle which is on a road solely for the purpose of a compulsory test; what is a compulsory test in these circumstances is defined in s 5(3) of the Act. Further exemptions are given to vehicles belonging to the Crown, vehicles used for special purposes, vehicles driven by certain classes of disabled persons, and vehicles used for civil defence or by police authorities (Road Vehicles Registration and Licensing) Regulations 1971, SI 1971/450, regulations 24–27, as amended by the Road Vehicles (Registration and Licensing) (Amendment) Regulations 1972, SI 1972/1865).

In terms of s 6 of the Act a vehicle acquired by an overseas resident may in certain circumstances attract exemption from duty.

8.15:5   Using and keeping vehicles without a licence

In terms of s 8(1) of the Act:

If any person uses or keeps on a public road any mechanically propelled vehicle for which a licence is not in force, not being a vehicle exempted from duty under this Act by virtue of any enactment (including any provision of this Act) he shall be liable to the greater of the following penalties namely –
(a) An excise penalty of £50; or
(b) An excise penalty equal to five times the amount of the duty chargeable in respect of the vehicle.

Accordingly it is an offence to use or keep a mechanically propelled vehicle on a public road for any purpose whatsoever when a licence is not in force in respect of that vehicle (*MacNeill v Dunbar* 1965 SLT (Notes) 79).

An offence in terms of s 8(1) can be proved by the evidence of only one witness (Road Traffic Offenders Act 1988, s 21(2)(e)). Accordingly, even a broken down vehicle or one which is not capable of being moved still may require to have a licence. Section 38(2), as above indicated (paragraph 8.15:2) makes it clear that the only qualification which the Act applies to the requirement is that the vehicle must be mechanically propelled. However, in *MacLean v Hall* 1962 SLT (Sh Ct) 30, a van which had neither an engine nor a gear box and which was being towed along a public road on its way to a scrap yard was held not to be a mechanically propelled vehicle within the meaning of the Act.

In terms of s 8(2)(c), 14 days of grace are usually allowed after the expiry of the normal term which appears on the licence.

8.15:6 Vehicles excise: general provisions

Sections 9(1), 10 and 11 of the Act provide that a further liability may exist for the keeper of a licenced vehicle on the amount of unpaid excise duty. It is a separate offence to keep on a public road a vehicle on which duty is chargeable without fixing and exhibiting the appropriate licence (s 12(4)).

In terms of s 13 of the Act, temporary licences may be issued. The issue of temporary licences by motor dealers is covered by ss 14 and 15 of the Act. Section 16 of the Act makes provision for trade licences to be taken out by a motor trader or a vehicle tester. The vehicles covered by a trade licence are, in the case of a motor trader, all mechanically propelled vehicles which are from time to time temporarily in his possession in the course of his business as a motor trader, and all recovery vehicles kept by him for the purpose of dealing with disabled vehicles in the course of that business. Whether a vehicle is a recovery vehicle is a question of fact but the term includes vehicles which are equipped to tow or raise disabled vehicles. In the case of a vehicle tester, the licence covers all mechanically propelled vehicles which are from time to time submitted to him for testing in the course of his business as a vehicle tester; and in the case of a motor trader who is a manufacturer of mechanically propelled vehicles, the licence covers vehicles kept and used by him solely for research and development. In all these circumstances, however, only one vehicle may be used under a trade licence at any one time, and the vehicles so covered may not be kept on the road. In addition to the provisions of s 16(1) of the Vehicles (Excise) Act 1971, reference must be made to regs 28–40 of the Road Vehicles (Registration and Licencing) Regulations 1971, SI 1971/450 as amended by SI 1976/1680, SI 1986/2101 and SI 1987/2123. In particular it should be noticed that for a vehicle to be disabled, it must have broken down or in other words be incapable of movement because of some mechanical defect or as the result of an accident (see *MacNeill v Calligan* 1973 SLT (Sh Ct) 54; *Smith v Holt* 1986 SLT (Sh Ct) 49, 1983 SCCR 175). However, it has been held in *Smith v Holt* (*supra*) that more than one disabled vehicle may be carried at any one time by a recovery vehicle, and thus the decision in *Lockhart v Ayrshire Commercial Spares* 1983 SLT (Sh Ct) 74, 1982 SCCR 192 no longer applies. A motor trader or vehicle tester who has had an application for a trade licence refused may require the Secretary of State to review the decision in terms of s 25 of the Act.

If a vehicle is registered in terms of a particular class of duty because of its nature and composition but thereafter its nature and composition is altered, this may bring the vehicle into another class of duty which the keeper is obliged to pay (s 18; *Blaikie v Morrison* 1957 JC 46; 1957 SLT 290 and *Blue Band Motor Limited v Kyle* 1972 SLT 250). Section 18A of the Act (introduced by the Finance Act 1982, s 7(1)) provides for possible additional liability on the keeper of the vehicle in relation to the alteration of the vehicle or its use. See also paragraph 8.15:11.

Section 66 of the Road Traffic Act 1988 allows the Secretary of State to make regulations prohibiting the grant of excise licences for certain vehicles except in compliance with certain conditions.

8.15:7 Registration and registration numbers

Sections 19–23 of the Vehicles (Excise) Act 1971 provide for the issue of registration marks and numbers. These numbers must be clearly fixed on a vehicle and legible, and be capable of being properly illuminated during the hours of darkness (Road Vehicles Registration and Licencing Regulations 1971, SI 1971/450, regulations 18–22, as amended by SI 1975/1089 and SI 1984/814). Section 17 of the Act and the Roads Vehicles (Registration and Licencing) Regulations 1971, SI 1971/450, regulation 5 allows that a vehicle excise licence may be surrendered at any time, and on so doing the keeper is entitled to any appropriate refund or unexpired duty.

8.15:8 Forgery or fraud

In terms of s 26(1) of the Vehicles (Excise) Act 1971, it is an offence to forge, or to fraudulently alter or use, or fradulently lend or allow to be used by any other person any registration mark, trade plate or licence or registration document. In terms of s 26(2) it is an offence to make a false or misleading statement in respect of any application for a licence or registration mark, or in respect of a requirement to furnish particulars relating to a vehicle or the keeper thereof.

By virtue of s 27 of the Act any person who is the registered keeper of a vehicle or any other person in a position to do so, or the alleged user of an unlicensed vehicle, is obliged to give such information as he may be required on behalf of a Chief Officer of Police or the Secretary of State as to the identity of the person or persons involved in an alleged offence of using or keeping a motor vehicle on a road without a licence or in contravention of the requirements in respect of trade plates, or in respect of a vehicle alleged to have been altered so that a different rate of duty applies. It is an offence to fail to comply with any of these requirements. The institution and conduct of proceedings in Scotland relative to licensing matters is dealt with in s 29.

8.15:9 Evidence

Section 31(1) of the Vehicles (Excise) Act 1971 as applied to Scotland by s 31(4) contains an important provision on the admissibility of records as evidence. In particular, reading s 31(1) and (4) together, the Act provides as follows:

a statement contained in a document purporting to be–
(a) A part of the records maintained by the Secretary of State in connection with any functions exercisable by the Secretary of State by virtue of this Act; or
(b) a copy of a document forming part of those records; or
(c) a note of any information contained in those records, and to be authenticated by a person authorised in that behalf by the Secretary of State shall be admissible in any proceedings as sufficient evidence of any facts stated therein, so however that nothing in this sub-section shall be deemed to make such a statement evidence in any proceedings except where oral evidence to the like effect would have been admissible in those proceedings.

The Vehicle and Driving Licences Records (Evidence) Regulations 1970, SI 1970/1997, have effect as if made under s 31(3) by virtue of s 39 and Schedule 7, Part II, paragraph 1.

In *Cardle v Wilkinson* 1982 SLT 315, 1982 SCCR 33, 1982 CO Circulars A/3, a statement contained in a document as described in sub-section 1 and authenticated by a rubber stamp signature was held to be admissible in evidence.

8.15:10　Change of ownership

In terms of the Road Vehicles (Registration and Licencing) Regulations 1971, SI 1971/450, regulations 12 and 15, when a mechanically propelled vehicle changes ownership, the former owner is under a duty to deliver the registration book and any current licence to the new owner and intimate to the Secretary of State in writing that the change has taken place. An offence occurs if this notification of change of ownership is not made 'as soon as possible'. What constitutes 'as soon as possible' will be a matter of fact and circumstances in each case; in *A & C McLellan (Blairgowrie) Ltd v McMillan* 1964 SLT 2, a prosecution for failure to make proper notification failed because it had not been embarked upon within a six month period after it could be reasonably said that the former owner had failed to make notification as soon as possible. Further, the owner of a vehicle must intimate any change of address on the registration book or licence document and send it to the Secretary of State. In terms of regulation 14, the owner of a vehicle must notify the Secretary of State when a vehicle has been broken up and destroyed or sent permanently out of the country and in those circumstances the registration document must be surrendered.

A cherished number plate may be transferred from one vehicle to another on application to the Post Office and payment of a fee of £50.

8.15:11　Alteration of vehicle

In terms of regulation 11 of the Regulations and s 18 of the Act, where a vehicle licence has been taken out for a vehicle at a rate of duty specified in the legislation and the vehicle is at any time used in an altered condition, or in a manner or for a purpose which brings it under the description of vehicle to which a higher rate of duty applies in accordance with s 18 of the Act, the owner of the vehicle is under a duty to furnish the prescribed particulars to the Secretary of State and must send those details to him together with the licence and the registration book and the additional duty chargeable (*Blaikie v Morrison* 1957 JC 46, 1957 SLT 250; *Blue Band Motor Limited v Kyle* 1972 SLT 250).

8.15:12　Registration documents

In association with the issue of a licence in respect of a mechanically propelled vehicle, the Secretary of State also issued a registration document giving details of the vehicle and its owner, in terms of the Road Vehicles (Registration and Licensing) Regulations 1971, SI 1971/450, regulation 8. Although the document is associated with the vehicle rather than the driver, the owner must produce the document for inspection if he is required to do so by a police officer at any reasonable time or by anyone acting on behalf of the Secretary of State. Mutilation or alteration of the document except under the procedure provided for on the change of ownership is an offence.

8.16   CAR TAX

In terms of the Car Tax Act 1983, a car tax is charged in respect of vehicles made or registered in or imported into, the United Kingdom. The current rate is 10 per cent of the wholesale value of the vehicle and certain exceptions to the tax are provided. The vehicle will not be licensed if the tax has not been paid.

8.17   TEST CERTIFICATES (MOT CERTIFICATES)

In terms of ss 45–48 of the Road Traffic Act 1988, any motor vehicle other than a goods vehicle used on the road must have a valid and current test certificate, unless exempted. The requirements for goods vehicles are dealt with in chapter 9. It is an offence for a vehicle which must have a certificate, not to have one. It is submitted that a vehicle which is parked on a road is normally being 'used' in terms of s 47; however in the case of *Tudhope v Every* 1976 JC 42, 1977 SLT 2 it was held that a vehicle which had been immobilised could not be 'used' in this sense of the word.

The requirement to have a test certificate applies to all vehicles not less than three years old (Road Traffic Act 1988, s 47). The three year period follows on the date of the first registration of the vehicle. Small passenger coaches, taxis and ambulances need a certificate after one year (s 47(3)). The Motor Vehicles (Test) Regulations 1981, SI 1981/1694, provide exemption for vehicles being taken to or being retrieved from a prearranged test (regulation 6(2)). The regulations made by the Secretary of State in respect of the requirements of construction and condition of such vehicles and for the issue of the relevant certificates in all matters relating thereto are provided for in the foregoing regulations as amended by regulations of 1982

(SI 1982/783, SI 1982/814, SI 1982/1477, SI 1982/1715), 1983 (SI 1983/1434) and 1984 (SI 1984/815).

The examination of vehicles for the purpose of issuing a test certificate has to be carried out by duly appointed inspectors who receive their commission from the Secretary of State, and further such tests must be carried out in approved stations with approved apparatus (Road Traffic Act 1988, s 46).

Chapter Nine

Public service vehicles and carriage of goods by road

PART 1
PUBLIC SERVICE VEHICLES

9.1 TRAFFIC AREAS AND TRAFFIC COMMISSIONERS

The United Kingdom is split into various traffic areas and the Scottish traffic area serves as a single authority for the whole of Scotland (Public Passenger Vehicles Act 1981 (c14), s 3(1)). There is a single traffic commissioner for each such area who is appointed by and acts under the general directions of the Secretary of State (s 4(1) as amended by the Transport Act 1985, s 3(2)). The traffic commissioners are obliged to publish information in respect of their activities in terms of regulations made under s 5 (as amended *supra*). The traffic commissioner's office is a part of the Department of Transport: the Scottish commissioner's office is at 83 Princes Street, Edinburgh. In practice, the traffic commissioner uses that title when dealing with passenger vehicle matters, and is known as the 'licensing authority' when dealing with matters concerning goods vehicles. The commissioners have wisespread responsibilities in respect of the issue of HGV Licences, and also of operators licences for public service and transport of goods operations. The commissioners also have duties in respect of the supervision of public service and freight operations. A commissioner may hold an inquiry into any matter as he thinks fit in connection with the exercise of his functions (Public Passenger Vehicles Act 1981, s 54 (as amended by the Transport Act 1985, s 4)). Each Commissioner must report annually to the Secretary of State (s 55) and keep a record of all licences (HGV and operator's) granted by his office (s 56).

The traffic commissioner discharges his responsibilities in

practice through traffic and vehicle examiners appointed to his department. Like the police, the traffic examiners are entitled to carry out roadside tests and to require particular vehicles to undergo weight testing. In addition, the Vehicle Inspectorate, which is an executive agency within the Department of Transport, is the body which carries out day to day responsibility for the authorisation of MOT garages and mechanics, the testing and plating of goods vehicles, the licensing by certificates of initial fitness or certificates of conformity of public service vehicles and their annual testing; and the notifiable alterations for both public service vehicles and goods vehicles.

9.2   DEFINITIONS

9.2:1   Public service vehicle

In terms of s 1 of the Public Passenger Vehicles Act 1981 (and subject to the whole provisions of the section) '*a public service vehicle*' means –

'. . . a motor vehicle (other than a tramcar) which –
(a) being a vehicle adapted to carry more than eight passengers, is used for carrying passengers for hire or reward; or
(b) being a vehicle not so adapted, is used for carrying passengers for hire or reward at separate fares in the course of a business of carrying passengers.'

9.2:2   General

The phrase 'for hire or reward' is defined in s 1(5) and (6) of the Act; see also *Hawthorn v Knight* 1962 JC 31, 1962 SLT 69. The phrase 'separate fares' means payment by individual passengers in respect of any journey or journeys, whether the payments are made in terms of a fixed tariff imposed by the operator or under an arrangement between the passenger and the carrier (*Aitken v Hamilton* 1964 SLT 125). For the purposes of the Act a vehicle is deemed to be in use until that use has been permanently discontinued (s 1(2)). Section 1(3) provides exceptions for vehicles carrying passengers at separate fares in the course of a business of carrying passengers, under certain circumstances described in Parts 1 and 3 of Schedule 1 of the Act, unless the vehicle is adapted to carry more than eight passengers. Further, in terms of s 1(4) private motorists are allowed to make car-share arrangements, for a fare or for a consideration. A 'fare' need not be paid only to the driver or owner of the vehicle (*Hawthorn v Knight* 1962 JC 31, 1962 SLT 69).

9.3 PUBLIC PASSENGER SERVICE REQUIREMENTS

9.3:1 General

In respect of any such operation of public passenger service, there must be a certificate of fitness in respect of the public service vehicles which are used for the purpose of the service; the person or company who is the operator of the service must have a public service vehicles operator's licence; and the driver of the vehicle must have a public service vehicle driver's licence (see *infra*).

9.3:2 Deregulation

Under the previous system, a public passenger service operation required a road service licence for what were called stage carriage services, (in addition to an operator's licence), in terms of s 2 and ss 30–37 of the Public Passenger Vehicles Act 1981. These sections were repealed by ss 1 and 139(3) and Schedule 8 of the Transport Act 1985 which came into force on 26 October 1986 in terms of the Transport Act 1985 (Commencement No 6) Order 1986, SI 1986/1794. As a result of the repeal of ss 30–37 of the 1981 Act, such services were deregulated. In the place of the former road service licences, additional conditions may now be imposed by the Traffic Commissioner on the licences issued to public service vehicle operators in respect of what are now termed local services and which are defined in s 2 of the Transport Act 1985. The Commissioner's powers to impose these conditions in respect of registration and traffic regulation are found in ss 6–9 of the 1985 Act.

9.3:3 Certificates of fitness of public service vehicles

In terms of s 6 of the Public Passenger Vehicles Act 1981, any public service vehicle adapted to carry more than eight passengers cannot be used on a road unless there is in force in respect of such a vehicle a certificate of initial fitness or its equivalent (which is a certificate of conformity under a type approval scheme, see *infra*). Such a certificate may not provide a defence to a civil claim based on a failure to supply employees with safe equipment (*Donnelly v Glasgow Corporation* 1953 SC 107, 1953 SLT 161; but see also *Sullivan v Gallagher and Craig* 1959 SC 243, 1960 SLT 70). Such certificates of fitness are issued by a certifying officer or a public service examiner (now employed in the Vehicle Inspectorate) in terms of s 7 of the Act, and such officials have the right of inspection of all public vehicles by virtue of ss 8, 9 and 9A (as introduced by s 33 of the Transport Act 1985). Further, such officials may ban the driving of any vehicle if it appears that the vehicle is or is likely to become unfit for use (s 9 and s 9A). Exemption is allowed in terms of the Public Passenger Vehicles (Exemptions etc) Regulations 1987, SI 1987/1150.

A public service vehicle may not apply for hire generally (Transport Act 1985, s 30). Certain exemptions are given to school buses used in certain circumstances by a local education authority in terms of s 46(1) of the Public Passenger Vehicles Act 1981.

By virtue of s 6(1)(b) and (c) and s 10 of the Public Passenger Vehicles Act 1981, the approval by the Secretary of State of a vehicle as a type vehicle or a certificate of type of approval, may be treated as an equivalent to a certificate of fitness or as a certificate of initial fitness (see also Road Traffic Act 1988, s 54 *et seq*, and the relevant regulations 1981, SI 1981/257; 1982, SI 1982/1058, and 1984, SI 1984/1763).

9.4   PUBLIC SERVICE VEHICLE OPERATORS' LICENCES

9.4:1   General

In addition to certificates of fitness or equivalents relating to vehicles, the operator of any public service vehicle operation must have a licence granted to him in accordance with the relevant statutory provisions (Public Passenger Vehicles Act 1981, s 12 as amended by Transport Act 1985, Schedule 1, paragraph 4). The term 'operator' is defined in s 81 of the Act. Exemption may be granted to a school bus used by an education authority in terms of s 46. The licence relates to the operator rather than the vehicle and is granted by the traffic commissioner for the relevant area in which are situated the operating centre or centres of the vehicles used in the operation (s 12(2)). The power of the traffic commissioners to grant licences is contained in s 4(1) and the procedure to be followed by the commissioner is dealt with in ss 14 and 14A (introduced by s 25 of the Transport Act 1985). The commissioner also regulates the fees in respect of the issue of licences and must report annually to the Secretary of State and keep records of all licences issued (Public Passenger Vehicles Act 1981, s 56, as amended by the Transport Act 1985, s 3(5) and Schedule 2, Part II). Only one public service vehicle licence can be held by any one person in a particular area but there is no restriction on such a person holding such licences in other traffic areas (s 12(3)).

Licences can either be standard or restricted (s 13). There is a limit imposed on the number of vehicles that may be used under a restricted licence (s 16 as amended by Transport Act 1985, s 24). In terms of s 14(1) of the Act, the commissioner must be satisfied that the applicant for a licence is of good repute, of appropriate financial standing, and of the requisite professional competence. For a restricted licence the last of these qualifications is not required. Schedule 3 of the Act gives further details in respect of such applications. By virtue of s 14 the applicant must also demonstrate that he has sufficient facilities or arrangements for maintaining the vehicles which are to be operated in terms of the licences in a fit and serviceable condition and that he can provide suitably for observing the requirements of the legislation governing the driving and operation of such vehicles. The sort of conditions that may be applied to such licences are dealt with in ss 26 and 27 of the Transport Act 1985. The chief constable of the area or the local authority may object to the grant of such licences by virtue of s 14A, (inserted by the Transport Act 1985, s 25). The powers of the traffic commissioner to disqualify operators from holding a licence are described in s 28 of the Transport Act 1985.

A licence cannot be granted for a period in excess of five years and the duration is specified on the licence itself (s 15). Further, the licence normally indicates the maximum number of vehicles which may be operated together with further conditions where they are prescribed or otherwise (s 16); a description of the prescribed conditions to be attached to a licence is provided in the Public Service Vehicles (Operators Licences) Regulations 1986, SI 1986/1668. By virtue of s 17(4) and (5), the commissioner has the power to revoke, suspend or vary the conditions on a licence at any time. If the commissioner wishes to revoke a licence on the ground that the operator no longer satisfies the requirement of being of good repute or having the appropriate financial standing, or being professionally competent, a public hearing must first be held if the operator requires. The commissioner may appoint assessors in terms of s 17A (introduced by the Transport Act 1985, s 5).

By virtue of s 18, the operator has a duty to exhibit on each vehicle covered by the licence an appropriate disc issued by the commissioner. This disc gives particulars of the operator of the vehicle, his operator's licence and its date of expiry, but no details of the vehicle itself. Regulation 25 of the Goods Vehicles (Operators' Licences Qualifications and Fees) Regulations 1984, SI 1984/176, provides for the issue of a further disc in respect of any vehicle specified on the operator's licence. The requirements of the disc are given in the regulations. The operator must inform the Secretary of State of any relevant criminal convictions, or of any incident or damage relating to any of the vehicles covered by the licence, which might have a bearing on public safety (ss 19 and 20, as amended by the Transport Act 1985, s 29).

Certain exceptions to the requirements imposed by statute on the operation of public service vehicles by educational and other bodies, under a system of permits, is provided by virtue of ss 42–44 and 46 of the Act and a large number of regulations. Community bus services are dealt with under s 23 of the Transport Act 1985 together with other regulations and in general, reference should be made to ss 18–23 of the Transport Act 1985 in respect of these exemptions.

By virtue of s 57 of the Act an operator's licence is not assignable and ceases to be valid on the death, bankruptcy or mental incapacity of the holder, or in respect of any other event described in the licence by the commissioner. Deferment of termination may be granted in certain circumstances. The regulations covering the procedure for applications for such licences come in terms of s 59; current regulations are the Public Service Vehicles (Operator's Licences) Regulations 1986, SI 1986/1668; and Public Service Vehicles (Driver's Licences) Regulations 1985, SI 1985/214.

It is an offence to forge, or alter any licence, disc, certificate or document, or to make a false statement in any application connected with an operator's licence (ss 65 and 66). The registered keeper of a public service vehicle has a duty to disclose the identity of the driver of that vehicle at any given time (s 70).

9.4:2   Appeals

In the event of a traffic commissioner refusing an application for a public service vehicle operator's licence, or if a condition is imported into the licence which has not been included in the application, the appellant has the right to appeal to the Transport Tribunal (s 50 as amended by Transport Act 1985, s 31). The address of this body is Parliament House, Parliament Square, Edinburgh. Under previous legislation, the decision of the Secretary of State could be appealed on a point of law to the Court of Session (see, for example, *Strathclyde Passenger Executive v McGill Bus Service* 1984 SLT 377). Such an appeal is no longer possible.

Further, a person who has had an application for a certificate of initial fitness in terms of s 6, or a type vehicle certificate in terms of s 10, refused, may appeal to the Secretary of State under s 51 (as amended by the Transport Act 1985, s 31).

9.5 PUBLIC SERVICE VEHICLES DRIVERS' LICENCES

Any person who drives a public service vehicle also requires a licence from the traffic commissioner (s 22). Again exemption is granted to a local education authority acting under s 42. Any person refused a licence may apply to the commissioner for a personal hearing, and on a continued refusal has a right of appeal to the sheriff (s 23). Regulations may be made to govern the conduct of drivers, conductors and inspectors of public service vehicles, and also to regulate the conduct of passengers, by virtue of ss 24 and 25. The regulations currently in force are the Public Service Vehicles (Conduct of Drivers, Conductors and Passengers) Regulations 1936, (SR and O 1936/619), as amended by the Public Service Vehicles (Conduct of Drivers, Conductors and Passengers) (Amendment) Regulations 1965, SI 1965/461 and SI 1980/915). These regulations *inter alia* impose duties of care on the drivers of buses only in respect of persons entitled to board the bus and not in respect of anyone attempting to board while it is in motion (*Reid v MacNicol* 1958 SLT 42). These sections and regulations do not apply to tramcars and trolley buses, which are covered by the Stage Carriages Act 1832, s 48 (as amended).

9.6 LOCAL AUTHORITY SERVICES

By virtue of s 101(1) of the Road Traffic Act 1930 as amended by the Transport Act 1968, ss 31 and 37, a local authority may run public service vehicles on any road inside or outside its district as part of any operation of tramways, light railways, trolley vehicles or omnibuses which they undertake in terms of a local act or order.

9.7 PASSENGER TRANSPORT AUTHORITIES AND EXECUTIVES

The function of passenger transport authorities is to make general policy in respect of any unmet demand for public transport service in the area. The function of the Passenger Transport Executive is to secure services which will comply with that policy. The detailed provisions for these functions and in respect of local authority bus operations, are found in Part IV of the Transport Act 1985. The consequent financial provisions including those relating to travel concession schemes are dealt with in Part V of the Act. Part V covers general miscellaneous matters including

questions of competition law, the reconstitution of the Transport
Tribunal, the provision by British Rail of substitution road
services and the constitution of the Disabled Persons Transport
Advisory Committee.

9.8   TRAVEL CONCESSIONS

The local authority may make travel concessions to certain qualified persons who travel on their vehicles by either introducing free
travel or reduced fares. Persons who qualify for these concessions
may be men over 65 and women over 60 years of age; children
under 16; persons between the minimum school leaving age and 18
who are undergoing full time education; blind persons, disabled
persons and members of the local authority. Those provisions are
contained generally in the Transport Act 1985, ss 93 *et seq.*

9.9   INTERNATIONAL CARRIAGE OF PASSENGERS AND LUGGAGE BY ROAD

The convention on the above is given effect to by the Carriage of
Passengers by Road Act 1974, which is yet to come into force.

PART 2
CARRIAGE OF GOODS

9.10   GOODS VEHICLES

The legislation imposes certain requirements on the operation of
commercial goods vehicles and the carriage of goods on the roads
for hire or reward. The principal considerations met with in
practice are the requirement that anyone operating a goods vehicle
should have an operator's licence, the need to have a special licence
to drive the various classes of heavy goods vehicles, and the qualification of the amount of hours of work that a driver of a commercial
vehicle is entitled to do and the records which he must keep in
respect of that work.

9.11   GOODS VEHICLES OPERATORS' LICENCE

9.11:1   General

An operator's licence is required in respect of the use of certain
goods vehicles by the user of those vehicles (Transport Act 1968,

s 60, as amended). The licensing authority is the traffic commissioner (s 59).

The operator's licence is required when a vehicle is used on a road for the carriage of goods whether for hire or reward or for, or in connection with, any trade or business carried on by user (s 60(1)). A description of the phrase 'hire or reward' is given in paragraph 9.2:2. A vehicle is used for reward where a payment is made even although there is no legal obligation on the payer to make such payment (*Aitken v Hamilton* 1964 SLT 125).

For further definitions of the phrase 'hire or reward', reference should be made to the cases of *Wurzel v Houghton Main Home Delivery Service Limited* [1937] 1 KB 380 and *Albert v Motor Insurers Bureau* [1972] AC 301.

By virtue of s 60(2), small goods vehicles (which are defined in s 60(4) as amended by the metrication regulations) are exempted from these provisions. However, it should be noted that a small goods vehicle will be subject to all of these legislative provisions in respect of commercial vehicles if a trailer is added to the vehicle and the total weight of the vehicle and trailer exceeds the statutory minimum (which is currently 3.5 tonnes).

However, small trailers are excluded from the test for a small goods vehicle; a small trailer is one with an unladen weight not exceeding 1020 kilograms.

The licensing authority may specify in the operator's licence what vehicles the operator is authorised to use in terms of the licence (s 61). The remainder of Part V of the Act covers the procedures for the application for such licences, their conditions, suspension and curtailment. Additional provisions for the control of operating centres are now found in ss 69A–69G, all as introduced by the Transport Act 1982, s 52(2) and Schedule 4, Part 1. An appeal against any refusal of a licence by the Traffic Commissioner is available to the Transport Tribunal (s 70; see paragraph 9.4:2). In order to secure that the conditions of an operator's licence are being observed, traffic examiners and other authorised persons have powers of entry and inspection (s 82). Operator's licences are not transferable (s 86).

Operators' licences may be standard, which allow the vehicles to be used both for hire or reward, and in connection with the trade or business, and for international transport operations or national transport operations only. Alternatively licences may be restricted, which allows the vehicles covered by the licence to be used in respect of the operator's trade or business only. The nature of these licences and the qualifications which have to be met by an operator before a licence is granted to him (which relate generally to the applicant's reputation, financial standing and professional competence) are contained in regulations 4, 5 and 9 and Schedule 6 of the Goods Vehicles (Operators' Licences, Qualifications and Fees) Regulations 1984, SI 1984/176.

For more detailed and practical advice on the licensing of the operators of goods vehicles, the Traffic Commissioners' Office issue in association with the Department of Transport a number of useful booklets and guides on the subject.

9.11:2 Operators' licences: inspection and evidence

The operator of a goods vehicle has a duty to inspect the vehicle and a further duty to keep records of that inspection (Road Traffic Act 1988, s 74). In any proceedings for a failure to observe regulations under this section, or a failure to observe the construction and use regulations, such records are sufficient evidence of the matters stated therein (Road Traffic Offenders Act 1988, s 14).

9.12 GOODS VEHICLES DRIVERS' LICENCES

9.12:1 General

A special heavy goods vehicle licence (often abbreviated to HGV licence) is required by the driver to drive a heavy goods vehicle of any prescribed class on a road (Road Traffic Act 1988, s 110). It is also an offence to cause or permit another person to drive a heavy goods vehicle of any class on a road if that person is not so licensed to drive a heavy goods vehicle of that class (s 110(1)). 'Causing or permitting' is defined in paragraph 1.10:3. It is not only persons who have actual knowledge of the absence of an appropriate licence on the part of the driver who can be found guilty of causing or permitting the driver to commit an offence; constructive or imputed knowledge of the lack of such a licence may lead to conviction (*MacPhail v Allan and Day* 1980 SLT (Sh Ct) 136).

A heavy goods vehicle is defined in s 120 as '(a) an articulated goods vehicle, or (b) a large goods vehicle, that is to say, a motor vehicle (not being an articulated goods vehicle) which is constructed or adapted to carry or haul goods and the permissible maximum weight of which exceeds 7.5 tonnes.'

In terms of the definition of the term 'maximum permissible weight' contained in s 108 of the Road Traffic Act 1988, a rigid or articulated vehicle drawing a trailer may bring a vehicle into the category of HGV licensing if the total weight of the combination exceeds 7.5 tonnes.

9.12:2 Application for, and nature of, licence

An application for a licence is made to the traffic commissioners for the area in which the applicant resides (s 111). Heavy goods vehicles licences normally last for three years, before they have to be renewed (s 113). Generally, the principal requirements and conditions of such licences are found in Part IV of the Act, but there are also a number of important statutory instruments. Again the traffic commissioner issues booklets in respect of applications for such licences. In particular an applicant must pass a special driving test 112(1)).

The licensing authority has power to revoke a licence and to disqualify the holder (s 114). Considerations which may result in revocation and disqualification are the driver's conduct, his failure to keep records or a physical disability (see *Warrender v Scottish Traffic Area Licensing Authority* 1976 SLT (Sh Ct) 76). The disqualification may be indefinite or for such period as the licensing authority considers to be appropriate. The disqualification imposed by the licensing authority operates quite separately from any other kind of disqualification that may be imposed by the courts. Any heavy goods vehicle driver needs an ordinary licence to be on the road, just like any other motorist; the requirement of any HGV licence is additional. If therefore the courts have disqualified the driver in ordinary course, his HGV licence is rendered useless; however, if the licensing authority revokes the HGV licence, the driver is still entitled to use his ordinary licence.

If the test of competency to drive is alleged to have been unfairly conducted, or was not conducted properly in terms of the relevant regulations, the applicant may appeal by way of application to the sheriff for the area where he resides (s 115; see for example, *Crawford v Scottish Traffic Area Licensing Authority* 1974 SLT (Sh Ct) 11). An appeal to the sheriff is also available in respect of any refusal, revocation or curtailment of a licence (s 116).

9.13 GOODS VEHICLES PLATING AND TESTING CERTIFICATES

9.13:1 General

Section 49 of the Road Traffic Act 1988, and Part V of that Act generally provide that all goods vehicles which are used on the roads must have both a plating certificate and a test certificate. A plating certificate contains the plated particulars (including the plated weight) which are prescribed. The test certificate relates to requirements of construction and use. The Goods Vehicles (Plating and Testing) Regulations 1982, SI 1982/1478, as amended by SI 1988/338, make provision in respect of both types of certificate. Reference should also be made to Part III of the Road Vehicles (Construction and Use) Regulations 1986, SI 1986/1078, in respect of plating requirements, testing and inspection. Test certificates have to be renewed periodically.

9.13:2   Type approval schemes

The plating and testing certificates are required for all goods vehicles that are manufactured or produced and used. For practical reasons, they are implemented by means of type approval schemes. Manufacturers may submit to the Secretary of State a type vehicle for approval. The approval is intended to cover all matters of design, construction, equipment and marking. The Secretary of State then issues a type approval certificate, and this enables the manufacturer to provide other vehicles with a certificate of conformity to the effect that all such further vehicles conform to the type vehicle submitted to the Secretary of State. The plated particulars must be indicated on every vehicle. The principle of the scheme is extended to vehicle parts. There are a number of statutory instruments which implement the schemes in detail. A discussion of these details is not within the scope of this book.

9.13:3   Inspection

Authorised examiners have extensive powers of test and inspection of all kinds of motor vehicles. By virtue of s 67 of the Road Traffic Act 1988, such an examiner may test a motor vehicle on a road for a variety of purposes. The persons who may act as authorised examiners are described in s 67(4). Further provisions in respect of remedying defects discovered in the course of such tests are given in ss 67A and 67B, (added by Schedule 2, Part III of the Road Traffic (Consequential Provisions) Act 1988). Section 68 confers on goods vehicles examiners powers to inspect goods vehicles to secure proper maintenance, and ss 69 and 70 respectively allow prohibition of further driving of unfit or overloaded vehicles. Section 71 provides for the removal of prohibitions and s 70 creates the offences of driving vehicles which are unfit or overloaded in contravention of the prohibitions.

Prosecution for overloading or dangerous vehicles is dealt with in paragraphs 7.12:6, 7.12:7 and 7.12:15.

9.14   DRIVERS' HOURS AND RECORDS OF WORK

9.14:1   General

Section 95 of the Transport Act 1968 (as substantially amended) provides that drivers engaged in the road transport industry, whether engaged in the carriage of passengers or of goods, must observe certain restrictions in the hours worked. It should be noticed that the term 'working' used throughout this part of the legislation is not necessarily exclusively confined to 'driving'. The basic idea is that no driver of any vehicle engaged in the carriage of passengers or goods should drive for longer than certain periods (s 96(2)), and such vehicles should have installed and use prescribed recording equipment ('the tachograph') (s 97 as amended).

The purpose of these restrictions and provisions is specifically described as a protection of the public against the risks which arise when drivers are suffering from fatigue. The Secretary of State has extensive power to make regulations in respect of these matters and in practice makes regulations to take account of any requirement imposed by the rules of the European Economic Community. Numerous regulations have been made in terms of s 95. Part VI of the Act outlines the general framework of the scheme. Broadly speaking, there are two kinds of rules, those which apply to national and international driving, and those which, exempted from the first category, apply to what is called domestic driving. The international and national rules apply to most goods vehicles over 3.5 tonnes maximum weight. There are various exceptions from these requirements provided for in the regulations.

Generally, the requirements of international and national driving are at present as follows. A driver must not drive for more than nine hours in a day. This may be extended to ten hours twice a week. After four and a half hours of driving a driver must take a break of at least forty-five minutes. Weekly rest periods must be taken after six consecutive daily driving periods. The total period of driving per fortnight must not exceed ninety hours. A driver must have a minimum daily rest of eleven consecutive hours which may be reduced in certain circumstances. These general rules are subject to exceptions and revision.

Journeys to some European countries outside the Common Market are subject to an international agreement on drivers' hours.

These agreements (the AETR Rules) may also have to be observed. Further if a country is neither in the Common Market nor subject to the AETR Rules (like Switzerland) the domestic rules of that country have to be observed.

Certain operations are exempted from the international and national drivers' hours and tachograph rules when they are engaged in specific operations. In such cases, drivers of goods vehicles which are so exempted are subject to certain domestic rules. These are that no driver may drive for more than ten hours in a day or be on duty for more than eleven hours on any working day. There are also special considerations given to mixed domestic and common market driving and there are certain exemptions even from the domestic rules. Drivers governed by domestic rules do not have to install and use the tachograph.

9.14:2   Offences

In respect of offences in terms of these regulations, returns tendered by drivers as correct which show that driving has occurred for longer than the permitted hours are in themselves sufficient in the absence of any definite and further evidence, to constitute the offence; (s 97(D) of the Transport Act 1968 as amended by Passenger and Goods Vehicles (Recording Equipment) Regulations 1979, SI 1979/1746; *Adair v Craighouse Cabinet Works Limited* 1937 JC 89, 1937 SLT 499). In determining whether an offence has been committed, hours of driving outside the United Kingdom can properly be taken into account (*Fox v Lawson* [1974] AC 803, [1974] 2 WLR 247).

Tachographs must be kept regularly calibrated and periodic inspection every two and six years is required.

9.14:3   Keeping of records

There are numerous requirements relating to the keeping of records in terms of Part VI of the Act. Employers have a duty to provide their drivers with record charts of an approved type that can be used in the tachograph. The driver is obliged to enter certain information on the chart before inserting it into the tachograph. It is the driver's responsibility to see that recording by the tachograph takes place properly. Drivers are then obliged to return their charts to their employers who must keep them for a year. Only those drivers whose driving is governed by these EEC Rules require to operate the tachograph; other drivers are merely constrained by the domestic driving rules. However, the provision of the tachograph requirements as indicated above is complex and there are a number of exceptions.

The basic regulations are the Drivers Hours (Goods Vehicles) (Keeping of Records) Regulations 1987, SI 1987/1421; reference should also be made to s 98(4) of the Transport Act 1968 as amended by the European Communities Act 1972, s 4 and Schedule 4; the Road Traffic (Drivers Ages and Hours of Work) Act 1976, s 2(1)(c) and (d) and the Passengers and Goods Vehicles (Recording Equipment Regulations 1979, SI 1979/1746.

Any entry on a record sheet made by a crew member can be sufficient evidence of the matters appearing therein (s 97 and 97B) (as amended by Passenger and Goods Vehicles (Recording Equipment) Regulations 1979, SI 1979/1746.

9.14:4 Exemptions

Certain exemptions are granted in respect of both drivers' hours and the installation and use of the tachograph in respect of certain vehicles. For example: certain passenger and public authority vehicles; ambulances; vehicles in restricted use in agricultural, forestry and fishing enterprises, vehicles carrying animal carcases and waste unfit for human consumption are exempted (see Community Drivers' Hours and Recording Equipment (Exemptions and Supplementary Provisions) Regulations 1986, SI 1986/1456, regulations 2(1) and 4(1) and the Schedule thereto). Also exempted are vehicles in respect of operations carried out by specialised vehicles (paragraph 56 of the Schedule); this exemption applies to the operations which are carried out rather than the vehicles themselves (*Struthers (Lochwinnoch) v Tudhope* 1982 SLT 393, 1981 SCCR 329; *Stewart v Richmond* 1983 SLT 62 1982 SCCR 383, 1982 CO Circulars A/25). Police officers and other appropriate persons have an extensive power of inspection in respect of tachograph operations (Transport Act 1968, s 99) and exemption from all these requirements is given to the police and fire brigade, but not to armed service vehicles (s 102 as amended by the Transport Act 1982, s 64(2), (3)). Reference should also be made to Community Drivers' Hours and Recording Equipment Regulations 1986, SI 1986/1456; Drivers' Hours (Harmonisation with Community Rules) Regulations 1986, SI 1986/1458 and Drivers' Hours (Goods Vehicles) (Modifications) Order 1986, SI 1986/1459.

EEC Regulations 3820/85 provides (art 4) for similar exemptions in the equivalent EEC legislation. In particular, article 4(7) and (8) appear to extend the exemption to ambulance type vehicles, while the UK regulations do not. It is suggested that ambulances are exempt in terms of regulation 2 of the Drivers' Hours (Goods Vehicles) (Exemptions) Regulations 1986, SI 1986/1492.

9.15 FOREIGN GOODS VEHICLES AND PUBLIC SERVICE VEHICLES

9.15:1 General

By virtue of (1) the Road Traffic (Foreign Vehicles) Act 1972 as amended by the Transport Act 1978, s 9(1) and Schedule 3; (2) the Transport Act 1980, Schedule 5, Part II, and (3) the Public Passenger Vehicles Act 1981, Schedule 7, appointed examiners are entitled to inspect foreign goods vehicles and foreign public service vehicles to satisfy themselves that the relevant provisions of domestic road traffic legislation are being observed.

9.15:2 International carriage of goods by road

Special authorisation is required in respect of journeys by goods vehicles to certain continental destinations (International Road Haulage Permits Act 1975 and the appropriate regulations (SI 1975/2234)).

The International Carriage of Perishable Foodstuffs Act 1976 (as amended by SI 1983/1123) provided for the international carriage of perishable foodstuffs.

The conditions governing contracts for the international carriage of goods by road between a number of European states are now standard, reflecting the agreement contained in the convention for the international carriage of goods by road (known as CNR) which was drawn up in 1956. This was introduced into the United Kingdom by the Carriage of Goods by Road Act 1965 (as amended by the Carriage by Road Act 1965 and the Carriage by Road and Air Act 1979). The convention itself is given in the Schedule to the 1965 Act.

Appendix A

The Highway Code

The Highway Code is published by Her Majesty's Stationery Office, and may be purchased at HMSO Bookshops, HMSO accredited agents (which can be found in the Yellow Pages), and at most large bookshops. It is recommended that practitioners should have a copy of the Highway Code available for reference purposes. Some of the provisions of the Code are reproduced, with the kind permission of the Controller of Her Majesty's Stationery Office, for illustrative purposes. It must be emphasised that what follows is only a selection from the current edition.

The road user on wheels
(The Department of Transport's manual *Driving* deals with the following points in greater detail.)

GENERAL
26 Keep your vehicle in good condition. Pay particular attention to lights, brakes, steering, tyres (including spare), seat belts, demisters, windscreen wipers and washers. Keep windscreens, windows, lights, direction indicators reflectors, mirrors and number plates clean and clear. Do not drive with a defective or unsuitable exhaust system. If L-plates have been fitted, remove (or cover) them when the vehicle is not being used for driving instructions or practice.

27 You must ensure that any loads carried or towed are secure, and do not project unsafely. Do not overload your vehicle or trailer.

● ● ●

ALCOHOL AND THE ROAD USER
34 Drinking alcohol seriously affects driving ability. It reduces co-ordination, increases reaction time and impairs judgement of speed, distance and risk while inspiring a false sense of confidence. The risk of an accident increases sharply for drivers above the legal limit of 35 microgrammes of alcohol per 100 millilitres of breath. The driving of many people who feel perfectly sober is seriously affected well below this limit.

About one third of all drivers, motorcyclists and pedestrians who are killed in road accidents have alcohol levels above the legal limit for driving.

Driving above the legal limit means losing your licence for a long period and can mean a heavy fine or imprisonement. The safest course is not to drink and drive.

SEAT BELTS

35 If you are involved in an accident, wearing a seat belt halves the risk of death or serious injury. Drivers and front seat passengers in most vehicles must wear a seat belt. Those exempt from the law include holders of a medical exemption certificate, drivers carrying out a manoeuvre which includes reversing, and those engaged in making local rounds of deliveries and collections in a vehicle constructed or adapted for that purpose. It is your responsibility to wear the belt unless exempt. Make sure your seat belts are properly adjusted and that your passengers know how to use them.

36 The driver is responsible in law for ensuring that children under 14 are suitably restrained if they are travelling in the front. For a child under one year this means an approved child restraint designed for a child of that age and weight. A child over one may wear any approved child restraint or an adult seat belt. The safest place for young children to travel is in the rear seat of the car, wearing approved child restraints appropriate to their size and age. These are:
– for infants (0-9 months), a carry cot secured with special straps and covered with a net or stiff cover, or a rearward-facing infant safety seat.
– between nine months and four to five years, a child safety seat.
– for older children a child safety harness, or an adult seat belt used with a secured booster cushion of special design (not a loose household cushion).
If restraints are not fitted in the rear, it is safer for children to wear an adult belt in the front, with a booster cushion, than to travel unrestrained.

37 Do not carry children in the luggage space behind the rear seats of an estate car or hatchback unless the manufacturers have provided seats for this purpose. Ensure that child safety locks on doors, where fitted, are secured when children are being carried.

● ● ●

SIGNALS

39 Give signals if they would help or warn other road users. Give only the correct signals – those illustrated on pages 51 and 52 [of the Highway Code]. Give them clearly and in good time. Always be sure that your direction indicator signals are cancelled after a manoeuvre.

40 Watch out for the signals of other drivers, motorcylcists or pedal cyclists and take any necessary action promptly.

• • •

41 Always keep a special look-out for cycles and motorcycles, particularly when overtaking or turning. Bear in mind the two-wheelers are much less easy to see than larger vehicles and that their riders have the same rights to consideration as other road users and are more vulnerable. Drivers (especially of long vehicles or of vehicles towing trailers) should leave plenty of room for pedal cyclists in particular.

• • •

DRIVING ALONG

43 Keep to the left, except when road signs or markings indicate otherwise or when you intend to overtake, or turn right, or when you have to pass stationary vehicles or pedestrians in the road. Allow others to overtake you if they want to. You must not drive on a footpath or pavement by the side of the road.

• • •

49 You must obey the speed limits for the road and for your vehicle. Remember that, except on motorways, there is a 30 mph speed limit on all roads where there are street lights unless signs show otherwise. Bear in mind that any speed limit is a maximum. It does not mean that it is safe to drive at that speed – always take into account all the conditions at the time. (A table of speed limits, according to road and vehicle, is shown on page 48 [of the Highway Code].)

50 Never drive so fast that you cannot stop well within the distance you can see to be clear. Go much more slowly if the road is wet or icy or if there is fog. Drive more slowly at night. Remember – it can be especially difficult to see pedestrians and cyclists at night and in poor daylight conditions. Do not brake sharply except in an emergency.

51 Leave enough space between you and the vehicle in front so that you can pull up safely if it slows down or stops suddenly. The safe rule is never to get closer than the overall stopping distance shown below. But on the open road, in good conditions, a gap of one metre for each mph of your speed or a two-second time gap may be enough. This will also leave space for an overtaking vehicle to pull in. On wet or icy roads the gap should be at least doubled. Drop back if an overtaking vehicle pulls into the gap in front of you.

Shortest stopping distances – in metres and feet							
mph	Thinking distance		Braking distance		Overall stopping distance		On a dry road, a good car with good brakes and tyres and an alert driver will stop in the distances shown. Remember these are shortest stopping distances. Stopping distances increase greatly with wet and slippery roads, poor brakes and tyres, and tired drivers.
20	6	20	6	20	12	40	
30	9	30	14	45	23	75	
40	12	40	24	80	36	120	
50	15	50	38	125	53	175	
60	18	60	55	180	73	240	
70	21	70	75	245	96	315	
(See diagram on back cover)							

52   Make way for ambulances, fire engines, police or other emergency vehicles when their blue lamps are flashing or their bells, two-tone horns or sirens are sounding.

●   ●   ●

USE OF MICROPHONES AND CAR TELEPHONES
54   Do not use a hand-held microphone or telephone handset while your vehicle is moving, except in an emergency. You should only speak into a fixed, neckslung or clipped-on microphone when it would not distract your attention from the road. Do not stop on the hard shoulder of a motorway to answer or make a call, however urgent.

DRIVING IN FOG
55   When driving in fog:

a   Check your mirrors and slow down. Keep a safe distance. You should always be able to pull up within your range of vision.

b   Don't hang on to someone else's tail lights; it gives a false sense of security.

c   Watch your speed; you may be going much faster than you think. Do not speed up to get away from a vehicle which is too close behind you.

d Remember that if you are driving a heavy vehicle it may take longer to pull up than the vehicle ahead.

e Warning signals are there to help and protect; observe them.

f See and be seen. Use dipped headlamps or front fog lamps. Only use rear fog lamps when visibility is seriously reduced (Rule 120). Use your windscreen wipers and demisters.

g Check and clean windscreens, lights, reflectors and windows whenever you can.

h Remember that fog can drift rapidly and is often patchy. Even if it seems to be clearing, you can suddenly find yourself back in thick fog.

i Take particular care when driving in fog after dark.

j If you must drive in fog, allow more time for your journey.

THE SAFETY OF PEDESTRIANS
56 Drive carefully and slowly when pedestrians are about, particularly in crowded shopping streets, when you see a bus stopped, or near a parked milk float or mobile shop. Watch out for pedestrians emerging suddenly, for example from behind parked or stopped vehicles. Remember, pedestrians may have to cross roads where there are no crossings; show them consideration.

• • •

65 When turning at a road junction, give way to pedestrians who are crossing the road into which you are turning.

66 When entering or emerging from property bordering on a road, give way to pedestrians as well as to traffic on the road. Remember: pavements are for people – not for motor vehicles.

• • •

OVERTAKING
84 Do not overtake unless you are sure you can do so without danger to others or to yourself. Before you start to overtake make sure that the road is clear far enough ahead and behind. Use your mirrors and if you are on a motorcycle or pedal cycle look behind and to your offside. Signal before you start to move out. Be particularly careful at dusk, in the dark and in fog or mist, when it is more difficult to judge speed and distance.

• • •

88   Overtake only on the right, except:

a   when the driver in front has signalled that he intends to turn right and you can overtake him on the left without getting in the way of others and without entering a bus lane during its period of operation;

b   when you want to turn left at a junction;

c   when traffic is moving slowly in queues and vehicles in a lane on the right are moving more slowly than you are;

d   in one-way streets (but not dual carriageways) where vehicles may pass on either side.

● ● ●

LAMPS
119   You must:

a   make sure that all your lamps are clean, that they work and that your headlamps are properly adjusted – badly adjusted headlamps can dazzle road users and lead to accidents;

b   switch on your lamps at lighting-up time;

c   use headlamps at night on all roads where there is no street lighting, on roads where the street lamps are more than 185 metres (200 yards) apart and on roads where the street lamps are not alight;

d   use your headlamps or front fog lamps at any time when visibility is *seriously* reduced, that is, generally, reduced to a distance of less than 100 metres.

● ● ●

121   You should also:

a   use headlamps at night on lighted motorways and similar high-speed roads;

b   use dipped headlamps at night in built-up areas unless the road is well lit;

c   always drive so you can stop well within the distance you can see ahead;

d   slow down or stop if you are dazzled by approaching headlamps;

e   dip your headlamps when meeting other vehicles or road users and before they dazzle the driver of a vehicle travelling in the same direction in front of you.

● ● ●

WAITING AND PARKING

125   Also, do not let your vehicle stand:

● where it would cause danger to other vehicles or pedestrians, for example–
at or near a school entrance or a school crossing patrol – not even to pick up or set down passengers;
where it would hide a traffic sign;
on a footpath, pavement or cycle path;
at or near any bus stop;
on or near a level crossing;

● where it would make it difficult for others to see clearly, for example, near or at–
a junction, ie not within 15 metres of it;
a bend;
the brow of a hill;
a hump-back bridge;

● where it would make the road narrow, for example–
opposite a traffic island;
alongside another stationary vehicle;
opposite or nearly opposite another stationery vehicle if this would narrow the road to less than the width of two vehicles;
near roadworks.

Appendix B

Roadside Breathalyser Test Devices

There appear to be three such devices in current use in Scotland, the Lion Alcolmeter S-L2A, the Alcolyser, and the Alcotest R.80A.

Both the Lion Alcolmeter S-L2A and the Alcolyser are produced by Lion Laboratories Limited, Ty Verlon Industrial Estate, Barry, South Wales, CF6 3BE, who have kindly given permission for the following descriptions of their products to be reproduced.

1. The Alcolmeter

The Lion Alcolmeter S-L2A is a breath alcohol screening device based on an electrochemical fuel cell which generates a voltage in proportional response to alcohol vapour concentration. The alcohol detector, is unaffected by acetone, paint and glue fumes, foods, confectionery, methane and practically any other substance likely to be found in breath (apart from those which contain alcohol). No warm-up time is required for the device to be operated, and the temperature range is 0–40°C., although it is recommended that in very cold temperatures the device should be kept warmed in a coat pocket.

If the subject has consumed alcohol within the last twenty minutes, there may still be residual mouth alcohol which could give an inflated reading. Further, the operator must check that the fuel in the device is clear of alcohol from any previous test, and this is done by carrying out the 'Ready Check'. The procedure for conducting the 'Ready Check' is described in the manufacturer's handbook.

The subject should be instructed to fill his lungs, blow strongly into the mouthpiece to bring on the first breath sampling light (A), and continue to blow at that pressure until the second breath sampling light (B) comes on. If the driver fails to bring on one or both sampling lights, he will normally be deemed to have failed to provide a sample. The driver should also be instructed to keep his hands away from the sampling mechanism, as this may interfere with the reading.

A fresh mouthpiece must be removed from its wrapper and attached to the device for each test.

235

Appendix B(2)

1.2 Operator Controls: Alcolmeter S-L2A

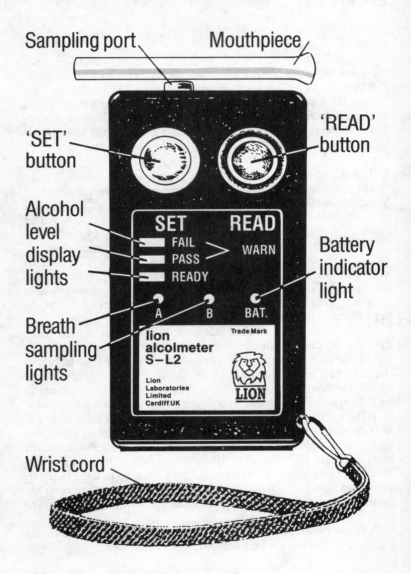

Sampling port   Mouthpiece

'SET' button

'READ' button

Alcohol level display lights

SET   READ

FAIL   WARN
PASS
READY

Battery indicator light

A   B   BAT.

Breath sampling lights

lion alcolmeter S-L2

Trade Mark

Lion Laboratories Limited Cardiff UK

LION

Wrist cord

Appendix B(2)(cont)

1.3 Description of Operator Controls

SET button	– This forms part of the sampling system. When fully depressed the button locks to set the instrument ready for sampling. When the button rises, the sample to be analysed is drawn into the fuel cell detector.
READ button	This has two functions:

1) to release the *SET* button – so taking the sample.

2) to switch on the amplifier and display system.

The button is spring loaded. Momentary depression will effect '1' but constant pressure is required for function '2'.

Battery Indicator Light – When the *READ* button is pressed and held fully down, the green light marked '*BAT*.' illuminates (with the *READY* light) to indicate that the battery has sufficient power for the instrument to operate.

Breath Sampling Lights – Light '*A*' illuminates to indicate that the subject is blowing hard enough.

Light '*B*' illuminates to indicate when the *READ* button should be pressed. It will only illuminate when the subject has provided a suitable sample of breath for analysis.

Alcohol Level Display Lights Three lights coloured green, amber and red –(marked *READY*, *PASS* and *FAIL*) illuminate to show the blood alcohol concentration of the subject.

Sampling Port – This forms the entrance to the fuel cell detector.

When inserted into the small hole in the side of the mouthpiece it allows a small portion of breath to be drawn into the instruments.

Mouthpiece – This is attached to the sampling port.

For reasons of hygiene the mouthpiece are supplied separately packed and are disposable. A new mouthpiece *must* be used for each individual breath test.

APPENDIX B(3)

2. The Alcolyser
The Alcolyser is a simple disposable device for measuring the alcohol content of a person's body by means of a breath analysis. The determination of blood alcohol concentration via expired breath is based on Widmark's principle; the alcohol in expired breath reacts with yellow crystals to change their colour to green. Expired breath (a mixture of tidal and deep-lung air) is blown through a tube into a 1 litre plastic bag in approximately 15 seconds. If the green stain in the tube containing the crystals extends beyond the red line at the centre of the tube then the alcohol level in the subject's blood exceeds the prescribed limit.

The instructions for use are simple; the assembly directions for the device must be correctly observed, and the driver must then be instructed to take a deep breath and blow steadily through the mouthpiece until the plastic bag is fully inflated (usually this takes between 10 and 20 seconds).

No test should be conducted if the driver has consumed alcohol within the previous twenty minutes.

3. The Alcotest R80A
The Alcotest R80A device operates in a similar fashion to the Alcolyser; it too has to be assembled in accordance with the manufacturer's instruction and the equipment has a 'use-by' date which must be observed. This device is produced by Drager Ltd, The Willows, Mark Road, Hemel Hempstead, Herts, HP2 7BW.

The Alcotest equipment is supplied in a box containing ten tubes, ten mouthpieces, and one plastic bag. Each tube has a yellow ring around its circumference; a blue arrow indicates the flow of breath through the tube, and the end marked with a green band is fitted to the plastic bag. Each bag may be used ten times, and so each box provides sufficient equipment for ten tests.

Before using the equipment, the operator must check the expiry date on the label attached to the box, and satisfy himself that the yellow crystals in the tube to be used are free from discolouration and cracks. The tube is shown in that condition to the motorist, and then broken open at each end. The green end of the tube is fixed into the collar of the plastic bag, and the other end is pushed into the mouthpiece, which has for this purpose been removed from its protective envelope. The mouthpiece should not be touched. The motorist is then asked to blow into the bag in one continuous breath of not less than ten seconds and not more than twenty seconds. Two exhalations have been allowed in an English case, but the manufacturers specifically advise that only one exhalation should be permitted to avoid the possibility of accumulation. If as a result, the yellow crystals in the tube turn green up to and beyond the centre line, the test is positive: up to the centre line is negative.

It should be noted that a false positive result will be obtained if the motorist has consumed alcohol within the twenty minutes which precede the test. Also, smoking immediately before the test should not be permitted, as tobacco smoke may cause the crystals in the tube to turn brown. A fresh mouthpiece must be used for each test.

Appendix C

The Camic Breath Analyser Device

This is the only instrument in current use in police stations in Scotland for the purpose of providing an analysis of a breath sample in terms of s 7 of the Road Traffic Act 1988. The machine is manufactured by Camic Car & Medical Instrument Co Ltd, Camden Street, North Shields, Tyne and Wear NE30 1OG, who have kindly allowed the following descriptions of their product to be reproduced from their Operator's Manual.

CAMIC BREATH ANALYSER

The Camic Breath Analyser is an instrument designed to analyse the alcohol content of a breath sample quickly and accurately.

Incorporated into the instrument is an automatic sequence to check the calibration of the instrument before and after each breath test. This allows the user to have full confidence in the final result.

The user operational controls of the instrument have been kept to the absolute minimum, with only one push button to initiate a full test sequence. After pressing the start button the analyser will run through its test sequence automatically with a lamp to tell the suspect when to provide a breath sample and a lamp to indicate when to stop blowing (normally set at 6 seconds).

If the suspect fails to provide a suitable breath sample the instrument will indicate the fault and revert back to the start of the sequence.

At the end of the test the Breath Analyser will provide printed copies of the test results including the date, time, calibration check results and analysis of the breath samples.

The Camic Breath Analyser operates on the Non-Dispersive Infra Red principle, measuring the absorption of the Ethyl Alcohol vapour in breath at 3.4 microns. Narrow band Optical filters are used to provide very high discrimination against possible interference.

A short path length analysis cell has been designed to provide easy breath sample requirements and has the advantage of giving a linear relationship between alcohol concentration and electrical output.

The analysis cell is held at a constant temperature to provide immunity against ambient temperature changes and also to prevent condensation from the breath sample obscuring the optical path.

The pipework of the instrument has been kept simple and any part of the pipework which may be susceptible to condensation problems is heated and all lines are back purged between samples to remove any residual gas.

A bench fixing kit is available from Camic to allow the instrument to be securely screwed to the bench top to prevent accidental damage. ONLY the Camic kit must be used.

OPERATIONAL INSTRUCTIONS

Check that the analyser and simulator units are both switched on. If the analyser has been switched off for any reason allow a 30 minutes warm up period to elapse before taking any breath test.

TO START TEST SIMPLY PRESS TEST BUTTON

The instrument will now calibrate itself and after approximately one minute the green 'blow now' lamp will come on requesting the subject to blow.

A CONTINUOUS breath of at least six seconds is required to provide an accurate sample and bring on the 'stop blow' lamp.

The subject has a total of 3 minutes to provide a correct sample. The subject may make as many attempts as necessary to provide a six second continuous sample.

If, after providing a correct breath sample, the subject attempts to suck the gas back out of the breath pipe, the instrument will sense this and immediately reset and print out 'Breath Invalid'.

After the first breath test has been completed the instrument will request a second breath sample exactly as before.

After the second breath test instrument will again check its calibration and if accurate then the results will be printed out, together with the date and time of test.

The instrument is set to calibrate at the reading of 35 Ug/100ml and a reading within the range 32–38 Ug/100ml will be accepted and allow the analyser to proceed with the test.

If the calibration check falls outside the 32–38 limits the analyser will print 'Calibration Out' and reset itself to the Ready for Test mode.

CAMIC BREATH ANALYSER
OPERATIONAL MODE

1. Instrument Switched on.
2. Front Panel Switch flashes on and off until the instrument reaches its operational temperature, when the illuminated switch stays on.
3. Initiate Test by pressing illuminated switch – the light will go out to indicate the automatic test sequence has started.
4. The analysis cell is purged with clean, alcohol free air, for 30 seconds.
5. Calibration gas is injected into the analysis cell and the readout for the gas is indicated on the digital display.
   If the calibration is within the allowed limits the test sequence continues:
   if the calibration is outside the preset limits the instrument will reset itself to the start of the sequence and printout that the reading was outside the required limits.
6. After calibration the analysis cell is purged for 30 seconds.
7. The instrument is now ready to accept a breath sample, as indicated by the green 'BLOW NOW' lamp illuminating. A continuous 6 second breath sample must now be provided within the next 3 minutes to allow the sequence to proceed. After a 6 second blow the 'STOP BLOW' lamp will illuminate. If no breath sample is provided within 3 minutes the analyser will print out 'BREATH INVALID' and reset itself to the start of the sequence.
   If a suitable breath sample has been provided the alcohol level will be displayed on the Digital Display.
8. The instrument purges for 30 seconds.
9. The instrument will now accept a second breath sample as No. 7.
10. The instrument purges for 30 seconds.
11. The instrument will now re-check its calibration as No. 5.
12. All test results are printed out in sequence as shown overleaf with test time and date.

POLICE STATION

NAME OF SUBJECT

SUBJECTS'S SIGNATURE

OPERATOR

OPERATOR'S SIGNATURE

· · RESULTS · ·

CAL CHECK NO.1
   037 UG/100ML
  · ZERO CHECK ·
   000 UG/100ML

BREATH TEST NO.1
   062 UG/100 ML
DATE   15/04/82
TIME   11:22 GMT.

BREATH TEST NO.2
   064 UG/100ML
DATE   15/04/82
TIME   11:23 GMT.

CAL. CHECK NO. 2
   035 UG/100ML

· · · CAMIC · · ·

Note

In practice, most forces appear to issue set instructions to Camic operators for use in every case. These normally include the reading by the operator to the motorist (after agreement by the motorist to provide two breath specimens) of the sequence of the operation of the test, with the operator indicating the relevant parts of the machine as appropriate during the explanation. The explanation is generally along the following lines.

The procedure begins by pressing a button which carries out a calibration check which should produce a figure of between 32 and 38 on the visual display panel. If the figure is between 32 and 38, the motorist will then be required to provide two specimens of breath. If the figure is not within these two figures, the device is not to be used, and an alternative procedure will be adopted.

When the green light comes on, the motorist has three minutes within which he must blow continuously into the tube for at least six seconds until the red light comes on. If the attempt is unsuccessful, further attempts may be made within the three minute period. Failure to provide a sufficient specimen within the three minute period will result in the machine printing 'Breath Invalid'.

If a proper and sufficient first specimen is given, the visual display panel will show the analysis of the motorist's breath and then reset itself. When the green light comes on again, a second specimen will be required. Any attempt to suck air out of the tube at any time will produce a 'Breath Invalid' printout.

Following two proper and sufficient specimens being given, a further calibration check is carried, which should again indicate a figure between 32 and 38. If this is correct, the machine will automatically print out the results of the analysis, and a copy will be given to the motorist.

Appendix D

Endorsement Offence Codes and Points

Drivers convicted of endorseable offences on or after 1.11.82 (and who are not disqualified for the offence(s)) will incur penalty points which will be endorsed on the licence. When a driver has accumulated 12 or more penalty points within 3 years he is liable to be disqualified. Endorsements imposed on the same occasion before 1.11.82 will count as 3 penalty points, unless the driver was disqualified on that or any subsequent occasion.

Aiding, Abetting, Counselling or Procuring
Offences as coded below, but with 0 changed to 2, eg UT10 becomes UT12.

Causing or Permitting
Offences as coded below, but with 0 changed to 4, eg PL10 becomes PL14.

Inciting
Offences as coded below, but with O changed to 6, eg DD30 becomes DD36.

Periods of Time
Periods of time are signified as follows: D = Days, M = Months, Y = Years. A consecutive period of disqualification is signified by an asterisk* against the period.
† 4 points if EXCEPTIONALLY disqualification not imposed.

Code	Accident Offences	Penalty Points
AC10	Failing to stop after an accident	5–9
AC20	Failing to give particulars or to report an accident within 24 hours	4–9
AC30	Undefined accident offence	4–9
	Disqualified Driver	
BA10	Driving while disqualfied by order of Court	6
BA20	Driving while disqualified as under age	2

Code	Accident Offences	Penalty Points
	Careless Driving	
CD10	Driving without due care and attention	3–9 ~~2–5~~
CD20	Driving without reasonable consideration for other road users	2–5
CD30	Driving without due care and attention or without reasonable consideration for other road users	2–5
	Construction and Use Offences	
CU10	Using a vehicle with defective brakes	3
CU20	Causing or likely to cause danger by reason of use of unsuitable vehicle or using a vehicle with parts or accessories (excluding brakes, steering or tyres) in a dangerous condition	3
CU30	Using a vehicle with defective tyres	3
CU40	Using a vehicle with defective steering	3
CU50	Causing or likely to cause danger by reason of load or passengers	3
CU60	Undefined failure to comply with Construction and Use Regulations	3
	Reckless Driving	
DD30	Reckless driving	10
DD60	Manslaughter or culpable homicide while driving a vehicle	†
DD70	Causing death by reckless driving	†
	Drink or Drugs	
DR10	Driving or attempting to drive with alcohol level above limit	†
DR20	Driving or attempting to drive while unfit through drink or drugs	†
DR30	Driving or attempting to drive then refusing to supply a specimen for analysis	†
DR40	In charge of a vehicle while alcohol level above limit	10
DR50	In charge of a vehicle while unfit through drink or drugs	10

Code	Accident Offences	Penalty Points
DR60	In charge of a vehicle then refusing to supply a specimen for analysis	10
DR70	Failing to provide specimen for breath test	4
	Insurance Offences	
IN10	Using a vehicle uninsured against third party risks	4–8
	Licence Offences	
LC10	Driving without a licence	2
	Miscellaneous Offences	
MS10	Leaving a vehicle in a dangerous position	3
MS20	Unlawful pillion riding	1
MS30	Playstreet offences	2
MS40	Driving with uncorrected defective eyesight or refusing to submit to a test	
MS50	Motor racing on the highway	†
MS60	Offences not covered by other codes	As appropriate
MS70	Driving with uncorrected defective eyesight	2
MS80	Refusing to submit to an eyesight test	2
	Motorway Offences	
MW10	Contravention of Special Roads Regulations (excluding speed limits)	3
	Pedestrian Crossings	
PC10	Undefined Contravention of Pedestrian Crossing Regulations	3
PC20	Contravention of Pedestrian Crossing Regulations with moving vehicle	3
PC30	Contravention of Pedestrian Crossing Regulations with stationary vehicle	3
	Provisional Licence Offences	
PL10	Driving without 'L' plates	2
PL20	Not accompanied by a qualified person	2
PL30	Carrying a person not qualified	2
PL40	Drawing an unauthorised trailer	2
PL50	Undefined failure to comply with conditions of a Provisional Licence	2

Code	Speed Limits	Penalty Points
SP10	Exceeding goods vehicle speed limits	3
SP20	Exceeding speed limit for type of vehicle (excluding goods or passenger vehicles)	3
SP30	Exceeding statutory speed limit on a public road	3
SP40	Exceeding passenger vehicle speed limit	3
SP50	Exceeding speed limit on a motorway	3
SP60	Undefined speed limit offence	3
	Traffic Directions and Signs	
TS10	Failing to comply with traffic light signals	3
TS20	Failing to comply with double white lines	3
TS30	Failing to comply with a 'Stop' sign	3
TS40	Failing to comply with direction of a constable or traffic warden	3
TS50	Failing to comply with a traffic sign (excluding 'Stop' signs, traffic lights or double white lines)	3
TS60	Failing to comply with a school crossing patrol sign	3
TS70	Undefined failure to comply with a traffic direction or sign	3
	Theft or Unauthorised Taking	
UT10	Taking and driving away a vehicle without consent or an attempt thereat	8
UT20	Stealing or attempting to steal a vehicle	8
UT30	Going equipped for stealing or taking a vehicle	8
UT40	Taking or attempting to take a vehicle without consent; driving or attempting to drive a vehicle knowing it to have been taken without consent; allowing oneself to be carried in or on a vehicle knowing it to have been taken without consent	8
	Special Codes	
XX99	To signify a disqualification under 'totting up' procedure	

June 1982

Index